MUSLIM EXTREMISM IN EGYPT

Muslim Extremism in Egypt

The Prophet and Pharaoh

GILLES KEPEL

Translated from the French by Jon Rothschild

University of California Press

Berkeley and Los Angeles

First published as
Le Prophète et Pharaon
by Editions La Découverte, Paris, 1984
© Editions La Découverte, 1984

This edition first published
in the United Kingdom by Al Saqi Books,
  26 Westbourne Grove, London W2
             and
in the United States by the University of California Press,
  Berkeley and Los Angeles
© Al Saqi Books, 1985

Afterword © The Regents of the University of California, 1986

Printed in the United States of America

Library of Congress Cataloging-in-Publication Data

Kepel, Gilles.
  Muslim extremism in Egypt.

  Translation of Le prophète et pharaon.
  Bibliography: p.
  Includes index.
  1. Islam and politics—Egypt. 2. Egypt—Politics
and government—1970–1985. I. Title.
BP64.E3K4413 1985   322'.1'0962   85-24590
ISBN 0-520-05687-6 (alk. paper)

1 2 3 4 5 6 7 8 9

Contents

To the memory of my friend
Richard P. Mitchell
who died in Cairo in
September 1983

Preface

Bernard Lewis

To the modern Western observer, the political role of Islam in the world today appears to be something of an anomaly. The heads of state or ministers of foreign affairs of the Scandinavian countries and West Germany do not from time to time foregather in Lutheran summit conferences, nor do the rulers of Greece, Yugoslavia, Bulgaria and some other countries, temporarily forgetting their political and ideological differences, hold regular meetings on the basis of their current or previous adherence to the Orthodox church. Similarly, the Buddhist states of east and south-east Asia do not constitute a Buddhist bloc at the United Nations, nor for that matter in any other of their political activities.

The very idea of such a grouping, based on religion, in the modern world, has been seen by some outsiders as anachronistic and indeed absurd. It is neither anachronistic nor absurd in relation to Islam. More than forty Muslim governments, including monarchies and republics, conservatives and radicals, exponents of capitalism and of socialism, supporters of the Western bloc, the Eastern bloc, and of a whole spectrum of shades of neutrality have built up an elaborate apparatus of international consultation and, on many issues, cooperation, hold regular high-level conferences, and, despite differences of structure, ideology, and policy, have achieved a significant measure of agreement and common action.

If we turn from international to domestic politics, the difference between the Islamic lands and the rest of the world, though less total, is still substantial. In that minority of countries which practise multi-party open democracy, there are political parties which call themselves Christian or Buddhist. There are, however, very few such, and religious themes play little or no part in their appeals to the electorate. In most Islamic countries, in contrast, religion is even more powerful in internal than in international affairs.

Why this difference? Some might give the simple and obvious answer that Muslim countries are still profoundly Muslim in a way that most Christian countries are no longer Christian. Such an answer, while not devoid of merit, would not in itself be adequate. Christian beliefs and the Christian clergy who uphold them are still a powerful force in many Christian countries, and although their role is no longer what it was in past centuries, it is by no means insignificant. But in no Christian country at the present time can religious leaders command the degree of religious belief and the extent of religious participation that remain common in Muslim lands; more to the point, they do not exercise, nor even claim, the kind of political role that in Muslim lands is not only normal but is widely seen as natural.

The far higher level of religious faith and practice in Muslim lands, as compared with those of other religions, is no doubt an element in the situation, but it is not in itself a sufficient explanation. The difference must rather be traced back to the very beginnings of these various religions, and to an intimate and essential relationship between religion and politics, creed and power, which has no parallel in any major religion besides Islam. The founder of Christianity is quoted as saying: 'Render unto Caesar the things which are Caesar's and unto God the things which are God's.' In this familiar and much cited dictum, a principle is laid down, at the very beginning of Christianity, which remained fundamental to Christian thought and practice, and which is discernible throughout Christian history. Always, there were two authorities, God and Caesar, dealing with different matters, exercising different jurisdictions; each with its own laws and its own courts for enforcing them, each with its own institutions and its own hierarchy for administering them.

Of these two different authorities, we normally use the words church and state. In the Christian world they have always been there, sometimes in association, sometimes in conflict; sometimes one predominating, sometimes the other – but always two and not one. The doctrine of the separation of church and state is now accepted in much though not all of the Christian or post-Christian world. In historic Islam such a doctrine was not only non-existent but would have been meaningless. One can separate two things; one can hardly separate one. For a traditional Muslim, church and state are one and the same. They are not separate or separable institutions, and there is no way of cutting through the tangled web of human activities and allocating certain things to religion, others to politics, some to the state and some to a specifically religious authority. Such familiar pairs of words as lay and ecclesiastical, sacred and profane, spiritual and temporal, and the like, have no equivalents in classical Arabic and the other Islamic languages, since the dichotomy which they express, deeply rooted in Christendom, was unknown in Islam until comparatively modern times, when its introduction was the result of external influences. In recent years those external influences have been discredited and weakened, and the ideas which they brought, never accepted by more than a relatively small and alienated elite, have begun to weaken. And as external influences weaken, there is an inevitable return to older, more deep-rooted perceptions.

The distinction between the political attitudes of Islam, Christianity and Judaism can be seen very clearly in the narratives of events which constitute the sacred foundation history of the three religions, and in which each of them perceives the very core of its religious message and historic identity. Moses led his people out of the house of bondage and through the wilderness, but was not permitted to enter the promised land. Christ died on the cross. Muhammad, the Prophet of Islam, suffered neither of these fates but on the contrary achieved worldly success during his lifetime, becoming a ruling head of state. As the Ayatollah Khomeini has recently reminded us, the Prophet Muhammad founded not only a community but also a policy, a society and a state, of which he was sovereign. And as sovereign, he commanded armies, made war and peace, collected taxes, dispensed justice, and did all those things which a ruler in power normally does. This means that from the very beginnings of Islam, from the lifetime of its founder, in the formative memories which are the sacred classical and scriptural history of all Muslims, religion and the state are one and the same. This intimate connection between faith and power has remained characteristic of Islam in contrast to the other two religions.

There are some further differences. Christianity arose amid the fall of an empire. The rise of Christianity parallels the decline and fall of Rome, and the church created its own structures to survive in this period. During the centuries when Christianity was a persecuted faith of the downtrodden, God was seen as subjecting his followers to suffering and tribulation to test and purify their faith. When Christianity finally became a state religion, the Christians tried to take over and refashion the institutions and even the language of Rome to their own needs. Islam in contrast arose amid the birth of an empire and became the creed of a vast, prosperous and flourishing realm, created under the aegis of the new faith and expressed in the language of the new revelation. While for St Augustine and other early Christian thinkers the state was a lesser evil, for Muslims the state – that is the Islamic state – was a divinely ordained necessity, established to maintain, defend and promulgate God's faith and to uphold and enforce God's law. In this perception of the universe, God is seen as helping rather than testing the believers, as desiring their success in this world, and manifesting his divine approval by victory and dominance. Muslims of minority and opposition sects form a partial exception to this; in radical Shi'ism in particular an almost Christian-style conception of suffering and passion combines with Muslim triumphalism to produce an explosively powerful social force.

These perceptions from the remoter Islamic past have certain important consequences for the present time, notably their effects on the shaping of Muslim self-awareness. Perhaps the most important and far-reaching of these effects is that for most Muslims, Islam rather than any other element is the ultimate basis of identity, of loyalty, of authority. In most parts of the modern world we have been accustomed, at different times and for different purposes, to define ourselves collectively in a number of ways: by country, by nation, by race, by class, by language, and by various other criteria. All of these have their place in Islamic self-perceptions as reflected in historical writings; sometimes that place is an important one. But over all they are seen as secondary. For most of the recorded history of most of the Muslim world, the primary and basic definition, both adoptive and ascriptive, is not country or nation, not race or class, but religion, and for Muslims that of course means Islam. In their view, it is religion that marks the distinction between insider and outsider, between brother and stranger. Whatever other factors may have been at work, in order to become effective they had to assume a religious or at least a sectarian form.

Since Islam is perceived as the main basis of identity, it necessarily constitutes the main claim to loyalty or allegiance. In most Muslim societies the essential test by which one distinguishes between loyalty and disloyalty is once again religion. What matters here is not so much religious belief or theological conviction, though these are not unimportant; what matters is communal loyalty and conformity. Muslims, unlike Christians, have not usually concerned themselves much with the meticulous definition of creeds, or the recognition and extirpation of heresy. Only God can judge the sincerity of a man's thoughts, and for that matter the correctness of his beliefs. But obedience to the law is a public and social act, and only in a society where the holy law is upheld can a Muslim fulfil God's purpose for mankind. And since religious conformity is the outward sign of loyalty, it follows that non-conformity is disloyalty and apostasy is treason. This insistence on conformity has meant, throughout history, a great stress on consensus, both as a source of guidance and as a basis for legitimacy. Despite the vast changes of the last century or two, Islam has clearly remained the most accepted form of consensus in Muslim countries, far more potent than political programmes or slogans; Islamic symbols and appeals are still the most effective for the mobilization of society, whether behind a government or against it.

Along with identity and loyalty, authority too is determined by Islam. In most Western systems of political thought or symbolism, sovereignty comes by inheritance and tradition, or in more modern times, from the people. In the Muslim view, the source of a ruler's authority is neither his predecessors nor the people but God. Since God is the sole source of authority, it is he who delegates and empowers the head of state, he too who is the

sole source of law and indeed of legislation. The principal function of government is to enable the individual Muslim to lead the
good Muslim life in this world and prepare himself for the next.
This is, in the last analysis, the purpose of the state, for which
alone it is established by God and for which alone statesmen are
given authority over others. The worth of the state, and the good
or evil deeds of statesmen, are measured by the extent to which
this purpose is accomplished. The basic rule for Muslim social
life, commonly formulated as 'to enjoin good and forbid evil' is
thus a shared responsibility of the ruler and of the subject, or in
modern terms, of the state and of the individual. The means by
which this purpose is accomplished is the holy law, which provides both the source and test of a ruler's legitimacy, and the sole
function of his office. If the ruler is God's ruler and the law which
he enforces is God's law, then obedience to him is a religious
obligation, and disobedience is a sin as well as a crime, to be
punished in the next world as well as this one. If the ruler does
not draw his power from God, and the law he administers is not
God's law, then he is a usurper. The duty of obedience lapses
and is replaced by a duty of disobedience. In the course of the
centuries Muslim jurists and theologians have produced a considerable literature discussing the questions of legitimacy and
usurpation. How does a ruler become legitimate? When does he
cease to be legitimate? In what circumstances does the subject
have the right or even the duty to disobey him – and ultimately to
remove him? Islam has its own corpus of revolutionary doctrine,
its own record and memory of revolutionary actions, which still
have a powerful evocative appeal. Recent events in Iran and in
some other countries have given them a new relevance.

Since early days there have been two levels of religious life in
the Islamic lands, one which might be called official, the other
popular. One is the kind of religion which is concerned with
dogma and law, and which generally enjoys the sponsorship of
the state. In many ways it is remote, having limited contact with
the people, and looking with disapproval on some of the less
official forms of religion. These latter constitute the other level of
Islam, that of the Brotherhoods and of other popular movements.
Some of the mystical fraternities tend to play down the significance of dogma, even at times of law, and instead stress the

intuitive and mystical aspect, the direct personal relationship between the believer and his pastoral guide, between the believer and God. Others, while sharing the mystic's impatience with the complexities and subtleties of theology and exegesis, do not decry the law but on the contrary make its restoration and enforcement, in the most rigorous form, their principal demand. Both the mystic and the purist share their opposition to state Islam, the one offering a critique of conservative Muslim regimes which pose as the upholders of the faith and the law, the other challenging the modernizing secularizing regimes which have committed the greater offence of setting the law aside and replacing it with other laws and usage of alien and infidel provenance. The two levels of Islam, the one official, the other popular in its various types, have always been present, sometimes associated in greater or lesser harmony, sometimes in conflict, but always mistrustful of each other. The latter, the popular traditions, have usually, with some reason, been regarded with suspicion by the state authorities, who recognized — and feared — the ability of popular leaders to control or release powerful pent-up religious emotions. We have seen examples of this in recent years.

From the beginning, Islamic history, tradition and law embraced two distinct and indeed contradictory principles, one activist, the other quietist. There are two stages in the career of the Prophet. In one, by far the better known and more frequently cited, the Prophet appears as the sovereign of Medina — as judge, general and statesman. But there was an earlier stage, before the *hijra*, that is, before the migration of the Prophet from Mecca to Medina. Before he became a ruler, the Prophet was the leader of an opposition movement against the pagan oligarchy of Mecca. While this opposition was primarily religious and moral in purpose, it inevitably took the form of political action. In this perception, the Prophet began as a critic and opponent of the regime in Mecca, left his homeland for Medina where he formed what in modern parlance might be called a government in exile, and from there waged war against Mecca until victory and conquest. In a sense, the advent of the new dispensation was itself a revolutionary challenge to an older leadership and an old order, both of which were overthrown and supplanted, the one by the Prophet and his companions, the other by Islam. In this as in so much else the Prophet was seen as a model, and his career as setting a pattern. Many later political aspirants attempted to follow his example; some of them succeeded, others failed. The two traditions, the Prophet as sovereign and the Prophet as rebel, often recur through the centuries of Islamic history. Both are still very much alive.

For some time past — more than two centuries in some areas, considerably less in others — the heartlands of Islam have been subject to the influence, at times the rule, of Europe. During this period of European impact and domination, there was a series of different Islamic responses, of acceptance and imitation, of rejection and revolt. What is surely significant is that whenever there was a genuine popular outbreak, involving the masses and going beyond a small educated leading elite, the movement expressed itself not in nationalist, not in patriotic, not in social or economic, but in Islamic terms. During the first major phase of European expansion into Islamic lands in the nineteenth century, when the British Empire was absorbing the Muslim northwest of India, when the French were invading North Africa, when the Russians were conquering the Caucasian lands, in all three places the most effective and persistent resistance was Islamic–organized in Muslim brotherhoods, led by Muslim religious leaders. The careers of Ahmad Brelwi in India, of Shamil in Daghistan and of Abd al-Qadir in Algeria all express the markedly religious character of this first major resistance of the Islamic world to the advance of imperial Europe in all three places.

In due course all three were crushed, and a period of acceptance, of accommodation followed. Muslim subjects of the three major empires began, despite some opposition, to learn the languages of their imperial masters, and even to adapt some of their cultural patterns. A second phase in Islamic resistance came towards the end of the nineteenth century, when for the first time we hear the word 'pan-Islam' to denote an explicitly political movement aiming at a greater unity of the Islamic world against European encroachment. Already at this time we see what became a characteristic feature of such movements — the distinction between two types, one state-sponsored and used mainly diplomatically, the other more popular and with more than a tinge of social radicalism.

The constitutional revolutions in Iran and in the Ottoman Empire in the early twentieth century brought a phase of liberal constitutionalism, which was reinforced by the victory of the Western Allies, the main standard-bearers of this form of government, in 1918. In the areas under their rule or tutelage, the British and the French, for a while the masters of the Middle East, set up new regimes in their own image, as presidential democracies and constitutional monarchies. Neither of these imported systems corresponded either to the past traditions or the future needs of the region. And both systems, after the departure of their foreign sponsors, fell in ruins. For a while, in the immediate aftermath of the First World War, there were some stirrings of a new Islamic militancy, notably in Anatolia and in Central Asia, but with the consolidation of the secularist Kemalist Republic in Turkey and of the Soviet Union in Transcaucasia and Central Asia, this phase of Islamic activity ended and a period of secular movements began — in some areas nationalist, in others socialist, in many both at the same time. Political models were still being drawn from the outside world, and as the Anglo-French hegemony was weakened, challenged and finally removed, these models were sought from a wider range of sources — from Central and Eastern as well as Western Europe, from South as well as North America. They did not work any better than the earlier range of imports.

Already before the outbreak of the Second World War, the first signs of a new kind of militant Islam could be discerned, which gathered strength during the war years and the immediate postwar period. But this phase came to a halt in the early fifties with the consolidation of two powerful rulers in Iran and in Egypt, which had been the main centres of militant Islamic activity at that time. The Shah and President Nasser differed in many significant respects, but they seem to have agreed in seeing militant Islamic movements as a threat to the kind of regime they were trying to establish, and in using whatever means were feasible to keep them under control. But there were still many signs of the active militancy under the surface, sometimes breaking out into the open, as for example in the Lebanese civil wars and the internal struggles in Iraq.

For a long time the importance of Islam as a political force was consistently — one might even say ideologically — underrated in the outside world. Indeed, until the upheaval in Iran, there was a general refusal to take cognizance of the fact that Islam was still a force in the Muslim world. Since then there has been a tendency in some circles to move to the opposite extreme, and those who previously could not see Islam at all now sometimes seem to have difficulty in seeing anything else. Both views are exaggerated; both are misleading. Islam is a reality, and its importance as a political factor is immense. But having accepted Islam as a fact, we should remember that there are still other facts. Muslims, like other people, seek ways to protest and rebel against political oppression and economic privation; Muslims, like other people, will react and respond in ways that are familiar to them. Whatever the cause — political, social, economic — the form of expression which Muslims most naturally find to voice their criticism and their aspirations is Islamic. The slogans, the programmes, and to a very large extent the leadership are Islamic. Through the centuries, Muslim opposition has expressed itself in terms of theology as naturally and as spontaneously as its European equivalents in terms of ideology. The one is no more a 'mask' or 'disguise' than the other.

At the present time we can still see many of the characteristic features of the classical Islamic situation. One is the dichotomy between official Islam and popular Islam. The first kind is expressed in governmental and diplomatic pan-Islamism, manifesting itself through summit conferences, inter-Islamic banks and development organizations, regional cooperation projects and the like. The second produces more radical forms of pan-Islamic activity, operating through underground movements, sometimes also supported by one or another radical Islamic government. These movements seek to achieve a renewal of society by ending the rule of alien infidels and domestic apostates, and returning to what they see as a pure and authentic Islamic order.

The philosophy and programme of these radical movements is well formulated in the name given to one of the religious opposition groups in Egypt — *al-Takfir wa'l-Hijra*. *Takfir* means to recognize and denounce an infidel, even if he claims to be a Muslim; its political implication is the rejection of allegiance to such a ruler. *Hijra* evokes the decision of the Prophet to migrate from Mecca to Medina — that is, to abandon a pagan society and create one that is truly Islamic. By present-day militant Islamic groups this migration is of course interpreted in a spiritual, social and political, not a territorial sense. To denounce, reject and, if possible, overthrow impious rulers, and to withdraw from a pagan and corrupt society, are seen as essential prerequisites to the establishment of God's kingdom on earth. At a time when imported institutions are breaking down and imported panaceas are failing to produce the promised and expected results, such doctrines have a powerful appeal.

Since 1978 the term 'Islamic revolution' has become a commonplace of writing on the Middle East, even among those who previously would have regarded the collocation of this adjective and this substantive as a contradiction in terms. The words Islamic revolution have been used to designate a wide variety of movements in various parts of Asia and Africa, whose common element is their combination of revolutionary purposes and tactics with religious belief and expression. In recent years Islamic revolutionaries have achieved two spectacular successes, the overthrow of the Shah in Iran and the assassination of Sadat in Egypt. Perhaps because it removed only the man but not the regime, the movement in Egypt has received far less attention than that in Iran. Even such basic questions as who killed Sadat and why are more often than not wrongly posed and answered in the Western world. Gilles Kepel's book, based on a study of recent Egyptian-Islamic movements that is at once extensive and profound, brings a new wealth both of information and of understanding.

Introduction

Journey to the Ends of Islam

> In order to preserve in political science the freedom of spirit to which we have become accustomed in mathematics, I have been careful not to ridicule human behaviour, neither to deplore nor condemn, but to understand.
>
> SPINOZA

Westerners have traditionally regarded Islam with a mixture of fascination and revulsion. This mix of sentiments was fully apparent when the Islamic revolution broke out in Iran. After first being attracted by the experience, exhilarated by its novelty, many leading intellectuals subsequently trumpeted their disgust at the Khomeinist state's thirst for blood and washed their hands of the matter: the phenomenon had proved too resistant to their categories of thought.

Disoriented by this experience, Western intellectuals have tended to take refuge behind a kind of Maginot Line of enlightened rationalism. From these entrenched positions they excoriate 'fanaticism', 'backwardness', and 'Muslim fundamentalism'. The West, they seem to be saying, has gone beyond all that: let it now go its own way and let Islam — irretrievably alien, intellectually inaccessible, and repugnant — wallow in its barbarism.

This attitude is pernicious. However healthy the reflex that engenders it, the result is facile misdirection. The sentiment of pity and its offspring, sympathy, are unworthy counsellors for the analyst. Unless they are resisted, one runs the risk of seeing reality only through the prism of one's own desires. When the consequent illusions suddenly fade, they are replaced by disappointment, and affability is supplanted by a bleak lack of

22

curiosity that stills the mind; understanding is renounced in favour of the stodgy comfort of time-honoured convictions.

This book seeks to take up the challenge to Western categories of thought posed by contemporary Islam in its most spectacular, most *monstrous* manifestation (in the strict sense of the word): the 'Islamicist movement'. [1] The term is meant to designate that collection of 'inflammations' of Islam (more easily listed than analysed) that have led — though exactly how is not yet clear — to such disparate events as the Iranian revolution, the attack on the Great Mosque in Mecca, the attempted assassination of the pope, the assassination of Sadat, and even Colonel Qadhafi's African intrigues.

The effects of these events have been real enough, while their causes, presumably complex and entangled, resist analysis. To unwind the skein of all these phenomena in an exhaustive study of the manifestations of Islamicism from Morocco to Indonesia, from the North African districts of Marseilles to Samarkand, would require a work of encyclopaedic scope. It is far better to examine one particular case more restricted in space and time. I have chosen the Islamicist movement in Sadat's Egypt, whose most clamorous act was the murder of the president on 6 October 1981, before a world-wide television audience.

The choice of Egypt was determined by a number of considerations. To begin with, it was in Egypt, in 1928, that Hasan al-Banna founded the Society of Muslim Brethren (or Muslim Brotherhood), prototype of the contemporary Islamicist movement. This historical primacy affords us much invaluable sociological information. Moreover, it was in Nasser's Egypt, beacon of the progressive independent states of the Third World, that the regime violently smashed the largest branch of the Brotherhood. It was also in Egypt that an Islamicist movement was reconstituted, against that independent state, and sought, not without considerable success, to articulate social dissatisfaction.

Furthermore, if Egypt offers a choice terrain for the researcher, it is partly because the poor and oppressed masses of the Muslim world are now watching the fate of its fifty million inhabitants just as they once fixed their gaze on Nasser. Tape cassettes of the Friday sermons of Sheikh Kishk, an Islamicist

1. The term 'Islamicist' is used throughout to render the French 'islamiste'. The loan-word 'Islamist' did not gain currency until after this translation had been completed.

preacher in Cairo, are avidly passed from hand to hand in towns and cities from Casablanca to Kuwait, and in the neighbourhoods of Muslim immigrant workers in Europe as well, providing their listeners with an Islamicist view of the world.

Finally, and perhaps most important, it was in Nasser's concentration camps, symbols of pharaoh's despotic regime, that a man called Sayyid Qutb charted the renewal of Islamicist thought of which the contemporary organizations are to a large extent the legatees. These organizations presented a varied and richly shaded array of tendencies throughout Sadat's decade in power, including legalistic currents, sects that established isolated communities for resocializing their members, mass student organizations, and groupings preaching armed struggle.

The Egyptian example — which I was able to analyse on the scene and at considerable length — therefore stands as a kind of paradigm against which other manifestations of Islamicism can be measured. Perhaps that will enable us to penetrate appearances, as fleeting as they are spectacular, and grasp the underlying meaning.

Our journey to the ends of Islam will inevitably subject the reader to some intellectual dislocation. This is unavoidable. Nothing would be more specious than to assume *a priori* that the manifestations of contemporary Islam are no more than the usual sort of phenomena analysed by the social sciences, but veiled, in this case, by the mask of religious ideology.

In discussing the anti-Jewish polemics of the Islamicist journal *al-Da'wa* ('The Mission'), for example, we will encounter many of the stereotypes of European anti-Semitism, foremost among which is the imperishable *Protocols of the Elders of Zion*. Admittedly, in this case we are dealing with a Western tradition that has forded the Mediterranean. But our investigation must not end with that observation alone. Our aim is to understand how and why these stereotypes came to be used again in the contemporary Middle East: how is it that they 'make sense' to the Islamicist mind, to the semantic system of the bearded militants in their white gallabiehs? To discover this is to reconstruct that system's grammar and lexicon, and thus also the Muslim cultural tradition from which it issued and the contemporary Third World in which it functions. Here the tasks of the orientalist and the political scientist are inevitably interwined.[2]

2. The author enjoyed a three-year stay in Cairo under the auspices of the Centre d'études économiques, juridiques et sociales, and participated in its research programmes and seminars. I am most deeply grateful to the French–Egyptian team at the Centre. Nevertheless, the opinions expressed in this book are the outcome of personal research alone and are my responsibility alone.

I would also like to thank the many friends, Egyptians and foreigners resident in Egypt, who taught me to open my eyes in that country. Of all of them, I will mention only Maurice P. Martin, whose intimate knowledge of daily life in the Nile Valley is equalled only by his relentless curiosity.

Olivier Carré, Bruno Etienne, and Maxime Rodinson gave me precious advice and spotted many errors during the drafting of the thesis on which the present book is based.

My 'professor of grammar', Michel d'Hermies, was a demanding reader of a manuscript whose content owes much to him.

Finally, Rémy Leveau was unstinting in his kindness and support, in both Paris and Cairo. The research that led to this book could not have been undertaken without the confidence with which he honoured me from the very outset.

A Note on Sources and Spelling

I have chosen to transcribe the Arabic names and terms in this book according to a system that is both intelligible to those who know no Arabic and familiar to speakers of the language. The latter will find little difficulty recognizing the emphatic letters and long vowels, neither of which have been marked, and will not be confused by the rendering of both *'ayn* and *hamza* by an apostrophe.

The combination *th* is pronounced as in English; the *kh* corresponds roughly to the German *ch* or the same letters in the Scottish *loch*; *dh* represents the sound *th* in the English word *then*; the *gh* is the rolled Parisian *r*. Other letters and combinations of letters are pronounced more or less as in English.

The thesis on which the present book is based contained some six hundred footnotes, most of which referred to Arabic sources, and a bibliography of about five hundred works, more than two-thirds of which were also in Arabic. These have all been eliminated to make the book more accessible. A brief list of works referred to directly in the text has been preserved, on pp. 241–43; it is followed by an equally brief list of periodicals. Numbers that appear in brackets in the text refer to sources in this list. The footnotes that remain are explanatory in nature.

Specialist readers who would like more detailed references may consult the above-mentioned thesis, *Le Mouvement islamiste dans l'Egypte de Sadate*, at the Ecole des hautes études en sciences sociales, Paris.

All quotations from the Koran in this book are taken from the translation by N.J. Dawood, second revised edition (1966), published by Penguin Books, Harmondsworth.

The author has made several revisions for the English edition.

1
From One Ordeal to Another: 1954–66

Nasser and his comrades took power in Egypt on 23 July 1952. On 9 December 1954, six leaders of the Society of Muslim Brethren mounted the gallows, while thousands of others languished in prison. Never in the quarter century since the founding of the Society by Hasan al-Banna in 1928 had the Brethren suffered such violent repression.[1]

The state built by the Free Officers after 1952 was nevertheless very different from the monarchy that preceded it. Nasser sought to mobilize civil society from top to bottom, to free Egypt from colonialism and its aftermath and turn the country into a modern, independent nation. Mobilizing society meant first and foremost ensuring that no discordant voices were raised to challenge the regime's objectives. On 16 January 1953, when all political parties were duly dissolved by decree, however, the Muslim Brethren were exempted from the measure. They were, of course, officially only an association and not a party; but more important, they represented the largest organized popular force in the country, and after only six months in power, the regime was not yet able to risk a direct confrontation.

A conflict was nevertheless inevitable, even though the Brethren had initially hailed the coup of 23 July. The officers had no intention of allowing the Brotherhood to express popular demands, which were instead to be channelled through a single party whose task was to rally the masses behind the government. After a number of incidents, relations between the state and the Muslim Brethren broke down irrevocably on 26 October 1954,

1. The principal dates in the history of the Muslim Brotherhood are listed in the chronology on pp. 263–73.

when a member of the Brotherhood tried to assassinate Nasser while the president was delivering a speech in Alexandria. The entire country heard the shots on the radio. The Brethren countered the regime's charge of conspiracy by claiming that the attack had been a police provocation. But no one listened. Their headquarters were burned down, their leaders were arrested and tortured, and government agents inflamed the populace against their members.

Immediately after 26 October, the state destroyed the last independent organization standing between society and itself. The rulers hoped that their action had been definitive.

As it turned out, however, during the three decades of rule by Nasser and Sadat, the state had to resort to firing squads and the gallows to silence Islamicist militants on four other occasions: in 1966, 1974, 1977, and 1981. The destruction of the Society of Muslim Brethren in 1954 had failed to extinguish the current of thought inaugurated by Hasan al-Banna and his epigones.

In the seclusion of the Nasser regime's concentration camps, new strategies were developed to fight against a state whose totalitarian character the imprisoned Brethren quickly perceived. Sayyid Qutb, the Islamicist thinker hanged by Nasser in 1966, produced a prison work that analysed the independent state in terms of Koranic categories. It also generated diverse interpretations, on the basis of which the Islamicist movement fragmented.

The various tendencies sought to express Egyptian civil society's opposition to the state. The language and categories adopted by Qutb and his emulators captured the suffering, frustration, and daily demands of certain components of that society, translating them into a challenge to the post-1952 state. An examination of Islamicist discourse may therefore help us to understand how significant sections of society viewed the state.

In the Beginning Were the Camps

Islamicist thought was reconstructed after 1954 primarily in the concentration camps, which were felt by Qutb and his disciples to symbolize the relationship of the state to society. The camp experience must therefore be assessed, before considering Qutb's major writings.

Most of the leaders of the Muslim Brotherhood were held in Tura prison, in Cairo's southern suburbs. Conditions there were appalling. Qutb, who was consumptive, lived more or less permanently in the prison infirmary.

The Brethren lived in terror of the 'final solution' to the problem they posed for the regime. At the end of May 1957 various developments convinced them that they were about to be exterminated. Fearing that they would be killed if they reported for the normal daily work detail (rock-breaking), they refused to do the forced labour, locking themselves in their cells on 1 June. Armed soldiers broke into the cells and massacred twenty-one of them. The authorities said that they had put down a rebellion.

These twenty-one new martyrs — added to the victims of the 1954 hangings and to Hasan al-Banna himself, the martyr *par excellence*, who was assassinated by King Farouk's police in 1949 — made a deep impression on the man who sat writing relentlessly in his sickbed. Sayyid Qutb was horrified by the barbarism of the camp guards, by the inhumanity with which they had let the wounded die. Various witnesses report that it was then that he lost his last remaining illusions as to the Muslim character of the Nasser regime.

In this he agreed with another young Muslim Brother who was also ill and who shared his cell: his name was Muhammad Hawwash, and he was executed along with his master in 1966. One night, according to the Islamicist historian Jabir Rizq [33], Joseph appeared to Hawwash in a dream and said: 'Tell Sayyid Qutb that in my sura he will find what he seeks.' Verses 35–41 of the sura (or chapter) of the Koran entitled 'Joseph' recount Joseph's imprisonment along with two other young men. In the sura, Joseph tells his fellow prisoners that all that man reveres but God are idle words and that God alone wields real power.

Qutb believed that the guards and torturers in the concentration camp had forgotten God. They no longer worshipped Him but revered Nasser and the state in His stead. They were ignorant of the principles of justice laid down by Koranic ethics and had placed themselves outside Islam. In other words, they were pagans. Only the imprisoned Brethren were still true Muslims.

While Qutb was busy interpreting events in the camp so as to weld them into the view of the world that he later expounded in his book *Ma'alim fi'l-Tariq* ('Signposts'), sympathizers of the Muslim Brethren outside the prison walls began to meet again. An unofficial mutual aid and relief organization was founded outside the camps to aid families whose breadwinners were incarcerated. Apart from its charitable and humanitarian aspect, this grouping enabled those who had been members of the Brotherhood to keep in contact with one another.

Towards the middle of 1956 those of the imprisoned Brethren who had never been brought to trial were released; they were destitute. The Society of Muslim Ladies, led by Mrs Zaynab al-Ghazali, assumed the charitable task of providing for the released prisoners. Her network of relations among Brotherhood sympathizers enabled the leader of the Muslim Ladies to act as a link in the secret reconstitution of the organization that had been formally dissolved in 1954. In 1957, while on the pilgrimage to Mecca, al-Ghazali met various Egyptian exiles, with the approval of the Saudi leaders, who were then encouraging opposition to the Nasser regime. In Mecca she was introduced to 'Abd al-Fattah Isma'il, one of the leaders of the Brotherhood, and they decided to pool their efforts [32].

While Mrs al-Ghazali organized a series of seminars in her home [12], 'Abd al-Fattah,known as 'the man who says his five daily prayers in five different governorates', began seeking out and galvanizing Brotherhood sympathizers the length and breadth of Egypt. Hasan al-Hudaybi, al-Banna's successor as Supreme Guide of the Brotherhood, had been spared by the regime in 1954 because of his advanced age. He was aware of the reorganization efforts and approved of them, though he did not participate directly.

Although the group which met at al-Ghazali's home was supposedly engaged only in 'Muslim education', the same was not true of several other nuclei that had arisen independently in various governorates. They included former Brethren, mostly

young men, who had escaped the previous police round-ups:
they had been recruited only recently and therefore had not had
much training [18].

The first assemblies of these scattered nuclei were held in 1957.
Their purpose was to hold collective discussions about the
causes of the ordeal of 1954. The reorganization took shape as
early as 1959, but only in 1962 did the new organization acquire
the features it would have three years later, during the next
'ordeal' inflicted by the regime.

The young activists who dreamed of avenging 1954, as well as
others who attended the seminars in Zaynab al-Ghazali's home,
all became acquainted with the latest literary productions of
Sayyid Qutb — in other words, with the initial drafts of *Signposts*. Mrs al-Ghazali visited Sayyid Qutb's two sisters regularly,
and through this link Qutb received reports about the work of
the 'seminar', sending his own writings in return. The first
pages of the work were greeted enthusiastically when they
arrived in 1962. Hudaybi himself (whose opinion became far
more measured after 1966) declared that the book vindicated all
the hopes he had placed in Sayyid Qutb, who now embodied
'the future of the Muslim mission' (*da'wa*).

The most active nuclei of young militants were in Alexandria,
Damietta, Buhayra, and Cairo. The leaders of these groupings
had formed a four-man operational directorate and were seeking
a thinker, an ideologue. It was against this backdrop that Sayyid
Qutb was released from prison in May 1964.[2] He joined with the
four members of the directorate, who told him of their plans to
overthrow the regime by force. According to subsequent confes-
sions (extracted under torture), they also told him that they were
expecting arms from Saudi Arabia. Whatever the truth of the
matter, it is known that an organization was secretly reconstituted at the end of 1964 and that Qutb's book *Signposts* was its
manifesto.

2. Officially, Qutb's sentence was suspended 'for reasons of health', on the
occasion of a visit to Cairo by the Iraqi head of state. His friends now say that his
release was a trap.

The 1965 'Plot'

Little is known of the events of 1965 — or more accurately, there
are enormous contradictions between the versions of sources
close to the Muslim Brethren and those of historians or other
observers who consider themselves leftists. According to the
latter (in particular the Nasserist 'Abdallah Imam), the militants
dreamed only of assassination, sabotage, and destruction
[18,32]; the former claim that the organization itself was an
invention of the police and that the repression was the result of
orders given to Nasser by the Soviet and American secret services and by world Zionism [12,33].

A polemic about *Signposts* seems to have broken out within
Islamicist circles, in particular among the Brethren released from
the Qanatir prison in the Cairo area; it was this that attracted
police attention to the grouping of militants around Qutb. The
temerity of the young militants alarmed more seasoned Brethren
like Munir al-Dilla, who warned Qutb against the dangers of
youthful enthusiasm. The '1965 organization' was therefore
divided over how to seize power. The young activists favoured
the use of violence to bring down the 'Nasser dictatorship',
while at the other extreme Zaynab al-Ghazali held that the
organization could do no more than establish 'educational programmes' lasting thirteen years at a time; these would have to be
repeated until 75 per cent of the population were won over [12].
Although *Signposts* did not recommend the use of bombs and
guns, it did preach Muslim emancipation through the 'movement' and not through words alone.[3]

In short, the Brethren had come together again, but they could
not agree on a political strategy. They were easy prey for the
regime, for they were indeed conspiring, but they scarcely represented any real threat. In 1965, at a time when Nasser was facing
serious problems in foreign and domestic policy alike — with
the fiasco of the Yemen expedition[4] and the bulimia of a state
bureaucracy that devoured everything in sight and succeeded

3. See the analysis of the book in chapter 2.
4. The Egyptian army had been sent to (North) Yemen to support the repub-
lican side in a civil war against the partisans of the Imam, aided by the Saudis.
The Egyptians became bogged down and suffered heavy losses.

only in reproducing itself — the 'new conspiracy of the Muslim Brotherhood' offered an ideal scapegoat that would enable the leader to reunite the people behind him.

There is also some evidence that the discovery of the 'plot' was a by-product of internecine conflicts in the various secret services, which were scrambling to garner maximum authority among the *marakiz al-quwwa*, or centres of power (which were in fact no more than warring factions of presidential courtiers): each yearned to reveal to the prince a plot that rival services had been unable to uncover. In the event, the *Mukhabarat 'Askariya* (Military Security Services) of Marshal Amer were intent on proving that the *Mabahith 'Amma* (General Intelligence) of the Ministry of the Interior could not guarantee the president's security. The Military Security Services, under the leadership of Shams Badran, dealt with the entire affair.

It began on 29 July 1965 with the arrest of Muhammad Qutb, Sayyid's brother and disciple. The organization seemed unable to respond to this attack. On 9 August Sayyid himself was arrested, along with various other Muslim Brethren. On 20 August 'Abd al-Fattah Isma'il and 'Ali 'Ashmawi, the latter a young militant, fell into a random police trap. 'Ashmawi 'talked', and the entire organization was then arrested. The repression was merciless. On 22 August, troops invested the village of Kardasa.

This village, not far from the pyramids and traditionally a stronghold of the Brotherhood, marks the terminus of a network of trails that stretch deep into the Libyan desert and are travelled by the denizens of a netherworld that includes both smugglers trafficking with Libya and political dissidents. The Muslim Brethren had had a base there since the forties, when training camps for militants had been established in the nearby desert. The Brotherhood had been able to secure control of Kardasa by reconciling two rival families who had previously waged blood-feuds over control of the post of *'umdah* (a sort of mayor). Nasserism had made little if any impact on the strength of the Brotherhood in the village until 21 August 1965, when a commando of military police in plainclothes arrived to arrest al-Sayyid Nazili, suspected of membership of the '1965 organization'. When the police failed to find Nazili, they took his brother instead. The inhabitants of the village intervened to free him, routing the police patrol. The next morning, Kardasa was surrounded by troops, houses were sacked, and the village notables and their families were stripped and flogged in the public square. The entire male population was then led away to a military prison, where they suffered the customary torture. They remained there for a month [33].

This sort of dragooning is the traditional means of bringing recalcitrant villages to heel in Middle Egypt when they harbour criminals, refuse to pay taxes, or engage in some traffic that the state takes it into its head to halt. Its use in this instance to stamp out political dissent gives some indication of the strength of the Islamicist base in the town.

On 30 August Egyptian public opinion learned, through a speech Nasser delivered from Moscow,[5] that the Society of Muslim Brethren was the force behind a gigantic plot exposed by the intelligence services. Their accomplices, said the president, included Mustafa Amin, a leading liberal journalist arrested on 2 September on charges of 'spying for the United States', and a hired killer named Husain Tawfiq. The regime pulled out all the stops in tracking down the 'conspirators'. On 31 August the Cairo shanty town of Bulaq al-Dakrur was searched; most of the governorates were raided during the first week of September. After the raids, all the regime's religious functionaries, spokesmen, and writers were mobilized to denounce seditious elements. Hasan Ma'mun, the sheikh of al-Azhar mosque, delivered a radio speech condemning the Muslim Brethren as 'medieval terrorists'. Deputies to the National Assembly and members of the ruling Arab Socialist Union shouted themselves hoarse in their local constituencies, trying to arouse the enthusiasm of the 'voters', who were driven to mass meetings in army trucks. The media, fulfilling their allotted task, heaped abuse on defendants who were thus condemned even before any semblance of a trial, however farcical. After taking up the old chorus of 1954 about the assassinations and bombings planned by the

5. 'The capital of atheism', as the Islamicists never tired of pointing out. They saw the site of the speech as itself proof that the president had spoken on orders from his Russian masters, egged on by the Americans and Zionists, all united in their hatred of Islam.

criminals, the newspapers exposed the foreign links of the 'religious fanatics': Sa'id Ramadan, al-Banna's son-in-law, was said to be pulling the strings from Amman, Jordan, on orders from CENTO.[6] The two main leaders of the conspiracy in Egypt were the Qutb brothers, while copies of *Signposts* and *The Jahiliyya of the Twentieth Century*, veritable compendia of terrorism, were found in every police search. Police action, however, had annihilated all the cells of the organization, which was structured to make maximum use of the members' skills, the chemists assigned to make bombs, the pilots to fly arms and funds in from abroad, and so on.

The prisoners suffered the most varied forms of torture. 'Ali 'Ashmawi, one of the young members of the directorate, broke down and denounced all his co-defendants. The trial, at which General Dajwi distinguished himself, offered the accused all the guarantees of fairness characteristic of a military court in a dictatorial state trying defendants broken by torture. Despite a campaign in many Muslim countries to save Sayyid Qutb, he was hanged on Monday, 29 August 1966, along with his beloved disciple Muhammad Hawwash and 'Abd al-Fattah Isma'il, the Brotherhood organizer. Press photographs showed Qutb shortly before his death, his face illuminated by a thin smile widened by his slanting eyes.

Such were the main lines of the rebirth of the Society of Muslim Brethren during the first decade of Nasserism, a decade that ended as it had begun, with persecution. There were parallels between 1954 and 1965, of course, but there had also been a palpable evolution in the thought, if not the practice, of the Islamicist movement. The major parallel was that in both cases the regime had been able to strike at the organization while it was in the process of reconstituting itself, after it had attained some strength but before it had developed a strategy that could have enabled it to resist the attack. But whereas in 1954 the Muslim Brethren had been unable to analyse the Nasser regime or to understand why confrontation was inevitable, in 1965, after

6. Founded in 1955, the Central Treaty Organization (CENTO) included Britain, Pakistan, Turkey, and, until 1979, Iran. The United States was an associate member.

Sayyid Qutb's *Signposts*, they had a theoretical tool that provided them with an analysis of the state they were combating and charted the road to its destruction and its replacement by a Muslim state.

In 1965, however, the work was too recent, and probably too theoretical, to have had any real effect on the practice of the reorganized Brotherhood. Moreover, not everyone interpreted *Signposts* in the same way.

The martyrology of the Nasser period is of the utmost importance for the subsequent Islamicist movement. The halo of persecution suffered in defence of a faith and a social ideal confers a status of absolute truth upon Islamicist discourse. Within the movement itself, this martyrology sharpens the contradictions between competing tendencies, which are divided according to their ideological reading — or non-reading — of *Signposts*. Shukri Mustafa, for instance, preached *'uzla*, or withdrawal from society, as a means of avoiding the horror of the camps and gallows. Others took the road of political commitment in a multitude of ways, either collaborating with the regime in an attempt to Islamicize it or entering the world of politics as a sort of opposition, in the hope of avoiding, partly through ties with the regime itself, the spectre of torture and extermination. Still others organized for the forcible seizure of power, hoping that next time they would be able to act before the state could strike back. This was the view of the members of 'Abd al-Salam Faraj's group, who assassinated Sadat in October 1981.

2
'Signposts'

The death of Hasan al-Banna on 12 February 1949, Richard P. Mitchell wrote, had been 'a tragedy of incalculable proportions' for the members of the Society of Muslim Brethren. 'Nothing that befell the Brothers as individuals and groups at the hands of authority had a more debilitating effect on the movement than the loss of its leader' [30]. The subsequent designation of Hasan al-Hudaybi as al-Banna's successor was the result of various compromises between the Palace and the Brotherhood on the one hand and among the Brethren themselves on the other. These machinations adversely affected the Brotherhood's cohesion and also created an ideological vacuum, which in turn gave free rein to the expression of tendencies which, while claiming allegiance to al-Banna's doctrinal legacy, interpreted it in very different ways. The new Supreme Guide, who lacked great intellectual authority, was unable to do any more than bestow or withhold the organization's *imprimatur*.

Between 1949 and 1954 there was a proliferation of works by Muslim Brethren and their fellow-travellers: 'Abd al-Qadir 'Awda, Muhammad al-Ghazali, Sayyid Qutb, al-Bahi al-Khuli, and Muhammad Taha Badawi all sought to continue al-Banna's work in their own writings [7], for the late Supreme Guide had left scarcely a trace of his thought on paper. While he lived, the Brotherhood's founder had decided everything, setting the organization's line in accordance with the evolving political, social, economic, and religious situation. His only significant written works were his autobiography, *Mudhakirrat al-Da'wa wa'l-Da'iyya* ('Memoirs of the Mission and the Missionary'), and a collection of his epistles. This output was simply inadequate to deal with all the problems and challenges the Brotherhood faced after his death, especially when they suffered the persecution of 1954, which took them ideologically unawares. Until 1952, their literature had always identified the British as the enemy, some of the Brethren adding the Palace and capitalism. But it was the Egyptian and Muslim government of the Free Officers that now put them through the 'great ordeal' of 1954. They had no theoretical tools capable of analysing this new regime in terms of the categories of Islam.

It was Sayyid Qutb[1] who filled this ideological vacuum, through the books he wrote in prison between 1954, when he was first incarcerated, and 1964, when he was briefly released, only to be re-arrested, tried, and sentenced to death in 1966. Qutb's last work, *Signposts*, describes the Nasser regime in particularly severe terms, as seen from the vantage point of a man who knew only its concentration camps. The Nasserist state, Qutb argued, belongs to the Islamic category of *jahiliyya*, or pre-Islamic barbarism. That designation placed the regime beyond the bounds of Islam.

In a simple and lucid style, Qutb presented his analysis of the regime and his recommendation of how to destroy it and replace it with an Islamic state. Although conceived on the basis of Qutb's observation of the Nasser regime, the basic analysis of *Signposts* would retain its validity under Nasser's successor as well.

Signposts is therefore a major document offering a direct encounter with the ideology of the Islamicist movement. The actions of the major tendencies of that movement are implicit in the principles it presents, and ultimately it became a manifesto for most Islamicists.

The religious scholars (*ulema*) of al-Azhar and all the various Muslim dignitaries linked to the regime have condemned this last book of Sayyid Qutb as abomination and heresy. The most traditional of the Muslim Brethren consider it a simultaneously fascinating and repellent text, some of whose assertions they consider admirable, others beyond the pale.

1. Some authors transliterate Qutb as 'Qotb' and call *Signposts* 'Signs Along the Path'.

Signposts, in other words, is the royal road to the ideology of
the Islamicist movement of the seventies.

Sayyid Qutb, Author and Martyr

Unlike Hasan al-Banna, Qutb was neither a leader of men nor an
organizer, but an *adib,* or man of letters, who became an ideologue of the Muslim Brotherhood only during the last fifteen
years of his life. The main events of his life illustrate the typical
trajectory of a twentieth-century Egyptian who decides to join
the Muslim Brotherhood, but they also highlight the originality
of his work compared with the doctrinal production of the
Brotherhood's other militants.

Sayyid Qutb was born in September 1906 in the town of
Musha in the governorate of Asyut, in Middle Egypt [20,4]. He
came from a family of rural notables fallen on hard times. In this
large village, with its mixed Muslim and Christian population
and its plethora of small family farms, there were two parallel
education systems: the government schools on the one hand and
the Koranic schools, or *kuttab,* on the other. Although there were
two graduates of al-Azhar on his mother's side of the family,
Sayyid was sent to the state school. He had been horrified by a
brief sojourn in the *kuttab,* and it was on his own that he committed the Koran to memory, before his tenth birthday. His
father, al-Hajj Qutb Ibrahim, was a Musha delegate of Mustafa
Kamil's National Party and a subscriber to the party journal,
al-Liwa' ('The Standard'). Because of the frequent private and
public meetings held in his father's home, Sayyid became politically aware at an early age: sympathetic to anti-British
nationalism, he was a reader of both the press and worldly
works, which he obtained from the local travelling bookseller.
Because of the child's intellectual bent (and since money had to
be found quickly to buy back the family patrimony, which
Sayyid's grandfather had been forced to relinquish piece by
piece), when Sayyid graduated from the Musha school in 1918,
the family decided to send him to Cairo. But the breakdown in
communications caused by the nationalist revolution of 1919
meant that the project had to be postponed until 1921. Sayyid

spent the next four years living with a journalist uncle, a supporter of the Wafd Party, in the suburbs of the capital. Nothing is known of his life during that interlude. In 1925 he enrolled in a teacher-training college. In 1928 and 1929, after graduation, he attended preparatory classes at the *Dar al-'Ulum* (House of Sciences), a modernist teacher-training institute founded in 1872 to compensate for the deficiencies of the Azhar training college, then considered sclerotic. He was formally admitted to the institute in 1930 and graduated in 1933, at the age of twenty-seven. Hasan al-Banna himself had studied at the *Dar al-'Ulum* between 1923 and 1926.

For the next sixteen years, Sayyid was employed by the Ministry of Public Instruction. He began his career teaching in the provinces but was later transferred to Helwan, in the environs of the capital, and decided to make his home there, living with his mother, his two sisters, and his brother. From 1940 to 1948 he served as an inspector for the Ministry. During this time he drafted many projects for the reform of the education system, invariably consigned to the waste-paper basket by his superiors (one of whom, for a time, was the great author Taha Husain).

Sayyid had a kind of parallel career as a man of letters. In fact, his literary and intellectual life was deeply marked by an early encounter with one of the masters of the epoch, Mahmud 'Abbas al-'Aqqad. Unlike Taha Husain and other intellectuals educated in Europe, al-'Aqqad was a self-taught man whose culture was almost exclusively Arab. A journalist, essayist, and novelist, he initially devoted his talents to the cause of the Wafd Party and its leader, Saad Zaghloul. But he distanced himself from the Wafd when Zaghloul was succeeded by Nahhas Pasha, whom al-'Aqqad considered more inclined to demagogy than to democracy. Disenchanted with the masses, whom he considered the dupes of a political class for which he felt only contempt, al-'Aqqad decided to devote the best of his literary output to singing the praises of the great men of Islam.

Sayyid Qutb's evolution was similar to al-'Aqqad's: he began as a member of the Wafd Party, later abandoned it, but remained interested in party politics until 1945 [35]. Until the end of the Second World War, however, he wrote primarily literary criticism. He took an active part in the debates of the thirties and forties, his fiery style highlighting his talents as a polemicist (against Taha Husain, in particular). After 1946, he took his distance from al-'Aqqad and his school.

Sayyid Qutb was a journalist as well as a critic. As early as 1921 al-'Aqqad had given him access to the popular press, in whose columns he published his opinions. But his main interest lay in poetry and the writing of short stories and novels. At least three of his works were autobiographical: *Tifl min al-Qarya* ('Child of the Village'), *al-Atyaf al-Arba'a* ('The Four Apparitions', written in collaboration with his brother, Muhammad, and his sisters, Hamida and Amina), and *Ashwak* '(Thorns'), a veiled account of a deep disappointment in love, after which Qutb resolved to remain a bachelor. He was tormented by this romantic disillusionment 'until he discovered the road of fruitful and constructive action in the service of God's apostolate, as militant, fighter, leader, and finally master' [4].

In 1945, the year in which he abandoned political parties, which he now regarded as remnants of a bygone era, the principal subject matter of his articles shifted from literature to nationalism, political events, and social problems. He brought such ardour to his efforts that he irritated King Farouk himself. The king wanted to imprison him, and Sayyid escaped incarceration only thanks to his old Wafdist connections. Instead he went into a kind of *de facto* exile. In 1948 he was sent for an unlimited stay in the United States, assigned to study the American education system on behalf of the Ministry of Public Instruction. Apparently it was hoped that he would return a supporter of 'the American way of life', but the experience drove him instead closer to Islam, and then to the Muslim Brotherhood.

Standing alone on the deck of the liner carrying him to New York, suddenly cut off from his entire world, Sayyid Qutb rediscovered Islam. Not that his faith had ever really wavered, but he had been temporarily distracted from it by his immoderate love for literature. He began saying his prayers five times a day, and on Friday he assembled and preached to his coreligionists. No sooner had this change occurred within him than the first carnal temptation loomed: returning to his cabin after the *'asha* (evening) prayer, he was accosted by a drunken, half-naked woman who proposed a night's hospitality that our St Anthony refused.

In fact, throughout his stay in the Bogartian America of the late forties, Sayyid was repeatedly embarrassed by a sexual promiscuity that disgusted him. In this country so unforgiving to the disinherited, devoted to the worship of the dollar and devoid of any values that made sense to him, he witnessed outbursts of joy at the assassination of Hasan al-Banna. Upon his return to Egypt in the summer of 1951, he denounced American society so bitterly that he was forced to resign from the Ministry of Public Instruction. He then began frequenting the Muslim Brethren and was ultimately recruited to the Brotherhood by Salih 'Ashmawi late in 1951, at the age of forty-five.

For Sayyid Qutb it was a complete break with the past. 'I was born in 1951', he was later to say. In 1952 he was elected to the Muslim Brotherhood's leadership council (*maktab al-irshad*) and was named head of the department for the propagation of Islam (*nashr al-da'wa*). In the months immediately before and after the 1952 revolution, during the brief honeymoon between the Free Officers and the Muslim Brethren, Sayyid met regularly with Nasser. In August 1952 Sayyid chaired a conference on 'intellectual and emotional emancipation in Islam', attended by everyone who was anyone in revolutionary Cairo, and was warmly congratulated by both Nasser and Neguib, Egypt's first president after the coup. During the subsequent conflict between the Muslim Brethren and the Free Officers, however, he took the side of Supreme Guide Hudaybi, as a result of which he spent the first three months of 1954 in prison. On 3 July 1954 Hudaybi appointed him editor-in-chief of *al-Ikhwan al-Muslimun* ('The Muslim Brethren'), the newspaper that expressed Hudaybi's criticisms of dissident factions within the Brotherhood. Only twelve issues of the paper appeared.

On 26 October the Muslim Brother Mahmud 'Abd al-Latif tried to assassinate Nasser in Alexandria's Menshieh Square. Whether it was a police provocation or a deliberate act, the attack gave the president the perfect excuse for finishing off the Muslim Brethren. Like most of the Brotherhood's militants, Sayyid Qutb was arrested and atrociously tortured. On 13 July 1955, after a farcical trial, he was sentenced to twenty-five years' hard labour, which he began serving in Tura concentration camp, and later in its infirmary. His conditions of detention were relatively flexible, which enabled him to write (and even to have published in pamphlet form in Cairo) his Koranic commentary, *Fi Zalal al-Qur'an* ('Under the Aegis of the Koran'), as well as several other works. As we have seen, in 1962 he began drafting the first chapters of *Signposts*, circulating them among the groupings gathered around the Muslim Sister Zaynab al-Ghazali [12]. Released from prison at the end of 1964 thanks to the intervention of 'Abd al-Salam 'Arif, the Iraqi president then on a state visit to Cairo, Qutb became the pole around which the remaining supporters of the Muslim Brotherhood gathered. In November 1964 *Signposts* was published by Wahba Books. 'As soon as it appeared it was banned', wrote one dyed-in-the-wool Nasserist. 'But the president read all banned books. When he had seen a copy of this one, he summoned the censorship authorities and told them that there was no reason to place it on the forbidden list' [18]. *Signposts* was then reprinted five times in six months, at which point it was banned once again.

When Nasser announced on 30 August 1965 that a 'new Muslim Brotherhood conspiracy' had been uncovered, Sayyid Qutb, considered the ringleader, was arrested again. According to the police, copies of *Signposts* had been found in each and every search. After a summary trial at which the defendants sat broken by torture (which Qutb managed to denounce to the spectators), he and two of his companions were sentenced to death. The three men were hanged at dawn on 29 August 1966. 'If you want to know why Sayyid Qutb was sentenced to death', wrote the Muslim Sister Zaynab al-Ghazali, 'read *Signposts*' [12].

Signposts, then, is the seal of Qutb's life's work, the culmination of an enormous literary production much of which has nothing whatever to do with Islamic preaching. His first specifically Muslim book, 'Artistic Imagery in the Koran'[2] appeared in April 1945, and was preceded and succeeded by many works of fiction and literary criticism. It was not until April 1949, when the first edition of 'Social Justice in Islam' was published, that Qutb devoted the entirety of his writings to Islam, and it was only in 1951 that he became the leading ideologue of the Muslim Brethren.

2. A bibliography of Qutb's works has been appended to this chapter. See p. 68.

Between 1951 and his execution in 1966 Sayyid Qutb wrote eight works of Islamicist doctrine, five of them in prison. *Signposts*, in fact, was not an entirely new production: at least four of its thirteen chapters were taken from 'Under the Aegis of the Koran', the voluminous Koranic commentary written between 1953 and 1964, mostly in prison. Moreover, as we shall see, the concepts used by the author were borrowed from various thinkers. But let us now move to an examination of the ideological content of *Signposts*. How and why did this book become, to take up the metaphor of the Egyptian intellectual Tariq al-Bishri [8], the *What Is to Be Done?* of the Islamicist movement?

Islamicism or Barbarism

The introductory chapter of *Signposts* announces the work's meaning and intent with crystal clarity:

'Humanity today stands on the brink of the abyss . . . not because of the threat of destruction that hangs over its head (for that is merely a symptom of the evil, not the evil itself), but because of its bankruptcy in the domain of the "values" under which man could have lived and developed harmoniously.

'Such is the evidence. Let us consider the Western world, where the "values" held up to humanity as exemplary no longer hold sway. The Western world no longer possesses even that with which it convinces its conscience that it deserves to exist, since its "democracy" has become something that presents all the features of bankruptcy. So true is this that little by little, the West has adopted the system of the Eastern bloc, in particular its economic system: socialism!

'In the East, the situation is similar. . . . The collectivist theories, Marxism first of all, which initially attracted many people, as ideologies embodying a doctrine, have regressed, intellectually speaking, to the point of being reduced to the role of state ideologies, which state stands as far as can be from the doctrinal foundations of these ideologies!' (p.5).

'Humanity needs a new direction!' (p.6).

'In the final analysis, both individualist and collectivist ideologies have failed. Now, at this most critical of times, when turmoil and confusion reign, it is the turn of Islam, of the *umma* [the community of believers] to play its role. . . . Islam's time has come, Islam which does not renounce the material inventions of this world, for it considers them the first function of man, since God has accorded man his lieutenancy over the world, and as a means — under certain conditions — of worshipping God and of realizing the aims of human existence' (p.7).[3]

'Now, Islam can play its role only if it is embodied in a society, in an *umma*. . . . Humanity will not listen, especially in these times, to an abstract belief that cannot be corroborated by tangible facts. The *umma,* however, has been crumbling for several centuries now.

'But the *umma* is not a territory inhabited by Islam, nor is it a homeland whose ancestors are said to have lived according to an Islamic model at some time in the past . . .

'The Muslim *umma* is a collectivity (*jama'a*) of people whose entire lives — in their intellectual, social, existential, political, moral, and practical aspects — are based on Islamic ethics (*minhaj*). Thus characterized, this *umma* ceases to exist if no part of the earth is governed according to the law of God any longer . . .

'Nowadays, the entire world lives in a state of *jahiliyya*[4] as far as the source from which it draws the rules of its mode of existence is concerned, a *jahiliyya* that is not changed one whit by material comfort and scientific inventions, no matter how remarkable.

'The principle on which it is based is opposition to God's rule

3. The virtually Protestant accents of this formulation were remarked upon by the Nasserist functionary who authored *Ma'alim fi Tariq al-Khiyana wa'l-Raj'iyya* ('Signposts to Treason and Reaction', one of the official refutations of the work, published by the Arab Socialist Union). He saw it as evidence that Sayyid Qutb was a supporter of Protestantism, under whose influence he was said to have fallen during his stay in the United States.

4. The term *jahiliyya* can be translated into English only through approximations and paraphrases. As it is used in *Signposts*, it is one of the axes of Sayyid Qutb's view of the world. Derived from the Arabic root meaning 'to be ignorant', this word is used by Muslims to designate the pre-Islamic society of the Arabian peninsula. This society 'was ignorant' of God, until Muhammad's mission. As the orientalist Goldziher has remarked, the concept of *jahiliyya* plays a part in Islamic tradition much akin to that of 'barbarism' in the Western tradition. 'Islamicism or barbarism' would thus be the alternative posited by Qutb.

over the earth and to the major characteristic of the Divinity, namely sovereignty (*al-hakimiyya*): instead it invests men with this, and makes some of them gods for the others. This transference of sovereignty does not occur in the primitive manner of the pre-hegira *jahiliyya*, but by allowing man to unduly arrogate to himself the right to establish values, to legislate, to elaborate systems, and to take positions, all without regard to divine ethics (*minhaj allah lil-hayah*), but rather in accordance with what He has expressly forbidden! Now, to oppose the rule of God in this way is to be the enemy of His faithful.

'The degradation of man in general in the collectivist regimes, the injustice suffered by the individuals and peoples dominated by capital and colonialism, are only the effects of this opposition to the rule of God, the negation of the dignity that God bestowed upon man!' (p.10).

'As for us, we know, without the shadow of a doubt, something completely new which humanity knows not and which it knows not how to construct!

'That being so, this new thing must be concretized in practice and in deed, an *umma* must be brought to life through it . . ., which makes the resurgence of the Muslim countries necessary. This will be followed, sooner or later, by their conquest of world domination.

'How must this Islamic resurrection begin? A vanguard must resolve to set it in motion in the midst of the *jahiliyya* that now reigns over the entire earth. That vanguard must be able to decide when to withdraw from and when to seek contact with the *jahiliyya* that surrounds it.

'If this vanguard is to find its way, it needs signposts to point toward the commencement of its long road, to tell it what role it will have to play to attain its goal, to inform it of its real function. . . . These signposts will likewise tell it what position must be taken towards the *jahiliyya* that reigns over the earth. How should the vanguard define itself relative to that *jahiliyya*? When should it mix with people and when should it separate from them? How and in what terms should it speak the language of Islam to them? . . .

'It is for this long-awaited vanguard that I have written *Signposts*' (p.12).

As is clear from these few extracts, the book aspires to be both an instrument for the analysis of contemporary society and a guide for a vanguard whose task is to inaugurate the resurrection of the *umma*. In short, it is a manifesto.

The point of departure is the observation of the bankruptcy of the West, of both capitalism and socialism. This is a truism of Muslim Brotherhood ideology [30], as is the assertion that the resurrection of Islam holds the solution to humanity's problems. On the other hand, Sayyid Qutb's use of the term *jahiliyya* to characterize the society in which he lives is an innovation that departs from the traditional beliefs of the Muslim Brethren.

Jahiliyya, in fact, is the cornerstone on which the theoretical construction of *Signposts* rests. If it is true that contemporary society can be reduced to pre-Islamic *jahiliyya*, of which it is no more than a sophisticated copy, then Muslims must view it just as the Prophet and his companions viewed their society. Today's vanguard must derive its mode of conduct from their example. The tactic of alternately withdrawing from and seeking contact with the surrounding society, for instance, was used by the Prophet, who chose to emigrate from Mecca to Medina (the *hijra*, or hegira) when he found himself in a weak position, only to return as a conqueror to the city he had earlier abandoned.

Qutb's trans-historical use of the concept of *jahiliyya* marks a notable new departure in Muslim Brotherhood dogma. Al-Banna, for example, never dreamed of accusing the Egyptian society of his day of being non-Islamic. But times had changed, and Egypt — which had lost even its name and was now called the United Arab Republic — was ruled, structured, and corseted by the Nasserist state. The social control exercised by the monarchy and the British occupiers had been far less effective than that of Nasser, who was advised by Soviet experts, masters of the art.

Signposts was written in the concentration camp in which the author spent ten years of his life. He was well acquainted with the underside of 'Arab socialism', the barbed wire and the hangman's noose. In this universe, preaching (*da'wa*) of the kind practised by the Muslim Brethren with such success in the thirties and forties was no longer possible. The totalitarian state now represented the model of *jahiliyya*. Qutb's *jahiliyya* was a society ruled by an iniquitous prince who had made himself an object of worship in God's place and who governed an empire according to his own caprice instead of ruling on the basis of the principles inspired by the Book and the Sayings of the Prophet. It was irrelevant that the whims of the prince were decked out in judicial garb, for that did not make them any less whims. In a long passage of *Signposts* devoted to *jahiliyya* society, Sayyid Qutb offered this definition:

'Any society that is not Muslim is *jahiliyya* . . . as is any society in which something other than God alone is worshipped. . . . Thus, we must include in this category all the societies that now exist on earth!' (p.98).

Qutb then reviewed various types of society, explaining why each was part of the general *jahiliyya*. At the top of the list stand the Communist societies, which deny God and in which the 'object of worship (*'ubudiyya*) is the party, it being understood that in this system the collegial leadership is considered the source of truth'. In these societies, 'human needs are reduced to those of animals'. Next come the various idolatrous societies, in which 'the highest sovereignty (*hakimiyya*) is exercised in the name of the people, in the name of the party, or whatever'. Next come Jewish and Christian societies. Finally, 'the societies that proclaim themselves Muslim must also be placed in the category of *jahiliyya* . . . because in the course of their existence, they do not practise the worship (*'ubudiyya*) of God alone — although they have faith only in Him — but bestow characteristics that belong exclusively to the Divinity upon others beside God. They believe in a sovereignty (*hakimiyya*) other than His. From this they derive their organization, laws, values, judgements, habits, and traditions . . . and nearly all the principles of their existence' (pp. 98–101).

Throughout the text, there is a pairing of concepts that serve as the key to the relation between man and God, and for that very reason to the essence of society as conceived by Sayyid Qutb: *al-'ubudiyya*, or 'worship', and *al-hakimiyya*, 'sovereignty'. These are not Koranic terms. The former is derived from a root meaning 'to adore' or 'worship', the latter from one meaning 'to govern' or 'judge'. Both appear in a work by Abu'l-A'la Mawdudi entitled *al-Mustalahat al-Arba'a fi'l-Qur'an* ('The Four

Technical Terms of the Koran') [29], the aim of which is to trace the original and genuine significance of the Koranic terms *al-ilah, al-rabb, al-'ibada,* and *al-din* ('God', 'Lord', 'worship', and 'religion') as they were understood by the Arabs at the time of Muhammad's mission and not as they have been denatured throughout centuries of decadence. For the Pakistani Mawdudi, one of the causes of the decline of the countries of Islam is precisely that their inhabitants no longer understand the Koranic message as they did at the beginning of the Muslim era. To build a Muslim society therefore requires first and foremost that people learn to read the Koran in its proper context, without attaching excessive importance to the Tradition, which Mawdudi considered sclerotic.

Mawdudi's book was written in 1941 and was first published in instalments in his review, *Tarjuman ul-Qur'an,* in the same year that he founded the *jama'at i islami* in India. In the context, the book's aim was to clarify the association's doctrine and to specify its attitude toward the ruling parties. In other words, its objectives were not dissimilar to those of *Signposts.*

For Qutb, as for Mawdudi, the only legitimate sovereignty in a well-governed (that is, Muslim) polity is that of God (*al-hakimiyya li-llah*). Likewise, He is the sole object of worship (*al-'ubudiyya li-llah*). The regime can exercise sovereignty only in God's name, by applying the prescriptions of revelation (*al-hukm bima anzala allah*). The principle of divine sovereignty is a guarantee against the discretionary power of the ruler: only that which bears the divine seal is just; only legislation governed by the Book (*shari'at allah*) is immune to vitiation and to transformation into mere juridical machinery in the service of a despot.

Jahiliyya society, unlike Muslim society, confers *sovereignty* upon others than God and turns these sovereigns into objects of *worship*. It is characterized by the apotheosis of the holder of power, whether it be man, caste, or party, and by the people's worship of that holder of power.

These two terms, in the sense in which Sayyid Qutb understands them, originate in the writings of Mawdudi, though Qutb uses them as basic concepts in his analysis of *jahiliyya* and Muslim societies, and thus lends them greater force than the Pakistani author had done. Neither *'ubudiyya* nor *hakimiyya* are

Koranic terms, a point made against Mawdudi (and thus also against Qutb) by Supreme Guide Hudaybi. Nevertheless, I would argue that Qutb was quite deliberate in his use of these terms.

By attempting to restore the full connotations of the four Koranic themes, keywords of Islam, during the epoch in which they were first used, by reviving them after freeing them from the gangue in which they had been congealed by the Tradition, Mawdudi effectively declericalized them. At the same time, he sacralized other terms belonging to modern vocabulary and then presented them as equivalent to the terms he was discussing. What was meant by *'ibada* in the Koran, he argued, is far broader than what is understood by the same word today; *'ibada* therefore had to be reconstituted in its complete sense (*al-ma'na al-kamil wa'l-shamil*). To do this meant listing all its various meanings as they would be expressed in modern idiom. These modern words then acquire a sacred resonance, for if the Koran were revealed to a Muhammad today, it would be in these words.

The Koranic term *'ibada,* for instance, is understood by Muslims today in the light of the time-honoured commentaries of the treatises of the Tradition. In this interpretation, it means 'ritual', the codified procedures that express the living creature's relation to God. In Islam this means the profession of faith, prayer, fasting, the giving of alms, and pilgrimage.

According to Mawdudi, however, to grasp the real meaning of the Koranic term *'ibada* we require three equivalent words in current use. These, depending on the context, would provide the most faithful translation: *'ubudiyya* ('worship'), *ita'a* ('submission'), and *ta'alluh* ('deification').

The Koran contains many verses that enjoin Muslims from conferring *'ibada* upon anyone except God. Mawdudi comments as follows on these verses:

'In the verses in which the word *'ibada* has the sense of "worship" (*'ubudiyya*) or "submission", the object of worship is either the devil or rebels [against God] who have made themselves idols (*tawaghit*) and have transformed those who worship God into their own worshippers and servants — in other words, the *imams* and leaders who compel people to live according to rules that they themselves have confected out of whole cloth, while concealing the Book of God behind their backs.

'In the verses in which '*ibada* has the sense of "deification", the reference is to the *jinns*, prophets, statues, angels, and other objects that men have declared divine. The Koran holds that all these things are valueless and that the exclusive object of '*ibada* as "deification" must be God' (pp. 107–08).

Sayyid Qutb's use of the term '*ubudiyya* makes it plain that he has read Mawdudi. The iniquitous prince is the ruler who, in one form or another, has himself worshipped as an idol.

Mawdudi introduces the notion of sovereignty (*al-hakimiyya*) when dealing with the term *rabb* ('lord', with the twofold meaning, both religious and political, that the word also has in English). Here again, his aim is to restore the full semantic range of the original term, which he says has five principal meanings in the Koran. Examining the various erroneous conceptions of the meaning of *rabb* common among non-Islamic nations and tribes, Mawdudi notes:

'Over nearly all the earth, ruling families have relentlessly sought to associate themselves, to a greater or lesser extent, with the Divinity and the Lord, and to cast themselves as part of the supernatural, in addition to their possession of political sovereignty (*hakimiyya*). They seek to constrain their subjects to offer them a sort of worship ('*ubudiyya*), although they did not really aspire to the status of the heavenly Divinity, and actually sought only a pretext for consolidating their political sovereignty (*hakimiyya*). . . . [Pharoah] used to say that he owned Egypt and its riches, that it was his nature to exercise absolute sovereignty over it, and that his person was the linchpin of Egyptian society, wherein no legislation or right other than his own could hold sway' (p. 71).

Mawdudi's intellectual approach here is similar to his treatment of '*ubudiyya*. To be the lord means, among other things, to exercise sovereignty. But sovereignty properly belongs only to God, and the iniquitous prince who exercises it over his subjects has therefore usurped divine power.

The necessary and sufficient criterion for determining whether a given society is Muslim or belongs to *jahiliyya* therefore lies in the sort of '*ubudiyya* (or worship) and *hakimiyya* (or sovereignty) that may be observed within it. In Muslim society, God alone is worshipped and holds sovereignty; in *jahiliyya* societies that status is held by someone or something other than the One True God.

In a chapter entitled 'Civilization Is Islam', Sayyid Qutb expounds his views on societies that call themselves Muslim but are in fact *jahiliyya:*

'For Islam, there are only two kinds of society: Muslim and *jahiliyya*. The Muslim society is that in which Islam is applied. Islam means faith, worship [of God], legislation, social organization, [theory of] creation, [mode of] behaviour. *Jahiliyya* society is that in which Islam is not applied. It is governed neither by belief nor by the Islamic view of the world, nor by its values, [its conception of] equity, its law, its [theory of] creation, and the [modes of] behaviour [proper to it].

'Thus, a society whose legislation does not rest on divine law (*shari'at allah*) is not Muslim, however ardently its individuals may proclaim themselves Muslim, even if they pray, fast, and make the pilgrimage.

'A society that creates a made-to-measure Islam other than that laid down by the Lord and expounded by His Messenger — called, for example, "enlightened Islam" — cannot be considered Muslim either.

'*Jahiliyya* society can present various faces:

' — the negation of the existence of God in favour of explaining history through materialism and contradiction; in other words, the application of the system known as "scientific socialism";

' — the recognition of the existence of God while limiting the domain of His power to the heavens, to the exclusion of the here and now; such a society does not regulate its existence on the basis of divine law nor on the eternal values that He established as its foundation. Although it permits people to worship God in synagogues, churches, and mosques, it prevents them from demanding that divine law govern their existence: it thus either denies God's divine quality on earth or renders it ineffectual. . . . This is likewise a *jahiliyya* society' (pp. 116–17).

Those readers who discovered *Signposts* in the Egypt of the sixties had no difficulty identifying which *jahiliyya* society it was that presented the two faces of 'socialism' and a nominal Islam: it was Nasser's United Arab Republic. In unmasking both these faces, Qutb declared that the regime's claim to Islamic legitimacy was groundless so far as he was concerned.

This claim, in fact, was one of the propaganda themes of the Nasserist state, although most contemporary observers paid little attention to it, deafened as they were by the constant trumpeting of 'Arab socialism' by the local English- and French-speaking elites. Far from embarking upon the 'secularization' for which some yearned, the Nasser regime sought instead to modernize the institutions of official Islam, particularly al-Azhar, in an effort to turn them into the most effective possible transmission belt for state ideology. This was the 'enlightened Islam' upon which Qutb poured his scorn.

Sadat replaced 'Arab socialism' with 'economic opening' (*infitah*), but the regime's second face not only remained but even grew more important over the years. The president sought ever greater legitimation from the institutions of Islam. For the militant Islamicist readers of *Signposts,* however, the sheikh of al-Azhar could promulgate *fatwas* (legal judgements based on the Koran) to his heart's content in an attempt to legitimate the acts of the iniquitous prince, but that changed nothing in the *jahiliyya* character of the regime. The basic concepts laid down by Qutb thus lost none of their applicability with the death of Nasser, nor, for that matter, when extended beyond the borders of Egypt. From the depths of his concentration camp, Qutb was able to fashion categories that could be used to analyse all the world's Muslim states on the morrow of their independence. That was the reason for his considerable success.

What Is To Be Done?

After establishing the concepts of Muslim and *jahiliyya* society, Sayyid Qutb went on to consider the process through which *jahiliyya* could be destroyed and the Muslim state erected on its ruins. It was high time to act, he argued, and in any case 'humanity will pay no heed to abstract beliefs, especially nowadays'.

The restoration of Islam, he wrote, requires a genuine revolution, under the leadership of a 'vanguard of the *umma*' which must take as its example 'the sole Koranic generation', namely the companions of the Prophet. They had taken their intellectual sustenance from the Koran alone, and were thus able to build the ideal Islamic society during the golden age of the 'rightly guided caliphs', the Prophet's first four successors. The moment the Muslims turned their attention to the cultures of the Byzantine and Persian Sassanid empires, their thought was adulterated. The evils began with the fifth caliph, Mu'awiya, the founder of the Umayyad dynasty.

Today's vanguard, said Qutb, must contemplate the Koran and must shun non-Muslim culture. The vanguard must begin by purging its own consciousness of *jahiliyya*:

'We must return to and assimilate the Koran, in order to apply it, to put it into practice . . . in order to understand what it demands of us, in short, in order to be! . . . Next, we must sweep away the influence of *jahiliyya* on our souls, eliminating it from our manner of thinking, of judging, our customs' (pp. 21–22).

Once freed from the alienation caused by *jahiliyya* society and inspired by contemplation of the Koran alone, the vanguard will be ready to act:

'Our first task is to change society in deed, to alter the *jahiliyya* reality from top to bottom. . . . To start with, we must get rid of this *jahiliyya* society, we must abandon its values and ideology, and must not enfeeble our own values and ideology by even one iota to bring them closer to it! Certainly not! Our paths diverge, and if we took even a single step toward it, our ethics would vanish and we would be lost!' (p.22).

The process of transition from *jahiliyya* to Islam unfolds in this way:

'A man has faith in this credo, which emanates from a hidden source and is enlivened by the power of God alone; the virtual existence of the Islamic society begins with the faith of this one man. . . . This one man, however, receives the revelation not in order merely to turn in on himself, but to carry its spirit too: such is the nature of this credo. . . . The immense power that has carried it into this soul knows with certainty that it will carry it further still . . .

54

'When three believers have been touched by the faith, this credo means to them: "you are now a society, an independent Islamic society, separate from the *jahiliyya* society, which does not have faith in this credo . . .". From that moment, the Islamic society exists in deed. The three become ten, the ten a hundred, the hundred a thousand, and the thousand twelve thousand . . . thus the Islamic society emerges and takes root. In the meantime, the battle begins between this nascent society that has declared its secession . . . from *jahiliyya* society and the latter, away from which it has carried men. . . .

'What characterizes both the Islamic credo and the society inspired by it is that they become a movement (*haraka*) that will allow no one to stand apart . . .; the battle is constant, and the sacred combat (*jihad*) lasts until Judgement Day' (pp. 129–30).

For purposes of analysis, two stages may be distinguished in the procession from the birth of the vanguard to the establishment of the Islamic society: that of spiritual maturation (the phase of Koranic inspiration whose aim is to free the subject from *jahiliyya* alienation) and that of the battle against this *jahiliyya* society. The concept of *jihad* encompasses this flux in its totality, from the personal effort to contemplate the Book to combat arms-in-hand.

In a long chapter of *Signposts* entitled *al-jihad fi sabil allah* ('The Sacred Combat in the Path of God'),[5] Qutb explains that he intends this concept in its full range of meanings, unlike those 'defeatists' who would soften it either by reducing it to 'defensive war' (so as not to frighten non-Muslims) or by limiting it to the solitary inner combat of the believer against temptation (so as to avoid the tribulations of contact with the real world). Granted, he continues, Islam seeks to liberate man from the degradation into which he is cast by his passions, but it must also be a weapon with which he may free himself from the yoke imposed by certain of his fellow men.

5. Since 1981, this and the preceding chapter have been expunged from the most widely circulated edition of *Signposts*, published by the Egyptian-Lebanese company Dar al-Shourouk. They have been replaced by other, less vigorous pages of Qutb's writings. In citing extracts from these chapters I have used a different edition; this is indicated in the references by the letter *a*.

Such is the function of *jihad*, and it would be illusory to believe that it can be waged by discourse alone:

'To establish the reign of God on earth and eliminate the reign of man, to take power out of the hands of those of His worshippers who have usurped it and to return it to God alone, to confer authority upon divine law (*shari'at allah*) alone and to eliminate the laws created by man . . . all this will not be done through sermons and discourse. Those who have usurped the power of God on earth and made His worshippers their slaves will not be dispossessed by dint of Word alone, otherwise the task of His messengers would be far more easily done' (*a*, pp. 60–61).

The task of what Qutb calls 'the movement' (*al-haraka*) is to remove the material obstacles in the path of the vanguard:

'Discourse (*bayan*) opposes [erroneous] doctrines and concepts, while it is the "movement" that overturns material obstacles, the political system in the first place' (*a*, p. 61).

The insistence with which Sayyid Qutb reiterates that the establishment of 'the reign of God on earth' cannot be brought about 'through sermons and discourse' is revealing of the context in which *Signposts* was written: faced with the totalitarian state being created by Nasserism, Islamicist militants must not limit themselves to words alone. Qutb's contribution to the theoretical legacy of the more traditional Muslim Brethren was his clear perception of the structural change in the relation between the state and civil society that had been inaugurated with the Nasser regime. Before 1952, most Egyptian governments had not seriously impeded the preaching of al-Banna and his disciples. The Muslim Brethren were able to proclaim their hatred of British colonialism, their contempt for the local Westernized elites, and their hostility to the political parties. But once the independent state had decked itself in the colours of 'Arab socialism' and critics were forced to choose between silence, exile, prison, and the gallows, Brotherhood propaganda became impossible. Qutb held that those who chose silence or who muted their voices were in error. The mode of action had instead to be adapted to the form of state repression: against *jahiliyya*, the militants of the Islamicist movement, the 'vanguard of the *umma*', had to resort to a 'movement', to a struggle that would not be purely verbal.

By pairing the terms 'movement' and 'discourse', Qutb referred implicitly to the propagation of Islam by 'the sword' and 'the Book', the two being essentially complementary. Historically, each of these instruments had had its appropriate field of application: the sword served to subdue territories ruled by non-Muslims, and within those territories to compel pagans to convert, on penalty of death. Jews and Christians, on the other hand, were not forcibly converted to Islam. They were instead supposed to be brought to the faith by the power of the Book alone — in other words, by preaching. (In reality, conversions were probably motivated primarily by the fiscal advantages of membership of the Muslim community.)

In the context of twentieth-century Egypt, Muslim Brotherhood propaganda was generally addressed to the Muslim masses more than to the Coptic Christian minority, and still less to the Jews. The majority of the population, although Muslim, had forgotten that Islam was a total and complete system, and instead restricted religion to the domain of private piety. The objective of the Brotherhood's message was to lead them to a rediscovery of this broader significance of Islam.

But the Free Officers' coup, followed within a few years by the establishment of the Nasserist state, changed all that. The state persecuted the Brethren, and thereby became, in their minds, the quintessential enemy of Islam. For the author of *Signposts,* tha propagation of Islam now required a shift of both field of action and instrument. The Book was no longer indicated: it was time for the sword. It was a *jahiliyya* regime, which had to be fought in the way pagans were fought.

Sayyid Qutb incurred considerable risk in embarking on a step which the *ulema* had hesitated to take throughout the history of Islam. To declare that the prince stood outside Islam was to excommunicate him, and excommunication was a dangerous weapon indeed, for it could all too easily fall into the hands of sects beyond the control of the *ulema* and the clerics.

Sayyid Qutb's premature death on the gallows, however, effectively placed his ideas, with all the imprecision they still contained, in the public domain; the weapon of excommunication thus fell neatly into the hands of uncontrollable sectarians.

Moreover, Qutb had left his definition of *jahiliyya* open-ended. Were the iniquitous prince and his bureaucracy its sole representatives, or was the entire society thus condemned? In other words, could any individual still be considered a Muslim?

Questions like this may seem no more than casuistic controversies. But the various components of the Islamicist movement of the seventies formulated different strategies depending on how they answered them. In the real world, these took the form of *coups d'état,* resocialization, or agitation on the university campuses.

Sayyid Qutb's *Signposts* marked out the starting point of the road along which the militants of the Islamicist movement would travel. But his torture and death interrupted his philosophical speculation, and his readers continued on that road guided only by chance wanderings and ideological patchworks, often losing their way, drifting into impasse, and winding up on the gallows or behind prison bars.

When Sayyid Qutb wrote *Signposts,* he was observing the Egyptian independent state from the very special vantage point of one of its concentration camps. A product of these 'objective conditions', the manifesto of the Islamicist movement was also part of a long tradition of criticism of the established regimes in the land of Islam.

Although there had always been many *ulema* who acted in complicity with the rulers, a significant number of them had fearlessly stigmatized what they saw as the abuses of the various dynastic or military regimes that ruled the countries of the House of Islam. Though a minority, this category of clerics nevertheless provided Muslim society with its most celebrated and vigorous jurisconsults and traditionalists down through the years.

Since the *ulema* spoke in God's name and based their judicial pronouncements on the Koran, they had considerable power to confer legitimacy upon a ruler or to withdraw it. Any opponent of a ruler who obtained the support of the *ulema* gained considerable credibility, especially if he was himself recognized as one of the *ulema* and denounced in God's name the regime he sought to overthrow. This is why the *ulema* were gathered together in institutions whose function was precisely to control access to religious status and to delimit the number and quality of those who were recognized as competent to issue legal judgements based on the Book. But these institutions have not always succeeded in maintaining the independence from the executive power required by the sublime character of their functions. In the modern era, moreover, the corps of *ulema* as such has generally exhibited noticeable intellectual ossification. There has consequently been room for Muslim thinkers whose initial training was not controlled by the institutions that officially dispense religious knowledge. These institutions have tended to react to this phenomenon either by coopting these thinkers or by stigmatizing them as heretics.

Hasan al-Banna and Sayyid Qutb were both graduates of *Dar al-'Ulum*, a secular secondary school, and neither of them ever studied at al-Azhar, Egypt's leading mosque and university. But although al-Banna was ultimately accepted by the *ulema*, albeit posthumously, Qutb never received any such recognition. On the contrary, the author of *Signposts* was placed on the index, the most common method by which al-Azhar has dealt with the problem of the Islamicist movement. In fact, his heretical genealogy was traced all the way back to the Kharijites, and Qutb himself was declared a deviant (*munharif*).

The Kharijites were the members of Islam's oldest religious sect. They were originally among the supporters of 'Ali, the fourth and last of the 'rightly guided caliphs', during the battle of Siffin (July 657) between 'Ali and Mu'awiya, the governor of Syria, future caliph, and founder of the Umayyad dynasty. When Mu'awiya proposed to halt the killing and to resort to arbitration by two representatives who would settle the dispute 'in accordance with the Koran', the majority of 'Ali's army accepted. But one group of combatants refused, declaring that 'judgement belongs to God alone'. They abandoned 'Ali's army, and were ultimately joined by others of his former partisans who were embittered when the arbitrators decided in Mu'awiya's favour.

The Kharijites subsequently split into a multiplicity of sects, whose common denominator was their claim that believers had to denounce as illegitimate any *imam*, or Muslim leader, who no longer followed the line of the Koran. They also maintained that faith without deeds was devoid of validity, and that Muslims who sinned were apostates. They pronounced *takfir*, or excom-

munication, against such people. The history of Kharijism soon
became one of confrontation with the established powers, which
earned them the repression of the princes. The other side of their
permanent revolt against any infidel regime was their own in-
capacity to establish a viable state for any length of time. Against
the Kharijites, the *ulema* always chose the state, for the state —
however evil and iniquitous, and even if issued of violence or
dynastic succession — at least defended Muslim society against
infidels. It was up to the doctors of religion to correct the prince,
to rectify his practices through their sage advice, and to criticize
him when they felt it necessary. But the excommunication of the
prince, be he the worst of despots, was pronounced only excep-
tionally, for it opened the prospect of considerable disorder and
created dangerous jurisprudential precedents.

The thinkers of the contemporary Islamicist movement in
Egypt reacted variously to their placement on the forbidden
index. Qutb, for instance, and Faraj, the theoretician of the
group that assassinated Sadat, appealed directly to medieval
Tradition and denied any relation to the Kharijites. Shukri
Mustafa, the leader of the Society of Muslims, rejected the entire
Tradition and appealed directly to the Koran.

Such were the terms of an important debate about Islam as a
force that could legitimate or withhold legitimacy from the
political regime. This debate remains a burning issue in Muslim
countries in the second half of the twentieth century.

The Ulema Intervene

Nasser's opinion of the author of *Signposts* was clear enough.
The iniquitous prince, who had usurped God's sovereignty and
made himself the object of worship of his subjects, had the
Islamicist theoretician hanged on 29 August 1966. Sayyid Qutb
thereby acquired the status of *shahid,* or martyr, in the eyes of his
admirers. It became difficult to discuss his personality and work
in any but the most passionate terms. For the civilian and religious functionaries of the Nasser regime, no insult was too
strong to add to the already tarnished memory of this dead
reactionary, a traitor who had been justly punished. Among the

Muslim Brethren hagiography was the rule, despite the notorious differences some Brethren had had with the audacity of *Signposts*.

The furiously indignant reaction of the Egyptian Islamic establishment was given free rein in *Minbar al-Islam* ('The Rostrum of Islam'), the journal published by the Ministry of Waqfs (a *waqf* is a religious property), and in various books released during Qutb's trial. The most authoritative view was expressed, at the behest of Hasan Ma'mun, the sheikh of al-Azhar, by Sheikh Muhammad 'Abd al-Latif al-Sibki, the president of the *fatwa* commission. Sheikh Sibki noted that although at first sight *Signposts* might appear to be a work appealing for Islam, one was soon put off by its 'inflammatory style', with its disastrous effects on the young and on readers whose Islamic culture was deficient.

The book was contested chapter and verse. The sheikh declared that it was blasphemous to describe as *jahiliyya* any period except that which closed with Muhammad's mission. He then charged Sayyid Qutb with Kharijism:

'Like the Kharijites, Qutb employs the concept of *al-hakimiyya li-llah* to call upon Muslims to oppose any earthly sovereignty.' The sheikh, on the contrary, argued that the Koran preaches obedience to the Muslim sovereign, who in return causes justice to reign among his subjects. Moreover, 'most of the contemporary leaders of the countries of Islam are good'.

As for *jihad*, Qutb treats it as a declaration of war against all those who do not think as he does, in order to establish a Muslim society of which he would be the leader. Finally, 'although in style [the book] is packed with verses from the Koran and references to Muslim history, in truth it is no more than the style of the saboteur, of the sort of person who, in any society, mixes truth and falsehood the better to dissimulate'. This book, 'intended to delude the simple-minded and to turn them into fanatics and blind assassins', must be considered in the light of recent events (a reference to the Muslim Brotherhood 'conspiracy' of 1965):

'If we draw the connection between Sayyid Qutb's preaching (*da'wa*) and recent events, and if we view it in the light of the Egyptian revolution [meaning Nasserism] and the stirring triumphs it has registered in all domains, then it becomes clear that the message of the Brethren is no more than a plot against our revolution under the guise of religious zeal, and that those who act to propagate it or who pay heed to it are seeking to prejudice the nation, to cause it to regress and to inflict calamities upon it' [18].

This text ruled out any possibility of the regime's coopting Qutb's thought, which was not the case for some of the other currents of the Islamicist movement. It also bestowed upon *Signposts* the prestigious status of a work regarded as dangerous to the existing regime.

Of greater interest are the refutations of the work produced within the Islamicist movement itself, by members of its reformist component. In chapter 1 it was mentioned that the Supreme Guide had given his *imprimatur* to the text, telling Zaynab al-Ghazali that the book 'vindicated all the hopes he had placed in Sayyid' [12]. Nevertheless, the first major reaction to *Signposts* from within the ranks of the Muslim Brotherhood, in 1969, was a work by Hudaybi, the Supreme Guide himself, intended to correct the errors of 'certain' Brethren. *Du'ah, la Qudah* ('Preachers, Not Judges'), like *Signposts,* was written in one of the concentration camps in which the Brethren were imprisoned after 1965. The tortures they suffered there had nurtured the idea of *takfir,* or excommunication, among the youngest of the prisoners. In their eyes, neither their torturers nor the rulers who gave them their orders could be considered Muslims, nor could people who failed to revolt against these unjust rulers [5]. Hudaybi wrote his book in an effort to lead errant young Islamicists back to the straight and narrow. It contains explicit criticism of Mawdudi's 'The Four Technical Terms of the Koran', but reading between the lines, it is not difficult to detect a refutation of certain passages of *Signposts.*

Everyone was well aware of this, not least Muhammad Qutb, who in 1975 published a long letter in *al-Shihab,* the organ of the Lebanese branch of the Brotherhood, in which he defended the memory of his brother, Sayyid, against those who accused him of having expressed ideas contrary to the doctrine of the Muslim Brethren: 'I myself heard him say more than once: "We are preachers and not judges. Our objective is not to legislate against people, but to teach them this truth: that there is no god but God. The problem is that people do not understand what this formula requires of them." '

According to Hudaybi, the task of the Brethren was to preach Islam in the society in which they lived. He did not characterize that society as *jahiliyya*, but merely noted that many Muslims remained in a state of *juhl*, or ignorance. These two words, *jahiliyya* and *juhl*, stem from the same root, but whereas the former is rich in connotations for the Muslim mind, the latter means no more than ignorance of the sort that can be remedied by mere preaching. As Hudaybi recalled, all that was required to be a Muslim was to pronounce the two professions of faith, 'There is no god but God' and 'Muhammad is His messenger'. There are Muslim sinners, of course, but one hardly excommunicates a Muslim merely because he has sinned.

In recalling this principle, which he argued was based upon the Koran and various *hadiths* (sayings of the Prophet), Hudaybi contradicted Mawdudi, who maintained that the profession of faith was misunderstood today, for it had to be not merely pronounced but also translated into action before anyone uttering it could be called a Muslim.

Hudaybi also argued against Qutb's position in *Signposts* that no one is a Muslim simply by virtue of saying so: 'A society whose legislation is not based on divine law is not Muslim, however much its individuals may proclaim themselves Muslim and however much they pray, fast, and make the pilgrimage.'

Here we come to the crux of the problem that divided the Islamicist movement, at this time and throughout Sadat's rule: the 'revolutionaries' believed that Egyptian society was *jahiliyya* in the strong sense, meaning that the 'movement' was the proper instrument for the propagation of Islam, while the 'reformists' held that 'preaching' alone would lead Muslim society, now ignorant of the universal validity of the Koran's rules, back to Islam.

The problem assumed a more practical form in their divergent assessments of the nature of the Egyptian political system under Nasser and his successor. Would the Brethren be permitted to preach or not? Hudaybi and, after his death, the neo-Muslim

Brethren grouped around 'Umar Talmasani and the journal *al-Da'wa* responded in the affirmative. They held that the Nasserist state was not structurally different from its predecessor. Sayyid Qutb and the young Islamicists who read his works, however, answered in the negative. They held that the independent state represented the reign of *jahiliyya*, of barbarism under the aegis of an iniquitous prince. Words were of no use against such a regime, and Islam could now be propagated only by the 'movement'.

Jahiliyya is a Koranic term. For Hudaybi it therefore had the weighty status of a concept whose true significance had to be properly grasped. But things were quite otherwise with the term *hakimiyya* (sovereignty), which Mawdudi used as a contemporary equivalent of the Koranic term *rabb* (lord) in the expression *al-hakimiyya li-llah*, 'no sovereignty but God's'.

The Supreme Guide believed that Mawdudi's entire approach was misguided, that there was in fact no need to seek contemporary equivalents of the four Koranic terms, since the Tradition had continuously glossed them throughout the history of Islam. Their meaning was therefore perfectly clear. Moreover, it was senseless to define the credo of Islam on the basis of the criterion of *hakimiyya*, to state as a matter of principle that only those who believe that there is no sovereignty but God's are Muslims: 'There are some who base their faith on a term unattested by any passage of the Book or any of the sayings of the Prophet, a word of human fabrication, a word that is not sacrosanct and is therefore the repository of error and illusion' [15] .

Mawdudi is subjected to criticism throughout Hudaybi's book, but Qutb is never identified as his spiritual heir. The martyr was untouchable, and it was not until 1982 that Talmasani wrote, 'Sayyid Qutb represented himself alone and not the Muslim Brethren.' Throughout the sixties and seventies, the 'reformist' wing of the Muslim Brotherhood was both fascinated and embarrassed by Qutb's work. Indeed, the movement never again produced any thinker of Qutb's stature. Both *Signposts* and *Under the Aegis of the Koran*, Qutb's Koranic commentary, were massively and avidly read, but the young Islamicist militants interpreted them in a fashion that hardly conformed to the dominant current of thought within the Muslim Brotherhood.

After Hudaybi's contribution, a number of the older Brethren also sought to comment on Qutb's work. All these essays are variations on a single theme, first stated in the letter sent by Sayyid's own brother, Muhammad, to the Lebanese journal *al-Shihab*. This letter was a defence and illustration of the 'martyr's' thought and also provided a key for the reading of it in a minor mode. 'There is nothing in his [Sayyid's] writings', wrote Muhammad, 'that contradicts the Koran and the Sunna, on which the mission of the Muslim Brethren is based, . . . there is nothing in his writings that contradicts the ideas of the martyr *Imam* Hasan al-Banna, founder of the Brotherhood, in particular al-Banna's comment in his letter 'Teachings' (*Risalat al-Ta'lim*), chapter 20: "It is not permitted to excommunicate a Muslim who pronounces the two professions of faith, acts according to their requirements, and accomplishes the ritual obligations." '

As al-Banna's spiritual heir, Sayyid Qutb could never be the model thinker for those, like the twentieth-century Kharijites, who sought withdrawal from society. Only a misinterpretation of Sayyid's writings could sustain such a claim: 'As for the problem of "separation" (*al-mufasala*), his words make it clear that what is meant is the "spontaneous" mental withdrawal of the pious and practising Muslim (*al-muslim al-multazim*) from those who do not feel bound by Islam's obligations, and not actual material separation. It is to the society in which we live that we preach Islam, and if we removed ourselves from it, how could we preach to it?'

In this letter, Muhammad Qutb seeks to steer his brother's thought between two reefs: on the one hand, the 'extremists' of the Islamicist movement, in particular those of Shukri Mustafa's Society of Muslims,[6] whose *hijra*, or withdrawal from *jahiliyya*, could not be based on Qutb's views, and on the other hand the ultra-moderates, like Hudaybi, who resisted taking *Signposts* literally and skirted the questions it raised by directing their attacks against Mawdudi, whom they implicitly assimilated to Sayyid Qutb.

After the publication of this letter, the authors belonging to the 'reformist' current of the Islamicist movement made great efforts

6. See chapter 3.

to produce exegeses of Qutb's text. While not denying that the most extremist 'revolutionary' current was inspired by Qutb, they also sought to demonstrate that this inspiration actually arose from a defective reading of Qutb's work. It was therefore incumbent upon them to present the gloss that would restore its original significance.

The object of their interpretation of *Signposts* and *Under the Aegis of the Koran* was to deny any spiritual link between Qutb and the most extremist militants of the Islamicist movement of the seventies. Toward this end they used three main procedures. First, they compared what seemed to be the most 'heretical' passages of Qutb's work with other passages proclaiming adherence to dogma, and then tried to resolve the ambiguity of the former in favour of the clarity of the latter. Second, they analysed the controversial terms and expressions in such a way as to limit their devastating effects and to reintegrate them into the Tradition. Third, when parts of Qutb's work proved resistant to either of these exercises, they simply affirmed that the author of *Signposts* was after all only a man and not a prophet: he was therefore fallible.

The best interpretation of Qutb in this 'reformist' spirit was produced by Yusif al-'Azm, one of the most prominent personalities of the Jordanian Muslim Brotherhood and the author of a well-documented biography [4]. Al-'Azm argued that blind hagiography did no service to Qutb: the master was a man, and therefore fallible, and it was not sacrilegious to discuss his ideas. On the contrary, they had to be expounded clearly, so that there would be no mistake, and whatever was open to criticism had to be criticized. Passionate condemnation and stubborn defence of his errors were equally wrong. These potential errors were contained in two works which, Yusif al-'Azm points out, were written while their author was in prison suffering ordeals that few could have endured: *Under the Aegis of the Koran* and *Signposts*.

'Some think that he [Sayyid Qutb] excommunicated all Muslims who were not active in the ranks of his Society [*jama'a*] or of the "movement" that was working, through that Society, for Islam, and that he considered the contemporary societies of the Muslim world as societies whose individuals, governments, and organizations were part of *jahiliyya*.' In Yusif al-'Azm's view, a distinction had to be made between excommunication and *jahiliyya*. Qutb uses *jahiliyya* to refer to intellectual, moral, and ethical underdevelopment. In this sense, it is quite legitimate to call today's society *jahiliyya*, and preachers can do so, provided that it is quite clear that this does not mean that the society merits excommunication. In Yusif al-'Azm's exegesis the vanguard of the *umma* is not a sect that excommunicates society, but a group of elite individuals who 'care for' their fellow citizens, contaminated as they are by defects of non-Muslim origin. In the same vein, the *'uzla* — separation or withdrawal — preached by Qutb in his introductory chapter, where he writes that 'the vanguard must know when to separate itself from people', is reduced to the status of mere 'spiritual abstraction'.

But some of Qutb's concepts could not be tailored to fit al-'Azm's interpretation. In such cases, he argued, there must be no hesitation in admitting that Qutb made mistakes. For example: 'That the countries in which we Muslims live constitute the House of Islam and that their populations are Muslim are truths that cannot be denied.' Now, if Qutb declined to include the contemporary societies 'that claim to be Muslim' in *Dar al-Islam*, it was because of the circumstances in which he wrote, the outrageous torture to which he was subjected in the Nasserist concentration camps. In general, al-'Azm argued, the formulations of *Signposts* should not be taken absolutely literally. Qutb was an author and not a *faqih* (doctor of religious law), and he was sometimes carried away by his own style. That is why his works should never be published without commentary, and the man best placed to fulfil the task of exegesis is Sayyid's brother, Muhammad Qutb.

At bottom, Yusif al-'Azm's position reveals the ambiguous attitude towards Qutb of the most consistent of the Muslim Brethren. Al-'Azm's office in Amman is decorated with a large portrait depicting the 'martyr' behind bars, his face haggard and full of sorrow but illuminated by an intensity of expression. At the same time, commentaries in hand, he seeks to locate the author of *Signposts* in a line of descent from al-Banna and to absolve him of the sins of Shukri Mustafa's Society of Muslims, while also conceding that the martyr must be criticized on certain points.

This chapter has done no more than present texts and situate the protagonists of the ideological debate aroused by *Signposts*. The works of Qutb and his detractors, of course, could easily be read and re-read at greater length,[7] their Koranic quotations compared, the place of their views in the history of Muslim doctrine examined. But the purpose here is different. At this point we must examine how the visionary constructs of those texts were articulated with, and transmitted to, the social reality of Egypt in the seventies.

7. See, in particular, Olivier Carré, *Mystique et politique*, 'revolutionary reading of the Koran by Sayyid Qutb, radical Muslim Brother', Presses de la Fondation Nationale des Sciences Politiques and Editions du Cerf, Paris 1984.

Appendix
Works of Sayyid Qutb

Twenty-one works by Sayyid Qutb were published during his lifetime. The following list gives dates of publication when known, according to Khalidi. Pamphlets written for the Ministry of Public Instruction have been omitted.

1. *Mahammat al-Sha'ir fi'l-Hayah wa Shi'r al-Jil al-Hadir* ('The Task of the Poet in Life and the Poetry of the Contemporary Generation'), 1933, literary criticism.

2. *Al-Shati al-Majhul* ('The Unknown Beach'), January 1933, poetry.

3. *Naqd Kitab: Mustaqbal al-Thaqafa fi Misr* ('Critique of a Book [by Taha Husain]: the Future of Culture in Egypt'), 1939, literary criticism.

4. *Al-Taswir al-Fanni fi'l-Qur'an* ('Artistic Imagery in the Koran'), April 1945, literary and religious criticism.

5. *Al-Atyaf al-Arba'a* ('The Four Apparitions'), 1945, autobiographical narrative, in collaboration with his brother and sisters.

6. *Tifl min al-Qarya* ('Child of the Village'), 1946, autobiography.

7. *Al-Madina al-Mashura* ('The Enchanted City'), 1946, short stories.

8. *Kutub wa Shakhsiyyat* ('Books and Personalities'), 1946, literary criticism.

9. *Ashwak* ('Thorns'), 1947, romantic novel, autobiographical.

10. *Mashahid al-Qiyama fi'l-Qur'an* ('Aspects of Resurrection in the Koran'), April 1947, religion.

11. *Al-Naqd al-Adabi: Usuluhu wa Manahijuhu* ('Literary Criticism: Its Foundations and Methods'), 1948.

12. *Al-'Adala al-Ijtima'iyya fi'l-Islam* ('Social Justice in Islam'), 1949, politico-religious work.

13. *Ma'arakat al-Islam wa'l-Ra's Maliyya* ('The Battle Between Islam and Capitalism'), February 1951, Islamicist doctrine.

14. *Al-Salam al-'Alami wa'l-Islam* ('World Peace and Islam'), October 1951, Islamicist doctrine.

15. *Fi Zalal al-Qur'an* ('Under the Aegis of the Koran'), first instalment October 1952, Koranic commentary.

16. *Dirasat Islamiyya* ('Islamic Studies'), 1953, Islamicist doctrine.

17. *Hadha'l-Din* ('This Religion'), n.d. (after 1954), Islamicist doctrine.

18. *Al-Mustaqbal li-hadha'l-Din* ('The Future of This Religion'), n.d. (after 1954), Islamicist doctrine.

19. *Khasais al-Tasawwar al-Islami wa Muqawamatuhu* ('The Characteristics and Values of Islamic Conduct'), 1960, Islamicist doctrine.

20. *Al-Islam wa Mushkilat al-Hadara* ('Islam and the Problems of Civilization'), n.d. (after 1954), Islamicist doctrine.

21. *Ma'alim fi'l-Tariq* ('Signposts'), 1964.

3
The Society of Muslims

Between 4 July and 1 December 1977, the Egyptian press —
otherwise preoccupied with heaping laurels upon Sadat, the
'peace president', for his visit to Jerusalem in November —
offered its readers daily photographs of bearded young men
accused of belonging to a group of terrorist guerrillas called
Takfir wa'l-Hijra (Excommunication and Hegira).[1] A long list of
offences and crimes was attributed to the group, not the least of
which was the kidnapping and assassination of Muhammad
al-Dhahabi, a religious scholar and former minister of waqfs.

Both the particular form of the violence — hostage-taking was
unprecedented in Egyptian political life — and its fatal outcome
seemed inexplicable: in the name of what sort of fanaticism
would Muslims execute one of their own coreligionists? What
kind of Islam did they have in mind? Later, when the arrest and
interrogation of suspects enabled the public to form a clearer
idea of the sect's practices and mores, the ideology of its leader
(an agronomist named Shukri Mustafa), and the scope of its
recruitment, Egyptian society was scandalized.

The mere existence of this sect was a social phenomenon. But
the political consequences of the manner and timing of its conflict with the state came to constitute an important link in the
chain of events that made 1977 a watershed year for the Sadat
regime. The confrontation between the regime and the Society of
Muslims, coming as it did between the January riots against
price increases and the president's speech to the Knesset in
November, prefigured the battle the government would later

1. The group's real name was Society of Muslims (*Jama'at al-Muslimin*).

wage against the Islamicist movement, whose mass organizations refused to accept 'the shameful peace with the Jews'.

Before the onset of the peace process, relations between these two protagonists of Egyptian political life were fairly cordial. The regime treated the 'reformist' wing of the Islamicist movement — grouped around the monthly magazine *al-Da'wa* and represented on the university campuses by the *jama'at islamiyya* (Islamic Associations) — with a benevolence that was well reciprocated, as the Islamicists 'purged' the universities of anything that smelled of communism or Nasserism. Meanwhile, the marginal, sectarian wing of the movement was accorded a tolerance tempered by discreet police infiltration: the regime's aim was to offer Islamicist dissidents some outlet other than planning *coups d'états,* the dangers of which had been highlighted by the abortive uprising of April 1974 at the Heliopolis Military Academy.

In 1977, however, this mutual tolerance soured into antagonism. The enmity provoked by Sadat's trip to Jerusalem mounted steadily until it climaxed in the conflagration of summer 1981 and its sequel, the assassination of Sadat by Islamicist bullets on 6 October of that year. The confrontation between the regime and the Shukri Mustafa group, played for all it was worth by the government's media serfs, was a prelude to this process. Two voices were prominent in this clash, representing two institutions that challenged Shukri and his sect's claim to a monopoly on normative discourse: al-Azhar and the army. The latter eventually held sway over the former, and the military court that handled the case had the last word.

The court took care to circumscribe the affair, which had begun as social and religious in nature, and later impinged on politics. The judiciary, however, was determined to confine it to the criminal domain. The social, religious, and political aspects of the case were buried in a great flood of writings *about* Shukri, while his own words were distorted or concealed.

And God Came to Shukri

Signposts was a prison work, and it was prisoners who, between 1965 and 1971, made it their manifesto, or at least the source of their inspiration in the development of their own doctrine.

The aspiration for a Muslim society, the qualification of Egyptian society as *jahiliyya*, and the belief that this society had to be destroyed and a Muslim society erected on its ruins lay at the root of Shukri Mustafa's thought. Most Egyptian observers of the Islamicist movement attributed the doctrine elaborated by Shukri Mustafa during his imprisonment to the virtually instinctive reactions of an unjustly incarcerated prisoner. Were that the case, however, it would be hard to understand the longevity of these ideas after their author's release in 1971. Shukri and his followers preached and recruited in a country whose president had solemnly affirmed that the Nasser regime's concentration camps were a thing of the past. Sadat's Egypt no longer punished 'crimes of opinion' as Nasser's had, but the *jahiliyya* model remained meaningful nevertheless. As far as the Islamicists were concerned, the 'worship of man by man' and the 'sovereignty of man over man', still prevailed, albeit in an altered form.

The police raids of 1965 had swept up not only former Muslim Brethren who had been arrested before back in 1954, imprisoned, and finally released after serving their sentences (and who therefore had police records), but also an entire generation of people who had either escaped imprisonment, like Zaynab al-Ghazali, or had not yet reached the age of political consciousness at the time of the 1954 arrests. This was the case for Shukri, who was arrested for the first time in 1965 and imprisoned for distributing Muslim Brotherhood leaflets at Asyut University. A gulf soon opened between these two generations, young and old, the majority of the latter adopting a reformist orientation and seeking accommodation with the Sadat regime until 1977, while the most radical of the former declared the *takfir* (excommunication) of *jahiliyya* society and established the 'Society of Muslims' on its fringes.

Back in 1965, some observers had remarked upon the large proportion of young people, especially students, among the victims of the police raids. The leader of the Egyptian left, Khalid Muhieddin, noted that the Muslim Brethren had won the support of young intellectuals and that it was therefore increasingly urgent for the Arab Socialist Union to clarify its doctrine with respect to various ideological problems. This was, in fact, a new phenomenon: elements of a generation that had grown up under Nasserism and knew no other kind of society were now revolting against it in the name of Islamic values and were joining the Muslim Brethren. The arrests and repression, which were felt to be out of all proportion to the crimes of opinion allegedly committed, turned the young sympathizers of the Muslim Brotherhood into the new leaders of the Islamicist movement and furnished the generation of cadres that later led the movement's revolutionary wing under the Sadat regime.

Shukri Mustafa was born on 1 June 1942 in the village of Abu Khurus, some thirty kilometres south of Asyut, in Middle Egypt. (Musha, the Qutb family's home town, was only a few hours away on foot, and the villages of the region have generally been Islamicist breeding-grounds.)

His father was the *'umdah*, or mayor, of the heavily fortified village, which lies nestled in the foothills of the Libyan mountains at the outermost limits of the agricultural zone, alongside desert outcroppings riddled with innumerable ancient tombs and grottoes that have long provided hide-outs for smugglers, arms dealers, and hashish growers. In the late seventies a military road was opened along the ridge of the mountains so that the authorities could penetrate this traditionally delinquent district. But when Shukri was a child, the state's presence in the area was no more than episodic: the army would be sent into one or other village from time to time to confiscate taxes, track down highway robbers, or temporarily stamp out a ring of smugglers. At times like these, the inhabitants would take refuge in the grottoes, returning to their homes once the army had withdrawn.

Shukri was thus born in an out-of-the-way region traditionally resistant to the penetration of the central state, in a forgotten corner of Egypt where, for that very reason, many Christians lived. But Shukri soon had to leave the village: his father repudiated his mother, and she left for Asyut, the regional capital, taking the child with her.

In this town, with its sprawling colonnaded baroque villas in which Coptic and Muslim landlords lived lives of considerable luxury before Nasser's nationalizations drove them into exile (and turned their decaying homes into party headquarters and police stations), Shukri attended not the select college founded by American missionaries, but a school run by an Islamic charity. He obtained mediocre grades, barely won his diploma, and enrolled in the school of agriculture at the university. It seems highly probable that it was there that he came into contact with the Muslim Brethren. Apparently he joined them, for in 1965, at the age of twenty-three, he was arrested for distributing their leaflets on campus. That, of course, was the year of the great wave of arrests after Nasser's announcement from Moscow that a Muslim Brotherhood conspiracy had been unearthed.

Shukri was first incarcerated in Tura prison, but in 1967 he was transferred to the Abu Za'bal concentration camp. He was released on 16 October 1971 as part of the package of measures decreed by Sadat after the 'rectification revolution' of 15 May of that year.

Shukri had spent six years in the camps. At an age when his class-mates were memorizing their professors' mimeographed handouts, he was reading Mawdudi and Qutb and learning to call the society that had produced the camps and torturers *jahiliyya*.

The imprisoned Islamicist militants were divided in their reading of *Signposts*. While the old-guard supporters of Hudaybi defended established dogma against heresies by publishing 'Preachers, Not Judges', the youth soon split into various factions. These may be classified in two major currents, which disagreed as to the proper interpretation of Qutb's term *mufasala*, or *'uzla* ('separation', 'withdrawal'). One tendency held that withdrawal from society meant only spiritual detachment, while the other felt it meant total separation.

Those who preached 'spiritual detachment' from society called themselves the *jama'a al-'uzla al-shu'uriyya* (Spiritual Detachment Group). They argued that contemporary Egyptian *jahiliyya* society had to be excommunicated (*takfir*), but they were aware of the dramatic consequences any enunciation of *takfir* could have, since they found themselves in a position of 'weakness' (*istid'af*) relative to the enemy *jahiliyya* society.[2] Since they con-

2. They felt that during the time he lived in Mecca before the hegira, the Prophet was in a phase of weakness, which compelled him to avoid open confrontation with the ruling pagan Qurayshite tribe. After the hegira came the

tinued to live within that society, they concealed their views, pronouncing the *takfir* secretly in their hearts while awaiting the advent of the phase of 'power' that would enable them to excommunicate a society which they would then have the capacity to combat without being doomed to defeat. Not unlike the Shi'ite sects that practice *kitman* (concealment), every Friday they pretended to pray before an imam whom they actually held to be an infidel. Their apostolate would take effect gradually (*bi'l-tadrij*), according to the principle *al-haraka bi'l-mafhum,* an expression that may be called the *'larvatus prodeo* principle': in other words, a concealed advance, the nature of contemporary society and the group's objectives being revealed little by little to initiates alone, depending on their degree of initiation.

For obvious reasons, there was little talk during the Sadat presidency of the various sects issued of this current of thought, for they all believed they were in a phase of weakness and therefore were careful not to appear on the social scene. During periods of tension with the Islamicist movement, the police would arrest the known members. Some were in Tura in 1977 [1].

The other faction, which preached *mufasala kamila,* or 'total separation' from society, agreed with the first tendency that *jahiliyya* society had to be excommunicated. They were also aware of the danger of pronouncing this excommunication while they were still living in society in a 'phase of weakness'. But their method of averting the danger was to withdraw from society and to create, on its margins, a little Society of Muslims, which would then excommunicate *jahiliyya* society without 'concealment'. Shukri belonged to this second tendency, but he was not its original leader: that position was held by Sheikh 'Ali 'Abduh Isma'il, a young al-Azhar graduate who, until 1969, was the acknowledged leader of those who sought complete separation from society. All those fellow prisoners who refused to swear allegiance to the *jama'a* led by the young Azharist were declared to be *kuffar* (infidels). The young rival sect members in the Abu Za'bal camp, though by no means numerous, mutually excommunicated and refused to greet one another, and some-

---

phase of strength (*tamakkun* or *tamkin*), during which he was able to wage the fight against them.

times even came to blows. It was in this atmosphere of fragmentation that the leaders of the Muslim Brotherhood stepped in, endorsing Hudaybi's book.

The excommunication movement was slowed but not halted by the defection of Sheikh 'Ali, who was convinced by Supreme Guide Hudaybi's arguments and signalled his renunciation of *takfir* quite dramatically: one afternoon in the summer of 1969, after leading his group in prayer, he threw off his white gallabieh and declared that he was renouncing *takfir* just as he had cast off his robe. The sect soon fell apart.

Shukri was finally left as its sole member, until he was joined by his nephew Mahir Bakri. Thus did the weapon of excommunication pass from the hands of a graduate of al-Azhar to a young Sa'idi[3] whose culture was rudimentary and who was therefore powerfully influenced by the cultural, social, economic, and political pressure brought to bear on him by Egyptian society. But he proved able to use that weapon effectively in the social domain, gathering a wide following who identified with him.

Shukri was released from the camp on 16 October 1971. He returned to Asyut, where he finished his agronomy studies while continuing to preach his *da'wa*. He soon gained a reputation in Islamicist circles. Qutb Sayyid Husain, an Azhar graduate and one of the first members of the Society of Muslims, relates that he travelled from Cairo to Asyut to see Shukri and then, having been won over by his eloquence and by the way he practised the *sunan* (bearded, his head shaved, wearing a black gallabieh), he decided to stay with him.

Every Friday, Shukri and his first disciples would roam the environs of Asyut, preaching in the hamlets and villages and gathering young men who would join the group. Success came rapidly, and by 1972 the police were keeping a watchful eye on his activities.

At the beginning of 1973, some of his disciples were arrested, and texts written by Shukri seized. The group then wandered among the mountain grottoes, actually implementing *hijra*, or withdrawal from *jahiliyya* society. The state did not consider

3. A Sa'idi is an inhabitant of Middle or Upper Egypt, traditionally considered rustic in his mores and speech.

Shukri and his companions especially dangerous, however, and after the October war against Israel in 1973 those who had been arrested were granted a presidential pardon.

At the time, the group seems to have been considered a sect of cranks who sought to withdraw from the modern world, seeking exile in Yemen; its principal offence was to entice young women away from their families to live with the members.

In 1974 and 1975 Islamicist militants known to the police were systematically tracked down after an attempted *coup d'état* organized by a rival group to Shukri's.[4] In May 1975 the Cairo daily newspaper *al-Akhbar* published an article about Shukri and his disciples, calling them *ahl al-kahf* (people of the cave), an expression used in the Koran to designate the Seven Sleepers of Ephesus and, by analogy, any others who sought withdrawal from the real world. The group's wanderings in the mountains seem to have made an impression both on the authors of the police reports and on the journalists who copied them. In reality, however, the group had lived only very briefly in the grottoes. Most members lived together in furnished rooms in the poor neighbourhoods ringing Cairo and other cities.

Although they were placed under surveillance, Shukri and his friends were not systematically persecuted. But that changed dramatically in the autumn of 1976, when rival Islamicist grouplets tried to woo members away from Shukri's group, which now had some two thousand adherents in all. In the view of its leader, to quit the group was to abandon Islam as an apostate, and that was punishable by death. The police intervened during a punitive expedition Shukri was conducting against some dissidents, and made many arrests. Shukri himself was now a wanted man. The Egyptian media got hold of the story and depicted the Society of Muslims as a gang of fanatical guerrillas and criminals. They called the group *al-Takfir wa'l-Hijra* because it practised the excommunication of its fellow citizens (*takfir*) and withdrew into the mountains (*hijra*).

From his hideout, Shukri tried to issue communiqués correcting this caricature, and hoped at the very least to turn the trial of

4. This was the so-called Military Academy group, which we will encounter later.

his disciples into a platform for the dissemination of his views. But none of his communiqués was published and no trial was held.

On 3 July 1977 the group kidnapped Muhammad al-Dhahabi, a former minister of waqfs, hoping thus to elicit some response to their demands. But the only result was repression, and the members of the sect then killed Dhahabi. Within a few days, hundreds of them were arrested, including the entire leadership. After a rapid trial, five members, including Shukri, were sentenced to death and executed, and dozens were sent to prison.

Such are the broad chronological outlines of the public manifestations of Shukri's group. Nowhere in its entire treatment of the affair did the Egyptian press even mention the group's real name, Society of Muslims. Mendacious accounts of its ideology and social practices were published. The important thing was to ensure that Shukri was seen as an insane criminal; by holding him up to popular wrath, the state effectively announced that its alliance with the Islamicist movement had been broken.

Let us therefore try to shed some light on Shukri's deliberately concealed discourse, to reconstruct the sect's ideology and social practices on the basis of the fragmentary information we possess. This will allow us to understand not only the reality of the Shukri group, but also the state and society in opposition to which it was formed.

The New Hegira

The criminal trial of the Society of Muslims was held in three *in camera* sessions of the Military Court of State Security on the sixth, seventh, and eighth of November 1977. The principal defendant was asked by the judge to explain his doctrine, and he took the opportunity to present a didactic and coherent exposition structured by its own criteria of rationality and not by the court's questions.

For Shukri, *i'tizal* — the withdrawal from society that had shocked his contemporaries so deeply — was 'merely a consequence of Islamic thought taken as a whole'. It could therefore be understood only in the context of a comprehensive description of this whole.

To begin with, Shukri recalled, Muslims hold that there is no science except in God. This assertion, based on many verses of the Koran, is accepted only figuratively by most believers today, but Shukri maintained on the contrary that the following concrete meaning should be ascribed to it: 'The Muslim is obligated to seek his path and knowledge before God alone, and so-called knowledge, which is actually no knowledge at all because it is not founded in the Lord, is forbidden.' Indeed, the Koran teaches (Sura II, 'The Cow', verses 216 or 232) that *God knows and you know not*. This means, according to Shukri, that everything that came after the Book and the accounts of the Tradition of the Prophet (the Sunna), is excluded from the domain of legitimate knowledge. The four great legal schools of the Sunni *imams* Abu Hanifa, Ibn Hanbal, Malik, and Shafi'i in particular are null and void. According to orthodox Islam, these four schools of medieval theologians and annotators established the limits of legitimate interpretation of the verses of the Koran. After them, the doors of interpretation (*ijtihad*) were closed, as the Arabic expression has it. Shukri told the court: 'We would like to call your attention to the following fact: Islam has been in decline ever since men have ceased to draw their lessons directly from the Koran and the Sunna, and have instead followed the tradition of other men, those who call themselves *imams.*'

The interpretive works of the four *imams*, Shukri argued, were wholly unnecessary. The Koran was delivered in Arabic; it is therefore clear, and the only tool that may be needed for explaining the meaning of some of its terms is a good dictionary. In what way do the glosses of the *imams* make its meaning more accessible? And why do the glosses of the *imams* themselves not need to be glossed?

After thus appealing to the plain common sense of his interlocutors, Shukri told them why the *imams* had closed the door to *ijtihad*: so that they and their texts would become objects of veneration, and they had indeed become idols (*asnam*) worshipped like the deities of a pagan pantheon. They had therefore interposed themselves between God and the believers, and had thus placed themselves outside Islam. They belonged to *jahi-liyya*, to barbarism.

But the doors of *ijtihad* had not always been closed to everyone:

'Have those who sought to close the doors of *ijtihad* really done so? No, they have closed them for the *vulgum pecus* and the rest of the men of the *umma*, but for generations they held it wide open for the *ulema* of the princes, that they might issue *fatwas* tailored to fit the views of the sovereign — whoever he was, and whatever his views — in order to spread sin, to declare the illicit legal in the name of Islam. If we wanted to offer examples from the present or the past, no one could refute us, for there are obvious cases of the authorization of usury and fornication, of the legitimation of government based on principles other than divine law, and even of approval of prostitution and wine in the name of Islam!'

In support of his contentions, Shukri cited Mahmud Shaltut, the sheikh of al-Azhar during the Nasser period, who had delivered a *fatwa* declaring banking interest legal, though other Muslims consider it usury. He also cited Sheikh Sha'rawi, the most famous preacher of official Islam during Sadat's presidency, who stated that Treasury bonds did not contravene divine law, and Sheikh Su'ad Jalal, who declared that beer did not fall under the prohibition of alcohol (which earned him the nickname 'Sheikh Stella', after the Egyptian brand of beer).

As for fornication, far from being punished, it is accepted by those who recognize existing civil law, which does not call it a crime, not to mention those who, worse yet, act as apostles of 'women's liberation' or the mixing of the sexes, which is nothing less than incitement to fornication, which can be committed, Shukri affirmed — basing himself on a *hadith*, or saying of the Prophet — by the hand, the eye, or the ear.

Muslim medieval scholarship in its entirety must therefore be scorned. Since the closing of the doors of *ijtihad*, the history of Islam has been the story of the *ulema's* complicity with the princes. It now devolves upon Shukri, who has been chosen by God and is 'guided by Him on the Straight Path', to reopen these doors, to interpret the Koran and the Sunna as he understands them, and to derive a Law from them.

If Shukri makes a clean sweep of the past, abolishing the

history of Muslim civilization in favour of a direct appeal to the mythified epoch of its origins, he also attacks the contemporary symbols through which society — which he believes is equivalent to *jahiliyya*, to pre-Islamic barbarism — proclaims, or rather usurps, its Islamic character. At the top of the list of these symbols are the mosques:

'Mosques in which prayers are conducted must be called by their lawful (*shari'i*) name, which is "mosque of God". They must be constructed out of piety. One may not pray in mosques that have not been founded in piety.'

In Egypt, as in other Muslim countries, there are two sorts of mosque. *Hukumi* (public) mosques are controlled by the minister of waqfs, and the preacher who leads the daily prayers and delivers the Friday sermon is a state employee, usually a graduate of al-Azhar University, where he will have taken the religious studies course. *Ahli* (private) mosques belong to private individuals, who choose the preacher without interference from the state.

In reply to the court's question, 'Do you believe that it is permissible for Muslims to pray in the mosques that now exist in Egypt?', Shukri replied: '. . . I say that there are some private mosques that are not subject to political influences, that are not dominated by the four Sunni legal schools of *jahiliyya*; I do not forbid prayer there. . . . Nevertheless, I hold that my home and that of the Muslims [of Shukri's disciples, that is] are the most appropriate places for prayer.'

Shukri's affirmation of such a view was considered scandalous. He had desecrated a site that symbolizes Islam, calling the mosques mere temples in which idols were worshipped under the control of the political regime. But there is nothing reprehensible about praying at home. A Muslim can pray to his God anywhere, provided that he performs his ablutions, faces Mecca, removes his shoes, and does not stand directly on the ground. In Egypt today, for instance, countless Muslims bow down anywhere and everywhere at the times of the five daily prayers (dawn, midday, afternoon, sunset, and evening): on the streets, in work places or at home, standing on pieces of cardboard, folded newspapers, or, more rarely, small prayer rugs.

These daily prayers are an individual act, although one can of

course pray alongside other believers: they mark the relationship of the individual as such to God. On Friday at midday,
however, the faithful gather for a collective prayer behind a
preacher, who also delivers a sermon. This is supposed to take
place in a mosque.

Even though prayer is one of the 'five pillars' of Islam (along
with the profession of faith, the Ramadan fast, the giving of
alms, and the pilgrimage to Mecca), Shukri unhesitatingly told
his judges that the Friday prayer, which is meant to represent the
assembly of believers, is illicit in a *jahiliyya* society. 'Such is the
first condition for the accomplishment of the Friday prayer: it is
permitted for the Society of Muslims only if it can take place
publicly and openly (*zahiran*).' And this condition is met only
when the Society of Muslims is in its phase of power (*tamakkun*),
once it has shifted the relationship of forces with the surrounding *jahiliyya* in its own favour. In 1977, however, the Shukri
group was still in its phase of weakness (*istid'af*) and therefore
refused to attend Friday prayers. In support of his position
Shukri cited a *hadith* according to which Muhammad and his
companions, who were in a phase of weakness *vis-à-vis* the
polytheists in Mecca before the hegira, did not hold collective
Friday prayers, but did so only later, in Medina. Shukri explained the transition from phase of weakness to phase of power
in these terms:

'Power, like everything else, has degrees. The phase begins, in
my view, when the circle of oppression and weakness is broken;
it then progresses to conquest and expansion. There is no doubt
that when the Muslims made the hegira from Mecca to Medina,
they were already at the first stage of the phase of power, since no
one could impose anything on them any longer.'

Shukri was then asked, 'And did not your group attain this
lower stage in Egypt, so that you could pray anywhere on
Friday?' 'Absolutely not', he answered. 'The proof is that in five
years we have been defendants in more than fifteen trials and
have suffered imprisonment; this time again many of us have
been arrested. Where, then, is the power?'

This refusal to pay his respects to the mosque or to attend
Friday prayers during the so-called phase of weakness would
seem to reflect, in terms of great symbolic violence, the intran-

sigence of Shukri's notion of rupture (*'uzla*), a sort of constant reminder that the group found itself in a merely temporary situation, having not yet attained its goal, the reconquest of the *umma*. Only then would it be time to celebrate the glory of God collectively. Politically, this amounted to a refusal to accept the comfort, however relative, of the marginal toleration effectively accorded by the state until the end of 1976. It is this that explains the court's line of questioning. By building its own counter-society, however aberrant its practices, the Society of Muslims acted as a pole of attraction for young Islamicist dissidents; although members were turned inwards, they were at least diverted from potential *coups d'état*. Had they prayed in their own mosques, they would have thereby shown that although they were oppositionists, they believed that the times in which they lived were Islamic. But by rejecting both the Friday prayers and the mosque, the Society of Muslims was implementing its own project: the destruction of *jahiliyya* and the erection of the Muslim society on its ruins. The sect thereby reminded its adherents of their objective and thus showed that it represented a constant danger to the established order.

Shukri demonstrated in practice that as far as he was concerned, Egyptian society in the seventies meant *jahiliyya*, barbarism of the sort described by Sayyid Qutb in *Signposts*. He strove to unmask it, and to invalidate the meaning of the symbols that had been usurped by those who sought to pass it off as a Muslim society. In accordance with this view, he undertook to destroy the instruments of legitimation of the Egyptian regime one by one. After the religious institutions, the next target of attack was the army.

One of the major reasons for the omnipotence of military officers within the Egyptian regime was the state of war with Israel that existed until 1977. In fact, the war against the Jewish state is one of the principal issues mobilizing the Arab and Muslim people behind their various states, serving to justify a sacred unity in support of the autocratic layer that monopolizes power. In the vocabulary of Arab nationalism, the Jewish state is an enclave of imperialism on occupied Arab land; in Islamic categories, it becomes a land usurped from *Dar al-Islam* by the infidel, and therefore part of *Dar al-Harb* (the Domain of War), which must be attacked relentlessly by *jihad*, proclaimed and directed by the commander of the faithful.

While the first of these affirmations formed the heart of the vulgate of the Nasserist state until 1977, the latter was the favourite theme of *al-Da'wa*, the monthly magazine of the neo-Muslim Brethren, between 1976 and 1981. But Shukri now opposed this attitude, as Faraj was subsequently to do in 1981.

When the military judges asked Shukri what the attitude of the Society of Muslims would be if 'Jewish forces' invaded Egypt, this was his reply: 'If the Jews or anyone else came, our movement ought not to fight in the ranks of the Egyptian army, but on the contrary ought to flee to a secure position. In general, our line is to flee before the external and internal enemy alike, and not to resist him.'

It would be difficult to find a sharper expression of Shukri's rejection of the independent nation as it was structured by the Nasserist nationalist myth crystallized in the struggle against Israel. For the Society of Muslims, the Israeli army and the Egyptian *mukhabarat* (secret services) were equally and indiscriminately enemies. During the phase of weakness, the group's disaffection with the 'Zionist enemy' took the practical form of a refusal to be conscripted. The Society's members felt no allegiance to the state. They therefore not only refused to wear its uniform but also rejected anything else that was connected with the state or might serve it. For instance, Shukri also forbad his followers to be state employees, and those who worked in public services changed jobs upon joining the Society of Muslims.

Shukri also rejected education as dispensed in the Egyptian school system, as he explained in response to a question from the military tribunal:

Question. 'The tribunal would like to know your opinion of the teaching of writing.'

Answer. 'The teaching of writing for its own sake is illicit (*haram*). . . . The Prophet did not open *kuttab* (Koranic schools) and institutions to teach Muslims writing and arithmetic, but permitted them to be taught according to needs and necessities.'

This rejection of public employment and of useless education does not appear to me, as Shukri's detractors argue, to be based exclusively on a misinterpretation of the Koranic verse (Sura LXII, 'Friday', 2): 'He it is who has sent a Prophet among the unlettered people' (*ummiyyin,* or illiterates), from which Shukri is said to have concluded that illiteracy is the only hope. It would seem more pertinent to consider this rejection in the light of the conditions of public employment and literacy in Sadat's Egypt.

By law, every graduate in Egypt has the right to state employment. This measure, a powerful weapon against non-employment, is actually the purveyor of massive disguised unemployment in the offices of a swollen administration in which productivity is as low as the employees are badly paid. If the state employee lacks an additional source of income — either one or more 'moonlighting' jobs or assistance from his family — he can still manage to feed himself by buying the state-subsidized products on sale in the cooperatives, but he is unlikely to rise above this level of bare subsistence. Anything whose price is determined by the market is beyond his reach. Almost every state employee has a second or even third job which, though it owes nothing to his intellectual qualifications, being unrelated to his course of studies, assures the basic part of his income. Innumerable employees who sit all morning at desks in one or other of the countless ministry offices spend the afternoon working as plumbers or taxi drivers, jobs they perform so inadequately that they might as well be filled by illiterates, the competent plumbers having long since emigrated to the Arabian peninsula, where their spanners are worth their weight in gold. An illiterate peasant woman who arrives in the city and manages to land a job as a foreigner's maid will be paid more or less double the salary of a university assistant lecturer.

It is against this background that Shukri's initiatives must be seen: in forbidding the teaching of writing when it does not correspond to a need, and in ordering the members of the Society of Muslims to renounce public employment, he is not acting as a fanatic from a bygone century, as some have been pleased to claim. He is putting his finger — in his own way (and in a vocabulary that, while not sociological or Marxist, is quite meaningful and immediately comprehensible to the layers he is addressing) — on a crucial problem of contemporary Egyptian society. For many Egyptians it is indeed useless to learn to write, and they have forgotten, without apparent ill effect, the rudiments they learned at school.

Struggle against religious legitimation of the state; indifference to the anti-Zionist struggle led by the iniquitous prince; radical rejection of any collaboration with the institutions of *jahiliyya,* including public employment and the educational system: Shukri placed himself on the margins of society, flouting established custom. He challenged the social conventions of daily life, revealing them as actually political.

Living Together in the Prophet's Way

The institution of marriage did not escape the corrosive social practice of the Society of Muslims. In fact, the first extensive police operations against the group's adherents seem to have been initiated after complaints by families whose daughters had disappeared to join the group and had found partners there. In fact, Shukri's group, unlike most other more or less clandestine Islamicist organizations, had women among its membership; they were married within the group according to a special ritual and had children, thus assuring the survival of authentic Muslims.

This 'leading of women astray' outraged public opinion, and provided headline material and innumerable photographs for the Egyptian press. In the newspaper stories, the scenario never varied: seduced by the captivating words of Shukri or one of his disciples, a young girl deserts the paternal home and hearth, abandons her studies, and goes to live among the group. Here is one such story, recounted from the witness stand at the military tribunal by an aggrieved father, two of whose daughters had disappeared. The witness was a man of forty-five, employed by a cotton-threshing company in Fayyum province. He spoke in a rural dialect:

'Last year, a little before the Lesser Holiday [which marks the end of Ramadan], my daughter Samiha came with an acceptance from the university dormitory, and afterwards her little sister Rawaya came to me and said: "Take me with you so I can see Cairo." I took them to Cairo and brought them to the house of

their older sister, who is married and lives there, and I went back
to Fayyum for the holiday.

'Their mother said to me: "Go and find out why the girls
haven't come home." So I went back to Cairo and asked
Mahmud, their older sister's husband, "Where are the girls?"
"Their brother Sa'id took them back to the countryside", he told
me. "I've just come from the village; they aren't there", I said.
Then he said, "Maybe you passed each other on the way." So I
went back to Fayyum, and their mother said, "Where are the
girls? Bring them back immediately, even if the devil himself's
taken them." So I went back to Mahmud and told him, "The girls
still haven't come home." "What do you want me to do about it?"
he said. "Their brother took them." This went on for three
weeks, back and forth, until finally Mahmud told me, "If you
want to know where they are, go and see a fellow named Mustafa
al-Jamal in Umm al-Misriyyin" [a poor neighbourhood in
Cairo]. So I went, and he told me, "Forget it, they're married
now, and the men we married them to are Muslims." Then — it
was just too horrible — he said, "We separate Muslims from
infidels." So I said, "Well, I want to see them. How do I know
they're all right?" "Okay," he said, "come back in three days." I
did, and then he told me, "In another week." So I went home to
the village. But their mother couldn't stand it any more. I went
back to this Mustafa, and he says, "Wait a minute." Then this
other fellow called Abu'l-Fadl comes in. I talked to him and he
says, "What girls? They're married." So I said, "You call this
human? . . . They disappear from home and get married? One of
them is only fourteen!" So he says, "That's how it's done." . . .'
The father then went to the police. At the end of his testimony,
the son, Sa'id, shouted from the defendant's box, 'Aren't you
ashamed, father, to play along with this charade staged by the
cops?'

Marriage as practised in the Society of Muslims, of course, did
not entail the complicated contracts commonly drafted in
Egyptian society to assure the bride's family that the groom will
provide housing. It was 'Muslim' marriage, for which all that
was required was the presence of witnesses and the couple's
consent.

As far as is known, Shukri himself chose both partners. Sometimes the future groom was living outside Egypt, in an oil-producing country from which he sent back money orders to the Society of Muslims. His prospective wife would have seen no more than his photograph. Once the knot was tied, the couple would live with other members of the sect in furnished lodgings rented by the group. Because of overcrowding, there were several couples to a room; they protected their intimacy by hanging curtains.

These details, plus the *droit de seigneur* attributed to Shukri by public rumour, created a janus image of the veiled women of the group who so modestly hid their faces from the popping flash-bulbs of the paparazzi: their excessive religious devotion was seen as no more than a hypocritical disguise for the unchained debauchery of which Shukri was supposedly the coryphaeus.

Shukri maintained that if one of the partners of a couple but not the other joined the Society of Muslims, their marriage ties were null and void and a new union could be contracted. When it was the man who became a member — as in the case of the 'engineer' Fathi 'Abd al-Salam, who forced his wife to sell their refrigerator, cooker, and washing machine and then left her to go and live with a member of the Society in Mansura — the story might arouse some pity for the abandoned wife, of course, but no genuine reprobation. Islam permits every man to have four wives, and repudiation is a simple formality. The same step taken by a woman, however, is sacrilege. During the trial, the question of what would happen in such a case was raised. The woman, Shukri declared, would ask for a divorce on grounds of divergence of creed (*al-ikhtilaf fi'l-'aqida*), but even if that was refused her, she would not have to return to her husband. More-over, if she wanted, she could marry a member of the sect, since the matrimonial ties of *jahiliyya* are valueless in the Society of Muslims.

The Shukri group made marriage possible and provided the young couples with a place to live, albeit cramped, in a 'fur-nished flat'. To understand why it had to be 'furnished', one must remember that a prospective groom in Egypt has to provide his future in-laws with proof that he has some housing. In theory, anyone can afford to rent a flat, because the law fixes rents at their nominal levels at the time of the Second World War, which inflation has turned into a derisory sum. But the landlords make their profit by demanding that prospective tenants pay 'key-money', a practice as universal as it is illegal. The sum paid is more or less what it would cost to buy the property, and since a young man just starting out cannot get credit (nor can anyone else whose official salary is but a fraction of his real income), the only way to afford key-money is to emigrate to the Gulf for some years. That is why most Egyptian men leave the country between the ages of twenty and thirty. During that time, the young women wait.

But there is one category of housing that can be had without paying key-money: 'furnished apartments', which often contain little or no furnishing and whose rents are determined by supply and demand. These 'furnished' rooms are invariably inhabited by foreigners, prostitutes, people living on the margins of society, and others who are unable or unwilling to settle in one place on a long-term basis. The furnished flat provides temporary housing. As marginal elements, the members of the Society of Muslims could find lodgings nowhere else. Shukri settled his followers in flats like these, and there they lived communally.

This was the actual site of the *hijra*, the Society's hegira, its withdrawal from *jahiliyya* society. In their furnished rooms, the Society's members created a tiny, genuinely Islamic society of their own, based on their understanding of Islam. Here their lives changed radically: they married young, housing was immediately available without payment of key-money, and the values of Egyptian society no longer applied. Diplomas were considered mere scraps of paper, the mosques of the Ministry of Waqfs temples for the worship of medieval annotators, and Israel an enemy on the same footing as the iniquitous prince and his administration.

Having abandoned state employment on Shukri's orders, the members did manual labour, grew vegetables, and sold knick-knacks from pushcarts. But these activities did not earn enough to pay the rent for their furnished flats. Most of the group's resources came from money sent back from Saudi Arabia, Kuwait, or elsewhere by members whom Shukri had sent into emigration by turns.

There were thus two *hijras* for Society members: the internal withdrawal from *jahiliyya* society to their life in the furnished flats of the Society of Muslims, and physical emigration outside the country like other young Egyptians, except that the income they earned was redistributed to support the rest of the members back in Egypt. On his return home, it seems, each member would be entitled to a wife.

This, of course, was a caricature of the sort of emigration forced on Egyptian citizens by the underdevelopment of their country, but it would be wrong to demean Shukri's experiment for that reason alone. He was seeking to procure funds· by the only means open to the disinherited. The reformist tendency of the Islamicist movement, with its representatives in business circles, enjoyed financial backing from Egyptian capitalists.

The importance and originality of the concept of *hijra* and its practice by the Society of Muslims cannot be overestimated. In Muslim tradition, the *hijra* refers to the Prophet's hegira. It is therefore part of a political strategy for dealing with *jahiliyya,* and consists of fleeing from an enemy that cannot be fought with any reasonable chance of success during the phase of weakness. But *hijra* as internal emigration was a social phenomenon that reflected Egyptian society of the seventies like a distorting mirror at a fun-fair, exaggerating deformities and defects.

Shukri, with his unpolished conceptual language — shaped by memories of a dissident childhood in Middle Egypt, his reading of Qutb and Mawdudi, and the experience of concentration camps — was able to attract the lost children of a Third World independent state who were convinced, in effect, that life was intolerable. The social mores of Shukri and his members were a kind of outcasts' hodgepodge that expressed, sometimes in the most conformist terms, their disorientation at the painful changes wrought by modernity. Nevertheless, identification of social dysfunction generally seemed more bold, authentic, and innovative when expressed in Shukri's Islamicist categories than when stated in the wooden language of the Egyptian Marxists.

Marriage as practised by the Society of Muslims is a significant example of this apparent paradox. Shukri noted that in Egyptian cities today marriage inevitably comes very late and that young people suffer as a consequence. He thus reestablished early marriage for his members, as practised in the countryside. But it was also arranged marriage, decided by Shukri himself and imposed on the couple.

Hermetic as it may appear to Western observers, Shukri's language nevertheless expressed demands that arouse deep feelings among Muslims who, like him, flounder in a society sinking ever deeper into the abyss of underdevelopment. It was therefore imperative to silence Shukri. But that turned out to be far from easy, and the state had to resort to the army. The final victory of Shukri Mustafa, chosen by God to lead Muslims on the Straight Path, was no doubt to have compelled the military society to come out into the open to inflict his martyrdom upon him.

Death of One of the Ulema

The Society of Muslims was by no means the only Islamicist current, nor even the only underground group of Islamicist dissidents. Shukri's attitude towards the Muslim Brethren and their epigones of the magazine *al-Da'wa* was one of unmitigated hostility. He came forward, in effect, as an opponent of the Brotherhood's dominant line, set by Supreme Guide Hasan al-Hudaybi, the author of 'Preachers, not Judges', and he is said to have spoken these ungracious words about the Brethren: 'I accuse these leaders of the Islamic movement who have led their men to their doom, . . ., these leaders of the Muslim Brethren who have delivered them to the executioners, the gallows, the prisons, of high treason . . .: they have ruined their men's lives, toying with them irresponsibly' [1].

There is in fact little doubt that Supreme Guide Hasan al-Hudaybi's shilly-shallying and lack of tactical sense permitted the 1954 repression against the Brethren to attain greater breadth. After that date, however, all the various currents of the Egyptian Islamicist movement took great pains not to leave themselves open to repression. The reformist tendency around the magazine *al-Da'wa* sought legal recognition from the regime in order to ward off the spectre of the gallows and the concentration camps. The radical tendency, inspired by Qutb's work, opted for withdrawal from society or for the strictest clandestinity.

By choosing withdrawal and by expounding the theory of the 'phase of weakness', Shukri guided the lives of his flock without making any major compromise with *jahiliyya* as far as his ultimate aim was concerned: the erection of the Muslim state on its ruins. He had nothing but contempt for the strategy of the neo-Muslim Brethren of the *Da'wa* editorial board. He did not consider the Brethren, and still less their epigones, to be part of the Islamic movement, as he told the military tribunal: 'The Society of Muslims is the first Islamic movement (*haraka islamiyya*) to be founded in centuries. As for the Muslim Brethren, God did not grant them power, and that is irrefutable proof that they were not a true and legitimate Islamic movement, and that their apostolate was fraudulent.'

Although each denied the other's right to speak in the name of Islam, Shukri's group and the editors of *al-Da'wa* encountered one another only sporadically, since the former lived on the fringes of society while the latter manoeuvred within it. There were, however, clashes, sometimes violent ones, between the Society of Muslims and other more or less well-known Islamicist dissident groups. These clashes, and the so-called 'physical elimination of apostates', were the first signs of the Society of Muslims' violent bent.

But it was another Islamicist group that was the first to resort to violence in Sadat's Egypt. In 1974, a 'Military Academy' group led by a Palestinian tried to foment an uprising in the Heliopolis military school in the Cairo suburbs and to assassinate the head of state. The facts of the case remain murky even now, but it is of interest on various counts. To start with, the abortive rising was a kind of dress rehearsal for the frontal assault by the Jihad group in October 1981. Second, it was the work of a tendency of the Islamicist movement whose analysis of the state and society differed from Shukri's. Finally — though this is only conjecture — it seems likely that the secret services of Arab countries hostile to the Egyptian-American *rapprochement* that followed the October war of 1973 may have been in contact with the group's leader.

The latter had arrived in Cairo toward the end of 1971, about the time that Shukri left the concentration camp. His name was Salih Sirriya and he was born in Ijzim, near Haifa, in 1933. Ijzim was also the home town of an enigmatic figure of the Arab Islamicist movement: Taqi al-Din al-Nabahani, the founder of the Islamic Liberation Party. Sirriya was probably a member of this party, which was founded in 1950 as a reaction partly to the defeat of the Arab armies in the 1948 war with Israel and partly to the assassination in 1949 of Hasan al-Banna, the founder of the Muslim Brotherhood.

Unlike the Muslim Brethren, who sought to preach to the Muslim masses about the need to Islamicize society, Nabahani's party held that political power had first to be seized in a *coup de force*. Islamicism would then be instituted from above. Because of its objectives, the party was outlawed everywhere, its members hunted down.

Sirriya lived in Jordan until September 1970, when, like many other Palestinians, he left the country after the victory of King Husain's bedouins over the fedayeen in the civil war. He then spent a year in Iraq, but finally had to flee Baghdad, where he was sentenced *in absentia* in 1972 for membership of the party. He then moved to Cairo, where he worked in the 'education' section of the headquarters of the Arab League (he held a doctorate in education).

When he arrived in Cairo, Sirriya began frequenting the Muslim Brethren, especially Supreme Guide Hudaybi (who died in 1973) and Zaynab al-Ghazali, the movement's *passionaria*. He won her confidence and held regular discussions with her. At the same time, he began to assemble a group of young people, most of whom were students in Cairo or Alexandria.

Unlike Shukri, Sirriya created no counter-society and organized no *hijra* to Cairo's furnished flats. His disciples continued to lead normal lives, so as not to attract the attention of the authorities. In any case, they did not agree that all society represented *jahiliyya*, anti-Islamic barbarism, but held instead that the iniquitous prince alone blocked the spread of an Islamic mode of society.

Having organized a group of conspirators, Sirriya and his disciples then sought the most opportune moment for a *coup d'état*. They finally picked 18 April 1974. On that day several conspirators, students at the Military Academy in Heliopolis, were supposed to seize control of the school's armoury, attack the presidential cortège, which was scheduled to pass near by, and kill Sadat.

The plan was set in motion, but ground to a halt within the grounds of the Military Academy, whose guards opened fire on the mutineers.

The plot was officially blamed on Libya, and a trial was held, after which two defendants, Sirriya and his top aide, were sentenced to death and executed. Twenty-nine others received prison terms and sixty were released.

The government made great efforts to implicate foreigners in the conspiracy, for it had been caught unawares by the sudden eruption of Islamicist violence at a time when all the members of the movement who had been imprisoned by Nasser were being released and the Islamicist movement was growing on the university campuses — with the sanction of the authorities, as we shall see.

Thus it was that as soon as Egyptian gaols were emptied of Nasser's Islamicist prisoners, they were peopled again with Sadat's. These new 'martyrs' were soon being courted by the other underground Islamicist groups, and one of the leaders of the 'Military Academy Group', Talal al-Ansari, joined the Society of Muslims while in prison. On the other hand, one of Sirriya's disciples who had been released, Hasan al-Hilawi, tried to lure away some of Shukri's friends to found his own group. It was this climate of fragmentation of the movement into rival sects and of incidents between them that gave the police the opportunity to intervene in the internal affairs of the Islamicist movement.

In November 1976 the leaders of the Society of Muslims decided to react to various actions which they felt threatened their authority. Hilawi had managed to win over some of their members. More seriously, Rif'at Abu Dalal, who had been in charge of physical training in Shukri's group, also split away, taking several members with him.

Punitive expeditions to 'chastise the apostates' were launched against the homes of Hilawi and Abu Dalal on 18 and 22

November. Shukri felt that this was an internal matter, and he expected that the actions would bolster internal cohesion by dissuading potential future dissidents. But by resorting to attempted homicide against Egyptian citizens, he allowed the judiciary to take up his case, and therefore opened himself up to *jahiliyya* attacks while still in the phase of weakness. The police intervened to put a stop to the 'punitive expeditions' and fourteen members were arrested. A warrant for Shukri's arrest was issued.

This marked the beginning of a confrontation between the state and the sect that would end with the latter's destruction and the death of its leaders. Even now it is difficult to understand why Shukri risked this confrontation. Perhaps he believed that the assault on his authority represented by the dissident currents was an unacceptable challenge that threatened the future of the Society of Muslims. He may also have believed that the police would not intervene. Nor is the role of the police completely clear: it is not impossible that Hilawi and Abu Dalal were manipulated in order to draw Shukri into a trap. In any event, it is known that Egyptian General Intelligence was in contact with the Society of Muslims' second-in-command, Mahir Bakri, who had advocated collaboration between the Society and the state intelligence services against the other tendencies of the Islamicist movement, in particular the putschist disciples and admirers of Sirriya [1]. Although he had termed the Egyptian state *jahiliyya*, Shukri himself had a less theoretical view of daily relations with the state apparatus: 'There is no doubt that the Sadat regime is a thousand times better than Nasser's. Nasser would never have allowed us to act as we are now acting, nor to carry out our propaganda openly' [1]. One of Shukri's close associates answered that whereas Nasser had struck at the Islamicist movement with a hammer, Sadat was strangling it with a silken cord.

The leaders of the Society of Muslims therefore had no very clear tactics in their relations with the state, and clung instead to their general strategy of withdrawal, of *hijra*, during the phase of weakness. In this context, the imprisonment of fourteen of their members took them unawares, as did the denunciation of their 'group of fanatical criminals' on the front page of the semi-official Cairo daily *al-Ahram*.

Throughout the first six months of 1977, Shukri ceaselessly demanded that the fourteen 'martyrs' be released and that the press offer its readers an accurate picture of the Society of Muslims. He mobilized all the group's energies, explaining that they had now entered the 'stage of general proclamation' (*marhalat al-balagh al-'am*). They sent communiqués to the newspapers and tried to deliver statements to radio and television journalists. Shukri also wanted to publish a small book he had written, called *al-Khilafa* ('The Caliphate'). None of these initiatives worked, and Shukri's credibility within the group was threatened once again.

He then decided that some master stroke was needed to restore his authority, some direct challenge to the state. On the night of 3 July 1977, members of the group disguised as policemen kidnapped Muhammad al-Dhahabi, a former minister of waqfs. The next morning, they issued a communiqué claiming responsibility for the kidnapping and formulating the following demands:

'1. Immediate release of all our imprisoned brothers, first of all Talal al-Ansari [the recruit from the 'Military Academy group'] . . .

'2. Amnesty for all those among us who have been sentenced . . .

'4. Delivery to us of the sum of 200,000 Egyptian pounds in cash . . . in unmarked, used notes, without sequential serial numbers.

'5. The newspapers *al-Akhbar, al-Ahram,* and *al-Jumhuriyya,* as well as the magazines *Akhir Sa'a, Uktubir,* and *Majallat al-Azhar* to apologize to us for their lies, these apologies to be printed on page one.

'6. Authorization to publish our first book, entitled *al-Khilafa* and now ready for printing; no obstacle to publicity for it in the newspapers may be erected.

'7. A committee of experts to be set up to investigate the activities of the following organizations: the prosecutor's office of the State Security Court, the magistrates, the General Intelligence Services, the Mansura prosecutor's office.

'8. This communiqué to be broadcast on news bulletins at 8.30 p.m. on 3 July.

'9. This communiqué to be published in the three Egyptian dailies on Monday, 4 July, also in the dailies *al-Ba'th* in Syria, *al-Nahar* in Lebanon, and in the Saudi, Kuwaiti, Jordanian, Sudanese, Turkish, and Iranian newspapers, as well as in the *New York Times* in America, *Le Monde* in France, and the *Sunday Times* and *Guardian* in England, in their respective languages.

'10. As Muslims, we are bound by what we have said and by the conditions we have set, in accordance with what the *shari'a* prescribes . . . [followed by threats to kill the hostage if the police look for him or arrest the people delivering the communiqué].'

The communiqué itself is a strange mixture of some demands that might be satisfied and others which were completely unrealistic in Sadat's Egypt, such as the formation of a 'committee of experts' to investigate the activities of the secret police. It reveals Shukri's difficulties in correctly and effectively understanding the state apparatus.

Dhahabi was kidnapped while Sadat was on a visit to Morocco. Political leaders back in Egypt refused to deal with the Society of Muslims. Shukri, his back to the wall once again, had the hostage executed; his body was found on 7 July.[5]

There was great indignation in the country, and the press set to work amplifying it. Within a few days, most of the sect's members had been arrested in sweeping police raids. Sadat decided to convene a special military tribunal.

That a military rather than a civilian court was given jurisdiction, even though none of the accused had been members of the armed forces, aroused some dispute. Army discourse was thus accorded the force of law, to the detriment of other discourses on the Society of Muslims by institutions like the corps of *ulema*, which was thereby reduced to ancillary status. It was the military prosecutor, General Makhluf, who articulated the official view of Shukri and his group in the newspapers and at the hearings, while the sheikh of al-Azhar, Islam's highest authority in Egypt, was not even allowed to testify at the trial: in other words, the opinion of the group to which the victim belonged went unheard.

5. Some Islamicists claim that it was the police who killed Dhahabi. I do not believe so, although I cannot offer any absolute proof.

In an initial interview with *al-Ahram,* General Makhluf explained that this civilian case had been entrusted to the Military Court of State Security because public opinion, shocked by the odious assassination, was demanding rapid judgement. Since the civilian courts were in recess for the summer, only the military tribunals could set to work without delay. The preliminary hearings were indeed conducted with alacrity, being completed on 27 July even though there were several hundred defendants. In a second interview with *al-Ahram,* General Makhluf congratulated himself on his diligent accomplishment of this task, reassured any readers who might raise niggling objections ('all the officers who participated in the interrogations had at least masters degrees, if not doctorates, in law'), and began to establish the army's line on the Society of Muslims, a master line that was shaped by the indictment and would dictate its own truth and its own analysis of the problem, its causes, and the requisite solutions.

Shukri, the general explained, was a charlatan (*dajjal*). He claimed to interpret the Koran and the *hadiths,* but he knew no more about either than he did about Arabic grammar, of which he was wholly ignorant. To speak in the name of the Koran or to issue *fatwas* required certain qualities that were acquired by following a course of Koranic studies, which Shukri had never done. In fact, when Shukri was imprisoned in 1965, he was unable to recite a single verse of the Koran. During his detention, he read deviant (*munharif*) books,[6] which enabled him, after his release, to dupe and mislead some young people, with the aid of Mahir Bakri, 'the group's philosopher', whose educational career went no further than secondary school.

How was it, then, that someone so simple-minded could have hoodwinked educated people, *muthaqqafin,* of whom the group had many? To this question the general replied that if the members had any culture, it was limited to that conferred by university disciplines such as medicine or engineering, which were powerless to remedy religious vacuity (*al-faragh al-dini*),

6. The reference is to works by Qutb and Mawdudi, who were mentioned by name, the former in the deposition of 'Adil Mujahid, the secret police lieutenant-colonel in charge of surveillance of the Islamicist groups, the latter in the military prosecutor's indictment.

the fundamental bane of Egyptian youth. The cause of this evil was revealed only when the general delivered his opening statement on 11 October 1977: 'the youth are no longer educated in religion'. His proposed therapy: the religious training of youth, from pre-school age to university level, through the compulsory study of religious subjects,[7] complemented by an obligation on the part of journalists, authors, and other men of letters to defend and illustrate religion in their writings. As for the *ulema*, he directed the following two 'propositions' to their attention:

'That al-Azhar and the minister of waqfs undertake to investigate the deficiencies of Muslim preaching (*al-da'wa al-islamiyya*) and to seek out its causes, as well as the causes of the desiccation of the sources irrigating the fields of religious instruction . . .

'That measures be taken to raise the level of al-Azhar graduates in the departments of preaching and guidance (*al-irshad*), so that they may be capable of fulfilling the noble functions with which they are entrusted, in a straightforward manner that will allow them to reach the hearts and minds of young people.'

Such was the army's line on the Society of Muslims: Shukri, a criminal charlatan who sought the overthrow of the regime, had been able to dupe many young people by cloaking his felonious projects in the mantle of religion; this was possible because the youth were suffering from religious vacuity due to al-Azhar's deficiencies. Clearly, the *ulema* had failed in their task.

The *ulema* found themselves in a highly uncomfortable position. Not only had the victim been one of their number, but the Society of Muslims considered them no more than lackeys of the prince, 'pulpit parrots' [1], while the army effectively accused them of dereliction.

Shukri had not selected Dhahabi at random, but held him largely responsible for concocting the negative image of the Society of Muslims: in July 1975, when he was still minister of waqfs, Dhahabi had written the preface to an official pamphlet directed against the Society. In it he traced the sect's inspiration back to Kharijism, thus reproducing the stereotypical discourse

---

7. This was already the case in primary and secondary schools, where religious instruction is compulsory and tested by an examination.

of the Muslim religious establishment when faced with any new and important phenomenon. Instead of analysing it as it deserved, so as to enable the state to understand it better and thus to counteract it more effectively, Dhahabi managed only to focus the hostility of Islamicist youth on the *ulema*. The Muslim religious hierarchy thus showed the political regime that it was not a reliable institution capable of playing the role expected of it: to educate the youth in religion, or in other words, to make sure that Muslim practice was a force for social integration and not a mode of expression for revolt against society.

This ossification of the *ulema* has a relatively well-known history dating back to the rule of Muhammad 'Ali at the beginning of the nineteenth century. With the reform of al-Azhar in 1961 and that of the Ministry of Waqfs the following year, the Nasser regime had sought to open these institutions up to society, so that they would be able to act effectively as transmission belts carrying the regime's ideology to the masses. The *ulema*, dragging their feet as they had for the past century, thwarted the reforms of the sixties while seeking to preserve their special status and to avoid becoming mere religious functionaries of the state. Such was the cost of maintaining their popular credibility. In return, however, the state could not have complete confidence in them: admittedly, they served the state, but they had no intention of being lectured on their duties. It is in this context that we must understand the position of the sheikh of al-Azhar on the Dhahabi affair, and consequently on Islamicist dissidence of the sort expressed by the Society of Muslims.

The sheikh, 'Abd al-Halim Mahmud, was in London from the third to the seventh of July 1977. His contribution to the press campaign against *al-Takfir wa'l-Hijra* did not appear in *al-Ahram* until 16 July. Although the grand *imam* rejected the group's ideas, he nevertheless explained that the cause of the phenomenon lay in the fact that power in Egypt had long been held by people whose political philosophy was not rooted in the religious culture of the country. It was this that explained why disoriented youth perceived society as *jahiliyya*. This was not the line of the military prosecutor, who said instead that the sect had cloaked itself in a religious garb in order to conceal its crimes.

The court refused the request of Shukri's lawyer, made in his opening statement on 23 October, to summon 'Abd al-Halim Mahmud to testify at the trial; al-Azhar's line on the Society of Muslims was thus concealed.

Nor was the state inclined to allow the military origins of the regime issued of the 1952 revolution to be placed on trial. Censure of Shukri's activities and ideology had to be expressed with a single voice. The Azhar sheikh therefore had to keep silent and let the military tribunal issue the canonical denunciation of the Society of Muslims on its own. But the publication of the court record on 12 March 1978 placed the *ulema* in the dock yet again, charged with having failed in their tasks of education and training. A furious 'Abd al-Halim Mahmud drafted a communiqué in reply, which received wide coverage in the Arab press, though not in Egypt itself. The sheikh accused the military court of incompetence because it had not been careful to distinguish between the assassination of Dhahabi on the one hand and Shukri's ideas on the other. Moreover, the sheikh revealed, the court had sought to associate al-Azhar with its ill-starred enterprise: the religious institution was expected to 'criminalize' (*tajrim*) Shukri's thought — and solely on the basis of transcripts, without the *ulema's* even being granted access to the texts of the accused or contact with their author. But 'in a country in which freedom of opinion holds sway, freedom of which atheists and communists avail themselves, it is not al-Azhar's function to criminalize thought "on the sly".'

The extreme violence of the Azhar sheikh's tone reflects the awkward situation of the *ulema*: the army's line had been favoured over theirs in a field of their own competence, the determination of religious deviance.[8] Six years after the 'rectification revolution' through which Sadat claimed to have restored the sovereignty of law and the normal role of institutions, the regime was forced, just as during the Nasser era, to call upon the army, the only institution whose loyalty was beyond question.

8. On the competition among the various intellectual discourses in Egypt today, see my article 'Les oulémas, l'intelligentsia et les islamistes en Egypte. Système social, ordre transcendantal et *ordre traduit*', *Revue française de Science Politique*, vol. 35 (1985), no. 3.

The Society of Muslims was a unique phenomenon in Sadat's Egypt. By organizing a counter-society in the furnished flats, a world in which the dominant social practices were inverted, it allowed the Islamicist youth who followed Shukri Mustafa to live out their own utopia. Their impassioned revolt of the poor, the disinherited, and the hopeless was as clumsy as it was novel: their disconcerting theoretical hodgepodge bears the authentic imprint of those who suffer.

This tendency of the Islamicist movement sank into a kind of oblivion. But its achievements and errors gave others food for thought, in particular the group that hatched the conspiracy that led to Sadat's assassination. The confrontation between the state and the Society of Muslims and the latter's destruction invalidated the 'phase of weakness' strategy, the basis of which had been laid by Sayyid Qutb. The young Islamicists who came after Shukri would no longer avail themselves of it.

4
'Al-Da'wa': Legalists Despite Themselves

In creating the Society of Muslims, Shukri Mustafa had stretched the concepts presented by Sayyid Qutb in *Signposts* to the limit. Another tendency of the Islamicist movement chose a contrary approach, trying instead to prune the shoots *Signposts* had cast out in so many directions and to confine the mission of the Islamicist movement to the path originally charted by Hasan al-Banna, the founder of the Muslim Brotherhood.

This tendency had emerged as early as 1969, when Hasan al-Hudaybi, Supreme Guide of the Muslim Brethen, brought out his book 'Preachers, Not Judges'. The Brotherhood 'old guard' in Nasser's concentration camps, those of its leaders who had neither renounced their ideas nor fled abroad, rallied to this current. After Sadat released the Islamicists, the members of this old guard came together and asked the state to grant them legal recognition. Although Sadat never agreed to the reconstitution of the Society of Muslim Brethren, in 1976 he nevertheless gave them permission to publish a monthly magazine, *al-Da'wa*, which appeared regularly until September 1981, when the president banned all the non-government press just one month before his assassination.

This magazine became the organ through which the reformist wing of the Islamicist movement presented its positions to the general public on all social, political, economic, and religious questions, but it was also a sounding board for the various activities of the movement in its preferred fields of endeavour. Reading it therefore allows us to follow the Islamicist view of the news on a month-to-month basis, to apprehend world events as diffracted by the magazine's editorial board in column after column.

Al-Da'wa was not the only Islamicist journal published during the last years of the Sadat regime: two other magazines competed with it for readers, but without making any serious inroads. The first of these, *al-I'tisam* ('Adherence'), took its name from the Koranic verse 'Adhere to the tether of God and do not separate from it'. Launched in 1936, until September 1977 it was the organ of a Muslim charitable association, the *Jama'iyya Shari'iyya* founded by Sheikh Mahmud Khattab al-Sibki to build mosques all over Egypt. Its publisher, Ahmad 'Ashur, was generous in opening its columns to young writers belonging to non-clandestine Islamicist circles. He also improved its format, turning it into a magazine. Although it was at times more radical or violent in tone than *al-Da'wa*, it came nowhere near its rival in wide-ranging editorial scope and the regularity with which it appeared. The final journal of the Islamicist trinity, *al-Mukhtar al-Islami* ('Islamic Selection'), was conceived as a kind of Muslim version of the Arabic-language edition of *Reader's Digest*, whose typography and layout it copied. Its long and heavily documented articles were aimed at a readership of a higher intellectual level than its two competitors. Less directly concerned with topical issues, it tended instead to concentrate on broad Muslim themes. It appeared monthly for two years, from July 1979 to September 1981, when it was banned.

Al-Da'wa, then, did not represent the totality of the Islamicist press, but it appeared with absolute regularity for nearly five years,[1] with a virtually unchanging content, the backbone of which consisted of a number of regular features. Moreover, it expressed the views of the most 'reformist', the least 'revolutionary', tendency of the Islamicist movement, whose leaders were seasoned Muslim Brethren generally much older than the supporters of Shukri Mustafa. Although *al-Da'wa*'s caution enabled it to survive for five years, it also ensured that Islamicist groups seeking active intervention in fields that *al-Da'wa* dared not even discuss would arise outside it, and to a large extent against it.

Before the Free Officers seized power in 1952, *al-Da'wa* had been owned by Salih 'Ashmawi. After 1953, when his dif-

1. Only the May 1979 issue failed to appear, the result of a government suspension lifted the following month.

ferences with Supreme Guide Hasan al-Hudaybi led to his ex-
pulsion from the Society of Muslim Brethren, 'Ashmawi turned
his periodical into an independent Islamicist magazine. Nasser
took a favourable view of the rise of internal dissension in the
Brotherhood, for it embarrassed the leadership. Both al-Da'wa
and its owner were therefore spared the ordeals of repression
inflicted on the Brotherhood beginning in November 1954. In
fact, al-Da'wa continued to appear sporadically throughout the
Nasser era. It was never longer than a few pages, and to preserve
its legal status it 'published judgements', as the Arabic expression has it, meaning the judgements issued by the various
'people's' or military courts against the Islamicist movement.

When Sadat consolidated his power in 1971, he released some
of the imprisoned Islamicist militants. While Shukri Mustafa
returned to Asyut to form the underground Society of Muslims,
'Umar Talmasani, a lawyer, future editor-in-chief of al-Da'wa
and one of Supreme Guide Hasan al-Hudaybi's close associates,
went to the 'Abidin Presidential Palace to inscribe in the public
registry his own thanks and those of his friends to the president
for having released them.

The last of the imprisoned Muslim Brethren, however, were
not freed until 22 March 1975. On 8 July of that year a general
amnesty was declared for all those who had been sentenced to
prison terms for their political ideas before 15 May 1971, the date
of the 'rectification revolution' in which Sadat ousted his rivals
in the political establishment. But the defendants in the Heliopolis Military Academy trial soon replaced the released Muslim
Brethren behind bars, thus maintaining a continuous presence
of Islamicist militants among the Egyptian prison population.
Sadat kept up the pressure on the Muslim Brethren through his
policy of releasing Islamicist prisoners gradually. He probably
hoped that this would convince the Brotherhood to support him
publicly, but the Brethren claim that they avoided the trap and
continued to refuse to pledge their allegiance to Sadat. 'Hasan
al-Hudaybi', wrote 'Abd al-Rahman Khalifa, 'refused to allow
Anwar Sadat to manipulate the Brethren or himself. Indeed, the
president wanted them to endorse his regime, and [in exchange]
would have permitted each Muslim Brother to work individually
for the spread of Islam. But he would not permit the resurrection

of the Society of Muslim Brethren, for fear that it would oppose the rulers or exert pressure on the regime to be governed by Islam' [21].

When Hudaybi died in 1973, no official successor as Supreme Guide was named, but Talmasani became the chief public figure of the Muslim Brethren in Egypt. In 1976 Salih 'Ashmawi, who had been expelled back in 1953, came to see Talmasani and placed al-Da'wa at the disposal of the Brotherhood. A new format was designed, and the financing of the journal was entrusted to the Islamic Publication and Distribution Company, with Talmasani as chairman of the board. The regime made no effort to block this transaction, and the first issue of the new-style al-Da'wa was published in July 1976. In an interview several years later, Talmasani gave this answer to those who complained that the Brethren had struck a compromise with the Sadat regime: 'Al-Da'wa had appeared back in the forties, and it was no business of President Sadat's to grant us authorization to publish it, because Mr Salih 'Ashmawi had made sure that it was produced regularly, although quite modestly . . . it contained only two or three pages in each issue, as was stipulated in its legal authorization.'

This plea by the elderly lawyer, however, did not convince the intellectuals of the Egyptian left. In September 1976 one of their number, the historian 'Abd al-'Azim Ramadan, writing in the weekly Rose al-Yusif, stigmatized the 'reactionary tendency within the Brethren' that was in charge of the magazine and erroneously interpreted Islam, 'a progressive religion'. Ramadan held that the Brotherhood as a whole faced a decisive choice: 'either to stand on the side of the broad masses, with the Communists and Nasserists, or to ally with the reactionaries, the Zionists, and the United States'!

Regardless of the various accusations and the responses to them, the fact remains that the major part in the magazine was played by former Brethren whom the Supreme Guide had expelled in 1953 for their inclination to collaborate with the regime: Salih 'Ashmawi for one, but also Muhammad al-Ghazali, who held an important post in the organizational hierarchy of the Egyptian Ministry of Waqfs in the early seventies, a time when he was also in favour in Saudi Arabia.

These, then, were Muslim Brethren of a new type. They acted in the name of the legacy of the 'two Hasans' (al-Banna and al-Hudaybi), but they proved unable to reconstruct an organization with the scope of the Brotherhood destroyed by Nasser in 1954, and their role on the Egyptian socio-political scene in the seventies remained marginal. It could therefore be argued that the appellation 'Muslim Brethren' should be reserved for the *Jama'at al-Ikhwan al-Muslimin*, and that the tendency behind *al-Da'wa* should be called the 'neo-Muslim Brethren'. This terminology duly notes that although the one was indeed the descendant of the other, an important part of the heritage had nevertheless disappeared.

The Purse-Strings

Decked out in its new image, *al-Da'wa*, which now called itself 'the voice of truth, strength, and liberty', declared in its first issue (July 1976) that it would 'call for Islam, proclaim the Koran, and demand the application of the *shari'a*', meaning the abrogation of the Egyptian code of civil law (which was inspired by French law) and its replacement by a legislative code derived from the Koran and the Sunna.

The magazine found a 'niche', and its circulation quickly rose to 78,000, according to the sworn statement of its auditor, published in the January 1977 issue in an attempt to attract advertising. In fact the magazine had carried advertising from its very first issue — not only the modest notices of various Islamicist bookshops, but also multi-column displays by food companies, importers and distributors of foreign automobiles, and clothing importers. By the last year of its existence, *al-Da'wa* had established an advertising base that 'targeted' a particular layer of the population so effectively that the nationalized Bank Misr placed a full-page advertisement on the inside front cover of the July 1981 issue announcing the launch of its 'branch of Islamic operations', under the slogan 'your money grows in accordance with the rules of the *shari'a*.' The text of the advertisement explained that funds deposited with the branch of Islamic operations were completely separate from all other assets and that one of the *ulema* of al-

Azhar supervised the legitimacy of financial transactions so that clients who chose to invest in the branch could not be accused of usury, which is the term many Muslims still use to describe interest-bearing loans. Bank Misr was the most ostentatious of the public-sector companies to advertise in *al-Da'wa*, though it was by no means alone in doing so. At first, however, most of the advertising came from the private sector, representing a typical cross-section of the businesses that soared as a result of the policy of *infitah*, the 'economic opening' decided on by Sadat and implemented by his minister 'Abd al-'Aziz Higazi beginning in 1975. Out of the total of nearly 180 pages of colour advertising in *al-Da'wa*, 49 were bought by real-estate promoters and entrepreneurs, 52 by chemical and plastics companies, 20 by automobile importers, 12 by 'Islamic' banks and investment companies, and 45 by food companies. About a fifth of the total advertising space was bought by companies identifiable as belonging to the public sector, whose funds were therefore managed by state employees. Half of the remaining four-fifths was accounted for by just three advertisers: al-Sharif plastics, the Massara real-estate company, and Modern Motors, importers of Japanese automobiles. These three companies are controlled by Muslim Brethren who made their fortune in Saudi Arabia over the past thirty years and have invested heavily in Egypt since 1975, particularly in the import and general consumer-goods sectors, which enable them to accumulate significant profits rapidly without tying up large sums of capital in heavy equipment. This interpenetration of certain business circles and the neo-Muslim Brethren was acknowledged by Talmasani himself in an 'American-style' interview granted to journalists of the Egyptian weekly *al-Musawwar* in January 1982:

'Do you admit that most of the commanding levers of the policy of economic opening (*infitah*) are now in the hands of former Muslim Brethren who were in exile and have now returned to Egypt, having made their fortunes?'

'I do not doubt that some rich Muslim Brethren are helping to resolve the problems of *infitah* in the consumer sector, but I deplore this, for the economic opening must benefit production first of all.'

In other words, while Shukri Mustafa was financing the

Society of Muslims by sending its members to work in the Gulf countries, the neo-Muslim Brethren had wormed their way into the economic fabric of Sadat's Egypt at a time when whole sections of it had been turned over to unregulated capitalism. They were thus able to draw upon substantial subsidies. The entrepreneur 'Uthman Ahmad 'Uthman, the Egyptian Rocke-feller, had made no secret of his sympathy for the Brethren, and although his name appears only once in all the colour advertising pages of *al-Da'wa*, it is more than likely that he was generous toward those in whose ranks he had been active during his youth in Ismailia.

Some militants of the Islamicist movement linked to the *Da'wa* group were also able to combine certain lapses of the Egyptian justice system with the fear inspired by the violent bent of the Islamicist university groups, the *jama'at islamiyya* (see chapter 5). These militants had established a commercial company in Alexandria called al-Qadisiyya, named after a victorious battle of the early Muslim armies against the Persians. Apart from resell-ing imported items, they specialized in a robust and profitable form of real-estate transaction. When Sadat lifted the sequestra-tion orders his predecessor had imposed on the property of 'capitalists', the former owners legally recovered their assets. During the period of sequestration, however, the various nationalized insurance companies that had been in charge of managing the sequestered properties had rented, or even sold them to new tenants (or buyers). This created a daunting legal mess. Although the courts ruled in favour of aggrieved former owners seeking to recover their property or to evict tenants, no executive force was capable of actually implementing the court rulings. The former owners were therefore often unable physi-cally to recover their properties. Al-Qadisiyya had a proposition for such former owners. The company would purchase the lands or buildings in question for a sum roughly equivalent to a third of the market price. Once the agreed sum had been paid and al-Qadisiyya became the legal owner of the property, Islamicist militants would visit the unwanted occupants and manifest their new ownership by building a small mosque. Usually this was enough to convince the terrified occupants to move out bag and baggage without further ado, for they were far more afraid of the cudgels of the *jama'at islamiyya* than of the possible intervention of a police force whose members were easily bought. Once the site was no longer occupied, it was available for any number of development projects, advertisements for which appeared in *al-Da'wa*.

This scattered information about how the magazine was financed, however, gives us only an impressionistic view of it, one that allows no definite conclusions. Nevertheless, the different means of acquiring money employed by Shukri's group on the one hand and by Talmasani's friends on the other is striking, and illustrates two sorts of perceptions of the nature of the economic problems of Egyptian society. The propaganda of the neo-Muslim Brethren was more reformist than radical or revolutionary, in many cases being designed to repaint existing structures in Islamic green without any great upheaval. This is quite clear from a reading of all the issues of *al-Da'wa* during its sixty-four-month lifespan.

The Four Horsemen of the Apocalypse

It need hardly be emphasized that *al-Da'wa* was not the kind of magazine to report events without comment. The journal's commentary, its classification of events into the categories of Good and Evil, its value judgements and statements of position, constituted the bulk of its copy and offered readers a vast fresco depicting the triumph of Islam as understood by the neo-Muslim Brethren and identifying the innumerable enemies, overt or covert, whom the magazine's journalists tracked down and denounced relentlessly in their zeal to expose the equally innumerable plots against Islam. This omnipresent dichotomy between Good and Evil will guide our reading of the journal, for it allows us to specify some elements of the editorial board's typology.

Islam's universal vocation impelled the editors of *al-Da'wa* ceaselessly to remind their readers of the numerical strength of the Muslim world, and to print regular articles about it. A column entitled *Watanuna al-Islami* ('Our Muslim Nation') presented monthly news about the multiform battle between Islam and its myriad enemies.

But however numerous these enemies were, they could be reduced to four principal types, though these might combine and thus produce hybrids. These four horsemen of the apocalypse were: 'Jewry', the 'Crusade', 'communism', and 'secularism'. Let us note that 'imperialism', the generic term designating the principle of absolute evil throughout the Nasser period and still denounced by the Egyptian left as such, appears in *al-Da'wa* not as a category, but as a mere attribute of the 'Crusade'. Let us now try to explain the content of these four terms, drawing freely upon many issues of the magazine.

For the editors of *al-Da'wa*, 'Jewry' is the ultimate abomination. The word 'Jew' (*yahud*) is used indifferently to apply to both Israeli citizens and other Jews. Israeli citizenship, in fact, is seen as merely an attribute of the Jew, defined ontologically on the basis of racial, historical, and religious criteria. In the children's supplement entitled 'The Lion Cubs of *al-Da'wa*' (*Ashbal al-Da'wa*), a pull-out section inserted into the magazine, there is a column entitled 'Recognize the Enemies of Your Religion' (*Ta'arraf 'ala A'da' Dinika*).[2] Here is the text of an article headed 'The Jews', which appeared in October 1980:

'Brother Muslim Lion Cub,

'Have you ever wondered why God cursed the Jews in His Book — *Those of the Israelites who disbelieved were cursed by David and Jesus, the son of Mary* (V, 78) — after he had earlier preferred them to the rest of the world? *Children of Israel, remember that I have bestowed favours on you and exalted you above the nations* (II, 47). . . .

'But by this preference, God was testing the children of Israel to see whether they would be associationists [*mushrikin*: meaning those who 'associate' other gods with the One True God and therefore count as polytheists] or infidels: *We tested them with blessings and misfortunes so that they might desist from sin* (VII, 168). And what was the result? God grew weary of their lies. *God has heard the words of those who said: "God is poor but we are rich."*

2. This column is decorated by a border composed of what might be called the magazine's *bêtes noires*. From left to right we find Hafez al-Assad, Brezhnev, Begin, Nasser, a star of David turned into a poisonous snake, a statue of Liberty with a crown of thorns, a hammer and sickle, and Kemal Atatürk.

Their words We will record, and the fact that they have slain their prophets unjustly. We shall say: "Taste now the torment of hell-fire" (III, 181). They associated others with God, they were infidels: *The Jews say Ezra is the son of God*(IX, 30). . . . His preference was met with ingratitude and denial of divine power. *The Jews say: "God's hand is chained." May their own hands be chained! May they be cursed for what they say* (V, 64). It may happen that a man lies or falls into error, but for a people to build their society on lies, that is the speciality of the children of Israel alone! *The Jews who listen to the lies of others and pay no heed to you* (V, 41). *They listen to falsehoods and practise what is unlawful* (V, 42). Such are the Jews, my brother, Muslim lion cub, your enemies and the enemies of God, and such is the truth about them as told in the Book of God. . . . Such is their particular natural disposition, the corrupt doctrine that is theirs, . . . they have never ceased to conspire against their main enemy, the Muslims.

'In one of their books they say: "We Jews are the masters of the world, its corrupters, those who foment sedition, its hangmen!"

'They do not like you, Muslim lion cub, you who revere God, Islam, and the Prophet Muhammad . . . .

'Muslim lion cub, annihilate their existence, those who seek to subjugate all humanity so as to force them to serve their satanic designs.

'*God has power over all things, though most men may not know it* (XII, 21).'

Such is *al-Da'wa*'s definition of the Jew, intended for the edification of Muslim children. The race is corrupt at its root, full of duplicity, and the Muslims have everything to lose in seeking to deal with them: they must be exterminated. These are the principles that guided Talmasani and his friends' perception of Israel, and subsequently of the problem of the Egyptian-Israeli peace treaty. In fact, *al-Da'wa* sees Palestine not so much as 'Arab land' in the manner of the 'progressives', but as a part of the Islamic nation usurped by the Jews.

Al-Da'wa showed particular interest in the problem of the Dome of the Rock mosque, in the old city of Jerusalem. The cover of the May 1981 issue depicts the famous structure ringed by a chain and sealed by a padlock stamped with the star of David. A hand holding a hatchet is coming down on the lock. The message is clear. The Egyptian state can sign its treaty with the Hebrew state, but for Muslims the problem remains: one of their holy sites is under the control of the enemies of Islam, and the *jihad* for the liberation of Jerusalem is on the agenda more urgently than ever.

Beginning in October 1976 a column entitled 'Israel Today and Tomorrow' regularly exposed all aspects of 'Israeli ignominy'. It was recalled in particular that because of the essential nature of the Jew, it was futile to seek to establish relations with Israeli progressive forces, as Yasser Arafat, the chairman of the PLO, had proposed. In fact, 'all Jews, like Menahem Begin, have spilled the blood of the Arabs, usurped their lands and homes. . . . The inclination to betrayal and belligerence is deeply implanted in the soul of every Jew. There is no difference between Ben Gurion and Begin.'

As might well be imagined, the Egyptian-Israeli peace treaty was not well received by *al-Da'wa*. In 1978, during the negotiations, Talmasani published editorials recalling that Israel was part of *Dar al-Harb*, the Domain of War, and that if the regime wished to be worthy of the name Muslim, it had to proclaim *jihad*, holy war: 'If the Muslims renounce the effort to recover any part of their alienated land when it is possible for them to do so, they are all in a state of sin. History will judge the present generation harshly, rulers and ruled alike, for having preferred material well-being to honour and religion.' Thus it was that relations between the regime and the neo-Muslim Brethren of *al-Da'wa* broke down over Sadat's trip to Jerusalem. Throughout 1978 the magazine attacked the very idea of negotiations, therefore implicitly suggesting that the regime was governing in flagrant contravention of Islam. This placed *al-Da'wa* on the most sensitive ground, questioning the regime's Islamic legitimacy, which it had never before done in public. The legitimacy of the Egyptian-Israeli peace treaty was of course confirmed by an Azhar *fatwa*, based on the treaties Muhammad concluded with the Qurayshites (at Hudaybiyya) and with the Ghatafan tribes, as well as on a Koranic verse (VIII, 61): *If they incline to peace, make peace with them.* In the July 1978 issue of *al-Da'wa* (no. 38),

'Abd al-'Azim al-Mut'ani offered a detailed criticism of the assimilation of the Prophet's treaties to the treaty with Israel. The September issue (no. 40) published a response from the office of the sheikh of al-Azhar, 'Abd al-Rahman Bisar, who sought to refute al-Mut'ani's argument. The very fact that al-Azhar deemed it useful to publish a response in *al-Da'wa* shows that the prince's religious establishment was alert to any contradiction of its position by dissident Muslim voices.

There seems little doubt that various hidden pressures from the government gave the editorial board to understand that if the magazine was to continue publishing, it would have to stop this sort of questioning of the regime's Muslim character. In 1979, the tone of the editorials changed: peace is the supreme goal of Islam, Talmasani now said, and it was good to seek it. The problem was the partner, the Jews, who because of their very essence were not to be trusted.

The question of the existence of the state of Israel and of possible relations with it was therefore very strictly circumscribed by *al-Da'wa*'s understanding of 'the Jew', and thence traced back to a number of negative characteristics that *ipso facto* prevented any sort of relation other than fighting for his extermination. Between late 1977 and 1979, when euphoria for peace swept the Egyptian population, *al-Da'wa*'s arguments fell on deaf ears. But when the first clouds gathered over Egyptian-Israeli relations with the stalling of the talks on Palestinian autonomy, and later with the Knesset's declaration of Jerusalem as the reunified capital of the Hebrew state, *al-Da'wa*'s propositions gained some credibility, notably because the Egyptian government seemed unable to react to the Begin regime's various initiatives. In September 1980, when Talmasani wrote an editorial entitled 'Today Jerusalem and the Golan Heights, Tomorrow Jordan and Lebanon', many Egyptians who were not necessarily regular readers of *al-Da'wa* but who nevertheless agreed that the existing bilateral relations were a fool's game, took notice. The neo-Muslim Brethren's reading of events thus had some impact. A certain audience was convinced by its process of deduction, which explained the behaviour of Israel in terms of the essence of the Jew, and it gained a new and far broader audience through an inverse process of induction: to all those who felt that Israel had tricked Egypt but were unable to explain why, *al-Da'wa* offered a way to trace the phenomenon back to its essence, in accordance with an internally coherent schema. Begin had become *al-Da'wa*'s most effective propagandist.

The perception of the Jews, or more exactly of 'the Jew', the main lines of which have been summarized here, invites a few remarks about what might well be called Semitic anti-Semitism. The short text intended for the edification of Muslim children is of particular interest in that it is presented as a mere commentary on Koranic verses and on 'one of the books of the Jews' — in fact none other than the notorious *Protocols of the Elders of Zion*, whose evolution from its fabrication in the offices of the Tsarist secret police to its official use in Saudi Arabia during the reign of King Faisal is well known. The illustration printed on the children's supplement is taken straight from German-Russian imagery: one wonders what sort of effect it has in a country whose inhabitants' physical characteristics, as seen by Western caricaturists, scarcely differ from those of the Jew, who here wears the calotte and gallabieh, just like any pious Muslim.

But this influence of European anti-Semitism on *al-Da'wa*'s perception of 'the Jew' acts on a commentary on Koranic verses, and inflects it in a particular polemical direction. The Koran does contain some verses violently hostile to the Jews (and to the Christians too, for that matter). It also contains others which are not systematically unfavourable to them, notably those that grant them the status of 'people of the Book' who have the right to continue to practise their religion in the countries ruled by Muslims, in exchange for the payment of a special tax. Such people are called *dhimmis*, or tributaries; their existence has been used by Islamophiles as evidence of Islam's tolerance and by Islamophobes as evidence of its inegalitarianism, each side approaching the question in a thoroughly anachronistic manner.

In the mind of the editors of *al-Da'wa*, the Jews, like the Christians, have a right to exist because they are, so to speak, potential Muslims, believers who have not yet been moved by the Islamic message. On the blessed day that this message touches them, they will immediately become Muslims. (In the course of working on this book, I spent a good deal of time with

Egyptian Islamicists, who always began trying to convert me to Islam once our contacts had acquired some stability.)

What the 'people of the Book' are not allowed to do is proselytize for their religion, or erect any obstacle whatever to the movement towards their ineluctable conversion to Islam. By this reasoning, if the resistance of Western Christians is already viewed with disfavour, anything that smacks of a reconquest of territories ruled by Islam borders on abomination. The Spanish Reconquista of Muslim Andalusia is still a source of sorrow and a scandal, but although various associations urge Muslims to remember that one day they will have to reconquer the Iberian peninsula, the issue is no longer considered one of burning topicality. The settlement of Jews in Palestine and the creation of the state of Israel, on the other hand, are the fruits of a recent plot that it is not too late to thwart. Holy war must therefore be waged until the Dome of the Rock and the country in which it stands are again brought under Muslim jurisdiction. Since Israel is a Jewish state, the Jews occupy the vanguard positions in the front of the enemies of Islam.

There is nothing very new in Talmasani and company's use of hatred of the Jews as the vector of anti-Zionism and the struggle against Israel. The caricatures that used to appear in the Nasserist press and propaganda brochures in the sixties are no less violent than those of the neo-Muslim Brethren. The latter are now mining the same thematic and iconographic vein, but they reduce it to its essence: the Jew is Jewish, and therefore detestable; there is thus no reason, even as a mere stylistic concession, to distinguish between the Zionist and the non-Zionist, the Israeli and the Jew of the diaspora, and so on. Nor was the Nasser regime concerned with such nuances when Egyptian Jews were imprisoned in the concentration camps of Tura and Abu Za'bal alongside the Communists and Muslim Brethren, for no crime other than their confessional allegiance.

This 'anti-Jewish line' was one of the major thematic axes of *al-Da'wa*. Sadat's trip to infidel-occupied Jerusalem and the subsequent Egyptian-Israeli peace treaty were thus absolutely unacceptable to the neo-Muslim Brethren, and brought about a very clear hardening of their attitude to the regime.

The 'Crusade' stands only slightly beneath 'Jewry' in the hierarchy of infamy. Where the Jew is evil by nature, the Christian is evil only contingently. Although all Jews are evil, there are both good and evil Christians. The latter, however, are a majority, and they strive relentlessly to pervert the former in order to win them to their aims: the hatching of conspiracies to destroy Islam.

Only very rarely does the Crusade dare to resort to armed operations against the Muslims in the bastion of Islam that is Egypt. It works instead through evangelists, missionary activity (*tabshir*), congregations established in the country, and so on. In donning the prepossessing garb of eucumenism, for example, the Crusade seeks to sow doubt and confusion about their doctrine in the minds of Muslims. It also seeks, with the aid of orientalists, to spread rumours that discredit Muhammad. The baneful influence of the Crusade on the education system is especially pernicious: examining the standard history book used by twelve-year-olds in 1975 and 1976, *al-Da'wa* remarks that the second edition devotes too much space to the sites of Christian pilgrimage in the Middle East and not enough to the Muslim holy places. This, the magazine says, is related to the fact that the second edition was written by a Christian and a Muslim, whereas the first edition was written by three Muslims and just one Christian. Moreover, it is shameful to teach children the majority of whom are Muslims that Christ's sepulchre is in Jerusalem: this is a Christian belief, not a Muslim one.

The advent of the fifteenth century of the hegira in 1980 provided an opportunity for the neo-Muslim Brethren to present a sweeping recapitulation of the past history of Islam, in an effort to draw edifying lessons for the future. One of the phenomena that had to be taken into account was colonialism (or imperialism, *isti'mar*) in its various aspects:

'We must be aware from the start that the enemies of Islam are the gang of liars represented by today's colonialist trinity (*thaluth*): Jewry, communism, and capitalism. For fourteen centuries our Koran has warned that the community of infidels (*millat al-kufr*) was one: *You will please neither the Christians nor the Jews unless you follow their faith. Say: "The guidance of God is the only guidance"* (II, 120). *They will not cease to fight against you until they force you to renounce your faith — if they are able* (II, 217).'

Since the Crusade is not mentioned by name here, it is worth noting that the Koranic foundation on which the argument against the 'colonialist trinity' rests is a verse directed against the Christians. This ambivalence is never really clarified, for the basic distinction between the good and happy tributary Christian who prays in his church without trying to win converts and submits to the rules of the *shari'a* and the evil Crusader is eminently subjective, liable to all the vagaries of conjunctural shifts.

The work of orientalists constitutes one component of the Crusade conspiracy, as is indicated by a mysterious 'Richard document' supposedly passing instructions to Christians which featured prominently in the confessional incidents that occurred in Minya in 1980.' The 'Richard' in question is Richard P. Mitchell, an American orientalist and author of a major work on the Muslim Brethren, *The Society of the Muslim Brothers* (1969). At the origin of this affair we find the hand of Talmasani's friends, who in 1979 confected what might be called 'the Mitchell case'. Before that date, the neo-Brethren harboured no particular hostility to the American historian, and were even somewhat proud that a work of this quality had been devoted to the Society founded by Hasan al-Banna. At first the work was noted in *al-Da'wa* and even recommended to readers. Suddenly, in January 1979, while Mitchell was in Cairo for a year's sabbatical, the magazine published a 'document' written in Arabic and 'addressed by the writer to the head of the secret services of the American Central Intelligence Agency'; it called for the urgent destruction of the Islamicist movement by the Egyptian state. There was scant internal evidence of the document's authenticity. It was far from clear why the American professor, even if he had been a CIA agent, would correspond with an American official in Arabic. *Al-Da'wa* was unable to answer the denials issued by both Mitchell and the American embassy in Cairo. But the point had been made, and a year and a half later, in Minya, the 'Richard document' was said to be the ultimate cause of

3. See chapter 5.

persecution of Muslims organized by the Crusaders. Young readers of *al-Da'wa* in Minya felt that there could be no truth to the denials: Mitchell was a CIA agent and the Christians were his fifth column.

In June 1981 serious incidents broke out in al-Zawiyya al-Hamra, a poor neighbourhood in Cairo with a mixed Christian and Muslim population. For *al-Da'wa*, they were a perfect illustration of the Crusader conspiracy against Egyptian Islam.

Three articles published in July and August sought to establish the chronology and genealogy of the events. It seems that 'the Copts of Egypt are the happiest minority in the world; all their material and moral rights are not only protected, but extended'. They lived in perfect harmony with the Muslims and enjoyed the enviable status of *dhimmi*: 'Everything was for the best until Shenouda became patriarch of the Copts of Egypt. Then phenomena appeared the like of which had never before been seen: we heard it said that Egypt was Coptic and that there was no place for Muslims, and so on.' The articles in *al-Da'wa* denounced foreign powers, in particular Copts living in America, for having incited the world's happiest minority to arrogance and defiance. The traditional distinction between good Christians who submit to Islam and evil Crusaders was obliterated in the heat of the moment: one article went so far as to suggest an indiscriminate boycott of all shops belonging to Copts.

But the confusion between Copts and Crusaders, unlike the amalgamation of all Jews, is not structural, but conjunctural. It came at a moment of extreme tension, a few months before the assassination of Sadat, when the state's grip was shaky and the Islamicist movement as a whole was in a radical mood, believing that its time had come. A slogan like the threat to boycott Coptic shops amounts to a direct attack on Egyptian national unity, which is itself one of the keywords of state legitimacy. That was one of the pretexts for the repressive measures against the Islamicist movement taken by Sadat at the end of the summer of 1981.

The neo-Muslim Brethren excoriate communism as well as Jewry and the Crusade. According to the editors, 'it is no accident that it was in Moscow — the capital of atheism — that Nasser gave the speech in 1965 that led to the martyrdom of Sayyid Qutb and his companions.' For the neo-Muslim Brethren, communism is first and foremost atheism, and therefore the mortal enemy of Islam. The magazine gave many examples. The policy of de-Islamicization in the Muslim republics of the Soviet Union, atheist museums being built for this purpose, was trumpeted. Communism combated Islam throughout the world: in Eritrea and Somalia it made alliances with the Crusade to exterminate Muslims; in Syria it supported the dictator Assad, who massacred the Muslim Brethren; finally, in Afghanistan it massacred the Muslims in general. In Egypt it was the dominant system between 1961 and 1971:

'During these ten years the country was ravaged, the servants of God suffered destitution, and corruption was widespread. . . ; communism is like cancer, it is extirpated only at the cost of great efforts. . . . The Communists dominated what was called the "Arab Socialist Union". They were everywhere: in its political commission, in its various branches. Under their aegis the people lived as in the blackest of nights; the worker spied on his fellow worker, the student on his fellow student, and the official press became a gigantic prison whose inmates were stifled. The Communists also took control of two other sectors: the Organization of Socialist Youth . . . and the Higher Council of Islamic Affairs, whose watchword was the trinity, "Socialism is our road, the Charter is our constitution, Nasserism is our credo."[4] . . . The era of communism ended with the death of Nasser.'

If any further proof of the eminently evil character of communism were necessary, al-Da'wa supplied it for its readers, who were reminded that 'Marxism and Zionism have a common origin: Marxist thought is a Jewish elaboration (ijtihad), and Marx's grandfather was a well-known rabbi.'

Communism is thus discredited on various counts. To begin with, it is associated with abominable Jewry and the wretched Crusade; it is fundamentally atheist in nature; and finally, it has ravaged the countries over which it rules, including those it rules in a disguised form, like Egypt under Nasserism.

4. A paraphrase of the famous slogan of the Brotherhood: 'Islam is our road, the Koran is our constitution', and so on.

Al-Da'wa's denunciation of communism in all its forms —
real, symbolic, and imaginary — was in complete accordance
with the official ideology of the Sadat era. On several occasions
the government authorized neo-Muslim Brethren meetings to
denounce Assad, the Syrian president, with whom Sadat happened to be locked in conflict over the Egyptian-Israeli peace
treaty. Meetings and collections of funds in support of the
Muslim fighters in Afghanistan were also permitted. In the
fight against communism inside and outside Egypt, the positions of the regime and *al-Da'wa* were perfectly complementary,
the magazine attacking their common enemies — Nasserism,
for example — with arguments the regin   could not afford to
use.

The fourth and final principle of evil is secularism (*'ilmaniyya*).
Although less powerful than its three predecessors (which it
serves, in any case, as a sort of quartermaster), it is nevertheless
no less pernicious for Islam, since it undermines one of its basic
principles, namely *al-Islam din wa dawla,* or 'Islam is both religion and state'. In other words, Islam is meant to rule the affairs
of both this world and the next.

The promoter of secularism in the Muslim countries was 'the
traitor Mustafa Kemal Atatürk', who twice won first prize in the
'Recognize the Enemies of Your Religion' column of the children's supplement 'Lion Cubs'. In November 1980 the presentation of Atatürk's personality began thus:

'Brother Muslim Lion Cub,

'Islam is a total system that governs all aspects of life, your own
and that of society. *We have revealed the Book which manifests the
truth about all things* (XVI, 89). The caliphate is the political
system that was established for us by the Prophet in Medina, and
it endured for fourteen centuries, until the advent of a man called
Mustafa Kemal Atatürk, who overthrew the Ottoman caliphate
and turned Turkey into a secular state whose religion was not
Islam. . . . This is your enemy, Muslim lion club, and the enemy
of your religion; he had connections with the prime enemy of the
Muslims: the Jews. Moreover, he was himself a member of a
Jewish sect called the *dawnama,* Jews who have their own occult
doctrine, which they do not reveal. They used Islam as a mask to

conceal their apostasy, for fear of the strength and power of the
Ottoman caliphate. . . . [The caliphate was the major obstacle to
Jewish plans, especially in the person of the Sultan Abdul
Hamid, who refused to sell Palestine to the Jews. This explains
why Atatürk abolished the caliphate.]

'He sought to alienate you from your religion, from the Book of
God, from all that the Tradition has bequeathed . . . by forbid-
ding the use of the Arabic language and replacing it with the
Turkish language, with its Latin-European letters.'

The sort of reasoning used here to discredit Atatürk is reminiscent of that used earlier against Marx: just as Marx's grandfather
was a rabbi, Atatürk is said to have been a member of a Turkish
Jewish sect. Historically, the sect in question is known as the
Dönme, and was founded by disciples of the Jewish 'messiah'
Shabbetaï Zevi (1626–76); while publicly professing Islam,
members secretly paid allegiance to Judaism. Although it is true
that some of the cadres of the Young Turk movement did come
from this sect (notably Djavid Bey, Atatürk's minister of
finance), there is no evidence that Mustafa Kemal himself was a
member. The rumour apparently originates from the fact that he
was a native of Salonica, a city in which, along with Smyrna, the
Dönme were concentrated. It was subsequently inflated by those
of Atatürk's religious enemies who were forced into exile and
gathered in Egypt. That is how it found its way into the children's pages of al-Da'wa.

None of the Egyptians whom I asked to read this page of
al-Da'wa had heard of the Dönme, and all of them without
exception pronounced the name Dawnama, which meaningless
word has been preserved in the transliteration. What we have
here is the intersection of a culture transmitted by Turkish exiles
to the Muslim Brethren and an anti-Jewish polemic that is prepared to use any ammunition.

It is important to Talmasani's friends that Atatürk be a Jew, for
this makes him alien to Islam, which explains why he introduced
secularism and the Latin alphabet, which alienates the Muslim
lion cub from the Book of God. If it was admitted that Atatürk
was actually a Muslim, as is most probably the case, then the
measures he took would pose an insoluble problem: how could a
Muslim, who possesses a supreme intelligence precisely because

of his belief, renounce it in favour of Western cultural by-products? He therefore has to be deemed an apostate, a particularly tricky category because it opens the door to excommunication (*takfir*), of which the neo-Muslim Brethren were suspicious inasmuch as it was used by Shukri Mustafa and his group to unleash a spiral of excommunications that soon became difficult to control.

Once introduced into the Muslim world by Atatürk, secularism became a component of many conspiracies against Islam. In particular, it inspired pan-Arabism and Arab nationalism, 'which has always been, in each of its stages, a secular movement against Islam led by Lebanese or Syrian Christians, Westerners, and Jews'. The Ba'th Party, for instance, is part of the plot. In Egypt secularism stands at the root of the legal system imported from the West; it must be hunted down everywhere, and 'it is no accident' that it resurfaced in the course of the confessional incidents in al-Zawiyya al-Hamra.

In the 22 June 1981 edition of the semi-official Cairo daily newspaper *al-Ahram*, the staff cartoonist, Salah Jahin, devoted his regular drawing to the theme of 'incidents damaging to national unity'. The cartoon depicted a matronly woman, labelled 'Egypt', who stood before three children labelled 'unity', 'harmony', and 'secularism'. She is saying to a hulking monster labelled 'confessional sedition', 'These are my children and they are all good! Whose daughter are you?' The mention of secularism as a daughter of Egypt roused the ire of *al-Da'wa*, and Salih 'Ashmawi himself mounted the barricades to demand the government's resignation for having allowed publication of the cartoon.

Al-Da'wa's identification and lengthy elaboration of the four major categories of enemies of Islam and the Muslims is symptomatic of the particular cultural situation of those layers of Egyptian society whose sentiments are reflected in the magazine. The editors offer their readers a kind of seamless suit of Islamicist armour to protect them from the identity crises from which they suffer. It remains to be seen how effective a defence this is against the attacks of modernity and what constraints are imposed by its use.

By making Jewry, the Crusade, secularism, and communism the four horsemen of the apocalypse, *al-Da'wa* demonstrates that, in the eyes of its readers, the lands of Islam now face an apocalyptic situation. Although all tendencies of the Islamicist movement fully agree on this observation, they differ when it comes to identifying the four horsemen. It is significant that the neo-Muslim Brethren have settled on four archetypes that are generally foreign to Egyptian society. This relieves them of the task of analysing the internal causes of the difficulties of Islam, particularly as regards the relations between the state and civil society. But the most radical tendencies have raised objections to this perspective. While they make no secret of their hatred for the external enemy (and in particular for the 'prime enemy of all', the Jew), they maintain that the fight must begin internally against *jahiliyya*, whose major representative is the iniquitous prince who rules in contravention of God's injunctions.

But because it thus designated the external enemy, *al-Da'wa* found itself in a new situation once the state undertook to sign a treaty with Israel — or, to put it in the vocabulary of the magazine's editors, to make a pact with the Jews. They consistently challenged this decision of the regime, although they declined to explicitly contest the regime as such, and still less the state.

Making Good Use of Parliament

The reformist option of the editors of *al-Da'wa* was equally apparent in their defence and illustration of Good, in this case Islam as understood by the neo-Muslim Brethren.

The magazine strove to present both the history and the current activities of the Brethren in a very favourable light. A special column, entitled 'The Muslim Brethren in the Pages of the Past', was designed to heap praise on the association founded by Hasan al-Banna, equating it with absolute Good.

'Love is the symbol of the Society of Muslim Brethren', affirmed Talmasani, who denied that the group's creation on a religious basis had had the effect of arousing dissension between Egypt's Christian and Muslim communities. According to him, the Brotherhood's function was to bring people together, unlike the political parties, which split public opinion into antagonistic factions. If the Brethren were attacked, it was because they 'constituted the greatest obstacle on the road to Nasserist dictatorship'. Far from being the criminals so cavalierly depicted by the state information organs, they were martyrs who perished that the banner of Islam might wave. That is why they suffered prison, torture, and hanging. If the Society was dissolved in 1954, it was because it was a threat to Israel's existence. It was for this reason that Nasser banned it, on Soviet orders al-Da'wa imperturbably informs us.

Such was the past history of the Brethren. And if today is to become a better tomorrow, the Society of Muslim Brethren must regain a legal existence, for it alone can reform the nation. Never in the past had the Brethren sought to seize power (*qalb nizam al-hukm*); instead they had tried to reform the regime, Salah Shadi wrote. Likewise today, Talmasani explained, 'those who call upon God' do not confuse the movement (*haraka*) with demonstrations (*tazahur*):

'Every honest man knows that the ruling regimes in this country and ourselves will remain on opposite sides as far as programmes and orientations are concerned . . . until the day the law of God is applied and His commandments are in force . . . But if what is called *haraka* means the burning of means of transport, the looting of shops, and the pillaging of public establishments, then we shall not partake of that nourishment, for God forbids corruption . . . and moreover, what is pillaged is the property not of the head of state or the government, but of the people and of each one of us. . . .

'If what is meant by *haraka* is to conspire and foment *coups d'état*, then let it be known that this is the business only of those who seek power for its own sake. As for us, we are indifferent to the person of our ruler, for what matters most to us is the type of government, its form and constitution. . . .

'If what is meant by *haraka* is to confront the regime by force and violence, then we believe that this is a futile use of the people's strength which benefits no one but the enemies of this country.

'Our movement exists within the framework of the Muslim mission. And it is through words that our movement acts (*wa taharrakna fi kalimat*). To wit:

'1. We educate the people, in particular the youth, on the Islamic basis set by the Muslims, in accordance with which they have ruled.

'2. We proclaim the truth and urge all the people to rally to it and to support it in all circumstances.

'3. We gather people together to tell them what they must do and from what they must abstain.

'4. We warn the people against secularism masquerading in Islamic garb in an effort to alienate Muslim youth from their religion through discourse as mellifluous as it is poisonous . . . .

'5. In educating the youth, we base ourselves on God, through the Book, the Sunna . . ., and so on.'

Although he is not named, the target of Talmasani's criticism in this passage is Sayyid Qutb, for it was the author of *Signposts* who counterposed 'the movement' to mere discourse, arguing that while it was the latter's task to counter the ideology of *jahiliyya*, the barbarism oblivious to Islam, it was up to the movement to sweep away the obstacles to the actual establishment of Islam, the first of these obstacles being the political system.

The editor of *al-Da'wa* makes no mention of *jahiliyya*. Moreover, he insists that there is no question of seeking to overthrow the regime. The point, rather, is to present it with regular requests and petitions designed to improve it, to Islamicize it gradually. The major demand raised by the magazine is therefore the application of the *shari'a*, the legal system derived from the Koran and the Muslim Tradition, codified by the *ulema* of Islam.

This demand was actually taken up by the state itself, particularly in 1977, when Sufi Abu Talib, an astute jurist trained in the law schools of Paris, was elected president of the People's Assembly (the Egyptian parliament, composed, with very few exceptions, of government henchmen). Abu Talib repeated unceasingly that Egypt would apply the *shari'a* some day soon, but first, he said, a titanic labour of codification of this Muslim law was necessary in order to adapt it to the conditions of contem-

porary society. So great was the scope of this preparatory enterprise that by 1983 only the preliminaries had been reached, and
the *shari'a* had yet to be applied. But the principal demand of
Talmasani's friends had been defused, not unskilfully, by bury-
ing the elderly lawyer's arguments in procedural points.

In 1976 *al-Da'wa* expressed its satisfaction that the members of
the People's Assembly were examining the rules of the *shari'a*.
The editorial board seems to have believed that the Muslim
Brethren would soon be allowed to reconstitute themselves as a
legal organization which could have representatives in parliament. Since a 'left tribune'[5] had been created, whose members
were Marxists 'who denied the existence of God', it would be
inconceivable for there to be no tribune to represent the
Muslims, who formed the bulk of the population. And who
better than the Muslim Brethren, Salih 'Ashmawi asked, could
assure that representation?

This demand for participation in political life, first by entering
parliament and then by bringing repeated pressure on the
deputies to apply the *shari'a* instead of wasting precious time
quibbling about the process of codification, sharply differen-
tiated the strategy of the neo-Muslim Brethren from that of the
other tendencies of the Islamicist movement. By waging these
skirmishes with the People's Assembly, acting as a kind of
lobby, the editors of *al-Da'wa* made themselves a legal opposition within the existing political system, on which they sought to
exert enough pressure to achieve peaceful evolution towards an
Islamic state based on the *shari'a*.

By opting for this sort of relationship with the state, integrating
themselves into the Egyptian political superstructure, Talmasani
and his friends could not hope to represent the aspirations of
those layers of Egyptian society that regard this political superstructure as profoundly alien. The propaganda of the neo-
Muslim Brethren was directed at Egyptians who were well estab-

5. These 'tribunes' (*manabir*) constituted the showcase of Sadat-style 'democracy' at the time. In reality, the whole exercise amounted to the election of a few
dozen members of parliament who did not belong to the president's party. But
when they criticized the peace treaty with Israel, they were divested of their
seats.

lished in social life and wanted to Islamicize social relations by granting religious dignitaries or other elite groups more power than military officers or technocrats. This sort of demand was quite acceptable to the various business circles of which the largest advertisers in *al-Da'wa* constituted a cross-section. It was also supported by the oil monarchies of the Arabian peninsula, which had close links with such influential members of the editorial board as Muhammad al-Ghazali and Yusif al-Qardawi.

But by deliberately opting for moderation, the neo-Muslim Brethren failed to capture the spirit of the Society of Muslim Brethren of Hasan al-Banna's time. Talmasani's cavils are utterly devoid of the inspiration that breathed such life into the message of the Ismailia primary-school teacher 'who held the hearts of the Muslims in his hand and moved them at will'. In the ramshackle dwellings of the suburbs ringing the large Egyptian cities, people by-passed by progress and development turned towards other, more radical tendencies of the Islamicist movement.

5

The Vanguard of the 'Umma'

The *jama'at islamiyya* were the Islamicist student associations that became the dominant force on Egyptian university campuses during Sadat's presidency. They constituted the Islamicist movement's only genuine mass organizations. Although they were at first a minority within the Egyptian student movement (then dominated by the Nasserist left and Marxist currents) that arose just after the country's defeat in the 1967 war, the Islamicist students made their breakthrough during the period of relative calm that prevailed on the campuses after the October war of 1973. A mere four years later, they were in complete control of the universities and had driven the left organizations underground. Having managed to dominate the Student Union and the most important faculties, the *jama'at* now represented a threat to the regime, which had initially favoured them. They began to exploit opposition to the policy of peace with Israel on which Sadat, the 'peace president', had gambled his legitimacy and political survival. From that point onwards they suffered administrative harassment and later police repression by the government that had previously handled them with kid gloves. The *jama'at islamiyya* thus won recognition as an opposition force. From then on, their numbers rose steadily. The regime saw no way of heading off the danger except direct confrontation, dramatized by the 'confessional sedition' in al-Zawiyya al-Hamra in June 1981. In September of that year the *jama'at islamiyya* were dissolved (although they had never been legally registered in the first place); their infrastructure was destroyed and their leaders arrested. One month later, Sadat was killed by an Islamicist militant, Khalid al-Islambuli, whose brother, a leader of the *jama'at islamiyya* at the University of Asyut, had been maltreated during his arrest in September.

The *jama'at islamiyya* were therefore an important part of the Egyptian political scene during Sadat's presidency. Although they were a student movement, their actions had effects that reached well beyond the confines of the universities, and they intervened directly in political life.

The *jama'at islamiyya* referred constantly to the *umma islamiyya,* or 'Community of Believers' as it existed, in their view, at the time of the 'golden age of Islam' during the reign of the first four caliphs, the 'rightly guided caliphs' (*al-khulafa' al-rashidun*). Their objective was the renaissance of this *umma* through the restoration of the caliphate. The means they employed to achieve this aim were meant to offer a foretaste of what life would be like in the radiant future, while simultaneously manifesting their militant and exemplary break with contemporary Egyptian society.

The Student Revolt

In February 1968 Egyptian military courts handed down sentences at the end of two highly publicized trials. The defendants were the men centrally responsible for the crushing defeat suffered by the armed forces in the six-day war the previous year. The accused in the first trial, who included the commander-in-chief of the air force, were either acquitted or sentenced to short prison terms. The low-ranking officers and minor state employees who stood in the dock in the second trial, however, were given far more severe sentences, life imprisonment in some cases.

On February 21, workers at four factories in Helwan, the sprawling, Soviet-style industrial complex on the southern outskirts of Cairo, walked out in protest against the leniency the ruling military oligarchy had shown its own colleagues, while blaming the 'little guys' for the rout. The next day there were street demonstrations, and seventeen workers were wounded. On 24 February the students took to the streets, chanting 'Death to the traitors!', but also 'No socialism without freedom!' and

'Down with secret trials!'. On 25 February, the demonstrations turned into a riot. Order was restored only by a promise of new, more severe sentences.

It was the first time in more than a decade that organized masses, unsupervised by government supporters, had taken to the streets in a demonstration whose aim was not to express the people's unconditional support for the president's latest initiative. This sudden and uncontrolled expression of discontent was an alarm signal for the regime and 'convinced it to enact a series of immediate and long-term reforms . . . in order to reassert the basis of its legitimacy before it was too late' [10]. But it also set a precedent for the students, 'freeing them from their chains and showing them, for the first time since 1952, that they could protest against an official decision, that they could march in the streets proclaiming opinions opposed to the authorities and the government' [38].

These opposition street demonstrations turned the student movement into a political force of which the regime had to take account. In fact, some pro-government forces defended the students, while not actually taking their side. Muhammad Hasanain Heikal, the regime's chief ideologue and formerly Nasser's ghost-writer, endorsed some of the demands of the youth [10]. Between the 1967 defeat and Nasser's death in 1970, during which time Egyptian society — and even the regime to some extent — engaged in an examination of conscience, the voice of the student youth, of the generation shaped by Nasserism (which had significantly expanded the number of university places), managed to make itself heard. These students demanded not only a firm stand against Israel, but also internal reforms to make the country more democratic [10, 16]. They acted as a kind of collective observer, even a censor, of government policy. In short, a 'student movement' took shape.

But various tendencies and divisions arose within it very rapidly. The regime lost no time in giving maximum publicity to these fissures, denouncing the 'foreign elements' who subverted demonstrations, especially the 'Communists and Muslim Brethren'. The latter had managed to reconstitute some nuclei of agitators in the universities despite the severity of the 1965 repression (which had ended with the hanging of Sayyid Qutb) and despite the incarceration of all their known leaders. In Mansura in particular, they infiltrated the youth organization of the Arab Socialist Union, the sole legal political party. The regime was forced to dissolve the Mansura youth branch in February 1968 for 'having manifested far-right tendencies'. These Muslim Brethren led the demonstrations in that city in November 1968 against a university reform that stipulated a reduction in the number of students in an effort to ease the burden on the state, which is compelled by law to provide jobs for all of the twenty-five thousand annual graduates of the various faculties. The 21 November demonstration, which began from the Azharist Institute of Religious Studies in Mansura, resulted in four dead and touched off huge demonstrations during which angry students in the city of Alexandria vented their wrath for four days. But even though they were sometimes able to detonate massive actions, the Muslim Brethren remained relatively few in number among the students.

With Nasser's death in autumn 1970 and his replacement by Sadat, the Egyptian student movement gained greater weight. The new president lacked his predecessor's authority. To retain power he had to carry out a palace revolution (on 15 May 1971) in which he neutralized the leading political figures who were most closely associated with the Soviet Union. This operation, termed the 'rectification revolution', gave Sadat a stronger grip on his political apparatus, but it also gave rise to suspicion on the left that he was about to desert the camp of progress. In those days, the great cause of this camp was the demand for a war of revenge against Israel, to erase the humiliation of June 1967.

A war of nerves broke out between the regime, which had no intention of throwing the Egyptian army into battle in the midst of its process of reorganization, and the militant sections of public opinion that clamoured for an offensive to be launched. To gain time, the president found himself regularly compelled to announce an imminent offensive, but the lack of preparation of the troops led him to postpone it just as regularly. One instance of this occurred on 13 January 1972, when Sadat delivered a particularly maladroit speech claiming that the latest postponement of the ever-imminent offensive was due to the 'political fog

created by the Indo-Pakistani war', in which the Soviet Union
had been involved. This, he said, had prevented Moscow from
giving the green light to the Egyptian initiative. This confession
of weakness convinced the students to strike, and they took to
the streets on 24 and 25 January to confront the police. The
Student Union, a corporatist organ whose leaders were selected
through a procedure that favoured the regime's agents, was
discredited, and a Student Coordinating Committee elected by
rank-and-file students was set up instead. This body organized
general assemblies of students, as well as sit-ins and street
demonstrations.

The Islamicist students were still a minority in these assemblies, outnumbered by the big battalions of the Nasserist and
Communist left. They were content merely to register their presence by proposing amendments to the platform of the National
Student Coordination Committee: placing more emphasis on
religious values, demanding the closure of the cabarets on the
Avenue of the Pyramids, and so on. These amendments were
usually rejected, obtaining no more than a quarter of the vote.

The Islamicist students were not yet organized in the *jama'at
islamiyya*, but in special clubs (*usar*). Apart from clubs for poetry,
painting, and various recreational activities, there were also
Koranic reading clubs and clubs in which participants learned to
commit the Book to memory. These soon became recruiting
grounds for Islamicist militants. But since they were still too
weak to put forward slogans of their own, they preferred to give
the leftist slogans a slight twist, a Muslim cast. War against
Israel, for example, which the leftist students called 'the national
liberation struggle of the Arab peoples against imperialism's
policeman in the Middle East', was described by al-Banna's
disciples as the *jihad* that would put an end to the usurpation by
infidels of one of the lands of *Dar al-Islam*. On this kind of basis,
there were no major obstacles to united action.

During the second phase of the movement, after December
1972, the fortunes of the Islamicist students took a turn for the
better. After various false starts, they finally found the key to
success: discreet, tactical collaboration with the regime to break
the left's domination of the campuses. Agitiation began in the
middle of December 1972, when three medical students were

ordered to appear before the Cairo University disciplinary council charged with having put up 'insulting' wall posters. Demonstrations in their support, in the name of 'democracy at the universities', soon clashed with counter-demonstrations of students chanting *Allahu akbar!*, 'God is most great!'.

This time, instead of joining the movement, the Islamicist students opposed it from the beginning [39]. Observers agree in noting 'the evident fragmentation' of the movement, the conflict within it between 'activists' and 'reactionaries' [37]. Although at the time Sadat placed both currents on the same footing — calling them, in a 31 January 1973 speech, the 'adventurist left' and the 'reactionary right' — retrospectively there seems little doubt that the regime, which had consolidated its power in a struggle against political leaders with ties to the Soviet Union, did not look with disfavour upon students who could serve as a useful counterweight to the Egyptian left, which had a real base on the campuses. It was important to prevent the student movement from going over to the Nasserists, who still controlled parts of the party and state apparatus. The polarization of the movement around two extremes, and therefore its relative paralysis, thus served the government's interest.

Muhammad 'Uthman Isma'il, a close associate of Sadat's and a former lawyer who played an important part in the preparation and technical implementation of the 'rectification revolution' of May 1971, is generally considered to have acted as the 'godfather' of the *jama'at islamiyya,* in Cairo from late 1971 and throughout Middle Egypt beginning in 1973. Appointed governor of Asyut in that year, he broke most records of longevity by holding on to the post until his removal by Mubarak, Sadat's successor, in 1982. During those nine years, he 'encouraged the *jama'at islamiyya* to fight against the communists'. In 1981 a teacher from Asyut wrote an article in a weekly magazine complaining that the Islamicist students 'go to meet with the governor and the president of the university, who treat them as equals'. The prodigious development of the Islamicist university associations owed much to their own dynamism and cannot be reduced to their manipulation by the political police, as the Egyptian left has long claimed. But it is undeniable that for a time they were encouraged by the regime, which thereby nurtured the snake that would later strike it.

The 'University of Large Numbers'

Throughout this discussion, the term 'student' ought not to conjure up images of the campuses of the Sorbonne, Sussex, or Berkeley. Although Egyptian universities resemble their counterparts in the developed countries as far as the names of the faculties and the ages of the students are concerned, comparisons must not be pressed much beyond that point. Since the Nasser era, Egyptian universities have been caricatures more than copies of Western, or even Soviet, models.

More than one Egyptian educationist has admitted that it is more than a little misleading to call the Egyptian institutions of higher learning 'universities': the appellation 'establishments of long-term instruction' would be a more accurate designation for institutions that provide more than half a million students with courses of study rigidly compartmentalized into narrow disciplines and offering degrees governed by an examination system that yields little to the Koranic schools in its exclusive reliance on the routine memorization of manuals. Once the ex-student has acquired a diploma — after drawing hefty sums from his family to pay for the individual tutoring that is as necessary for success as it is illegal — he will have earned the right to prefix the sonorous title *duktur* ('doctor') to his name, and will then work each morning as an underpaid state employee, and spend the afternoon moonlighting as an amateur plumber, a taxi driver who knows neither the streets nor the routes, or some sort of jobber, until a friend of the family or local contact finally gets him a seat on a plane or boat headed for one of the oil-producing Arab countries.

Eloquent statistics testify to the roots of this catastrophic situation, which gives the universities such a perverse role in the country's development: the number of students rose from slightly less than two hundred thousand in 1970 to more than half a million in 1977. The Egyptian university is a mass institution — or as the Arabic expression has it, 'a university of large numbers'. In the absence of the necessary resources, the laudable democratic intention of providing free higher education for the greatest possible number of the country's youth in order to train experts for national development has produced a system of cut-rate education whose costs measured in the waste of time and energy considerably outstrip its advantages.

The students themselves are not unaware of these problems. But the *jama'at islamiyya* drew their considerable strength from their ability to identify them and to propose immediate solutions.

The Egyptian student is confronted first of all with insurmountable difficulties due to the deficient infrastructure: it is not unusual for two or even three students to share a seat in the packed lecture halls and laboratories. Considerable prowess is required even to hear the teacher's voice, especially when the microphone is broken or when there are power cuts. The ability to follow a demonstration on the blackboard is a privilege reserved for the occupants of the first few rows. Moreover, since the examinations merely ask the students to regurgitate the brilliant course lectures word for word, success depends not only on buying the manual sold by the professor, but also on industrious attendance of the special tutorials given by teachers during the two months preceding the end-of-year examinations. These courses, the perfect negation of the free education system, guarantee the survival of the teachers, whose salaries are derisory. Their cost depends on the floating market price of the various diplomas, the most onerous fields being engineering and medicine. First prize, however, goes to the exorbitantly expensive anatomy courses, which require the illicit acquisition of a freshly buried corpse — a task reserved for specialists who command top fees.

Another consequence of the packed lecture halls is the promiscuity that threatens the female students' modesty. Similar embarrassment is suffered during the daily journey to the campus in an equally jam-packed bus. In a prudish society in which relations between the sexes occur late and are strictly circumscribed by marriage, the jostling bus in which bodies are pressed one against the other becomes a site of furtive eroticism of which the female students feel themselves the victims.

Those who manage to escape the bus are lodged in equally overcrowded dormitories or at the homes of unscrupulous land-lords, the sleep merchants who haunt the immediate periphery of the campuses. In Asyut in particular there has grown up around the university what can only be called a 'belt', al-Hamra. An entire universe of poverty-stricken students is packed into it, cut off from their family milieu and highly receptive to any voices that manage to make themselves heard and promise an improvement in their conditions.

This rapid sketch of the Egyptian university would be incomplete without a mention of two additional features: on the one hand, the massive emigration of teachers, who flee their miserable working and living conditions to seek jobs in the brand new universities of the oil-producing countries of the Arabian peninsula (a phenomenon that aggravates the problem of overcrowding: in some disciplines the professor/student ratio has reached 1/100); and on the other, the rigid system of selection by discipline. Every year the newspapers publish the high-school diploma scores below which each particular faculty will refuse to accept first-year students. The highest scores in this university market-place are required by the faculties of medicine, pharmacology, and odontology in the physical sciences, by engineering in the mathematics curricula, and by economics and political science in the liberal arts. Year in, year out, the future elites (or at least those designated as such by their graduation scores) flock to those faculties. The other departments compete for the mediocre, even the inept: a brilliant student interested in the legal profession knows that if he opts for a law faculty when his grades make it possible for him to study pharmacology instead, both his classmates and the level of teaching will fall far below his expectations. Entire fields of knowledge are thereby relegated to what the Egyptians themselves call 'garbage faculties'. This is the status, for example, of the humanities, and especially of social studies, with the single, numerically insignificant exception of the political science faculty at Cairo University. Here, as elsewhere, we can detect the indelible stamp of Nasserism, which (mimicking its Soviet big brother) preferred to train technicians capable of repairing human bodies and machines instead of intellectuals who think about the problems of society. Officers who had risen through the ranks were there to do the thinking.

The *jama'at islamiyya* proposed colourful Islamicist solutions to the problems of this sombre picture, the grimness of which is regularly acknowledged even by the semi-official press. They spoke a language easily understood by the mass of students whose deepest cultural identities remain quite traditional, as has been noted by Maurice P. Martin, one of the most scrupulous and attentive observers of the contemporary Egyptian scene:

'The acquisition of university education is a desperate and hazardous undertaking. Desperate because, no matter how narrow the field of study, the number of students and the competition demand enormous efforts in which intelligence plays little part. Paradoxically, the disproportionate efforts are somehow "passive", for the student becomes a slave to the manual, with its limited and compartmentalized content. For most students, this "passive" acquisition of modern knowledge for professional purposes never challenges the cultural foundations of their traditional society. Modernization has no reflection on culture, particularly the inherited religious culture. This may well partially explain why students can maintain a kind of double, parallel behaviour: modern as far as acquired techniques are concerned, traditional in life-style and thought' [27].

In the Shadow of the Regime

To understand the means by which the *jama'at islamiyya* sought to respond to the crisis of the Egyptian universities, we must recapitulate the stages of their development from the point at which we left them: late 1972. At that time the Islamicist students were opposing the Nasserists and Communists, to the great satisfaction of the regime.

During the 1973 vacations the first big summer camp was organized by the *jama'at* of Cairo University. The following year, *al-Ahram* printed an account of the final day's ceremony at the

'Islamic camp' organized 'by the students of Cairo University'. The Cairo daily reported that the first secretary of the government party had personally attended the event and had saluted the project's success: five hundred students had spent two weeks contemplating the Koran and the *fiqh*, or Muslim jurisprudence. In 1975 the same newspaper carried reports of the Cairo camp and the one at Beni Suef. 'Abd al-Halim Mahmud, the rector of al-Azhar, inaugurated the Mansura camp.

Although the government-controlled press made no explicit mention of the fact, it was the *jama'at islamiyya* that organized these camps, which were simply a resurrection of the summer camps held by the Muslim Brethren Youth before their dissolution in 1954. They served as schools for the cadres and future cadres of the Islamicist movement. The participants did not spend all their time contemplating the Koran, as *al-Ahram* so benevolently reported, but also trained in various group sports and self-defence, prayed collectively, and, at dusk, listened to preachers expound Islamicist solutions to the bitter disappointments of contemporary Egyptian society. The camps were microcosmic experiments in Islamicist utopia, past and future. The mythified epoch of the 'four rightly guided caliphs' (the Prophets' successors), the golden age of Islam, was both relived and projected forward in time. The camps were meant to be a model of the future Islamic society that the young Islamicists intended to build on the ruins of *jahiliyya*.

In 1975, however, the Egyptian political authorities chose to regard the camps as no more than an effective antidote to the Marxistic ideology upheld by Communists and Nasserists. Around the same time, various revisions of the decrees on which the statutes of the Egyptian Student Union were based enabled the *jama'at islamiyya* to take over the Union and to use the considerable funds and facilities thereby placed at their disposal to set in motion a student policy that would later register great success. The Eighth Congress of the Egyptian Student Union, held in Alexandria 3-9 April 1974, was inaugurated with a speech by Sadat himself, who exhorted his 'children, the students of Egypt', to study the history of the student movement of the past three years carefully and, on that basis, to reject hollow ideologies and come to terms with the reality of the country. He recalled that the government was based on certain institutions, among them the Student Union, and promised a new and more democratic system. Since the days of Nasser, the Student Union had faithfully reflected the concerns of the powerful, acting as a sounding board for their slogans and watchwords. In 1963, for example, the prime objective of the various local student unions (there was as yet no national organization) was to encourage the Arab national spirit among members and to deepen their knowledge of socialism. In 1966 new statutes turned the unions into mere appendages of the Arab Socialist Union, the sole legal political party at the time. Their prime objective was now to serve the regime (art 2, para. 1). The teacher assigned to supervise the committees in charge of the various activities was chosen by the ASU executive bureau (art. 15). To top it off, any student candidate for a post of responsibility within the Union also had to be approved by the ASU executive board (art. 40, para. 4).

This fine edifice, alas, was brought down by Egypt's defeat in the 1967 war. During the three years of self-criticism and relative freedom of expression after the war and before Nasser's death, the students became a political force that the regime could no longer ignore. It therefore decided to create an institution for the students, issuing decree no. 1533/1968, which created the General Union of Egyptian Students.

The ASU no longer had the right to supervise the new body. Although autonomous, the Union still had the objective of struggling against reaction, colonialism, and world Zionism (art. 5, para. 3). This General Union quite obviously had far greater resources than the old faculty or university unions. Now headed by an elected president, it had five national committees (political action, inter-Arab relations, external relations, internal relations, and information and publishing: art. 25). This last committee was supposed to publish magazines and pamphlets for the edification of students (art. 26, para. 5).

These were the regulations that Sadat promised in 1974 to make 'more democratic'. Decree 335/1976 stated that the Union's prime objective was now 'to deepen religious values among the students' (art. 5, para. 1), although there were also the usual ritual references to deepening socialist concepts (para. 3) and to the struggle against the accursed trinity of reaction, colonialism, and world Zionism (art. 6, para. 3). The Union's bureau, which was now sovereign, comprised a president and twelve other members, all elected independently (art. 39), which enabled various currents to gain representation. The *jama'at islamiyya*, bolstered by the creation of a committee for 'religion and society', surged through this breach.

The establishment of *jama'at islamiyya* cells in the Student Union gave the Islamicists a remarkably effective tribune and resulted in soaring recruitment. Once they had gained control of the information and publishing committee at the national level in 1975, for example, they were able to use both government money and student contributions to pursue a vigorous policy of producing low-cost Islamicist pamphlets: the collection called *Sawt al-Haqq* ('Voice of the Truth', which also happened to be the subtitle of *al-Da'wa*) made available to every student not only the densest passages of *Signposts*, copies of which were still difficult to find in Egypt at the time, but also selections from leading twentieth-century authors of the Islamicist movement.

But the *jama'at islamiyya* did not become the dominant force in the student movement until the Union's March 1976 congress. The agitation and student strikes of January 1975 in solidarity with the workers of Helwan were still led by the Nasserist-Marxist left, but they marked the left's swan-song. In March 1976 the die was cast: the congress, held in the town of Shibin al-Kaum in the Nile Delta, was mainly concerned with the application of the *shari'a* and even organized a march to Mit Abu'l-Kaum, Sadat's home village, to present this request to him. The lists of complaints respectfully submitted to 'the believer president' were the sum total of political opposition to the regime openly expressed by the *jama'at islamiyya*, whose sharpest barbs were reserved for communism.

'Changer la Vie'

Although they enjoyed the covert encouragement of the regime, the *jama'at* did not owe all their progress to the directives of the Ministry of the Interior. The tactics of their search for a base among the masses of students were decisive.

It was by elaborating a strategy to transform campus life that the *jama'at islamiyya* were able to persuade the students that it was through them that they could take their own destiny in hand here and now, and not by parroting official slogans and government projects which were in any case fated to sink without a trace beneath the weight of mismanagement and corruption.

In the February 1980 edition of *al-Da'wa*, the section entitled 'News of the Youth and the Universities' — a column that allows us to follow the month-to-month activities of the *jama'at islamiyya* (though filtered somewhat by Talmasani and his friends) — contains an article on 'the major difficulties facing the young'. The first of these is the mixing of the sexes, 'a Western weapon of corruption designed to make us to abandon our Islamic personality'. A student (male) declares that 'mixing of the sexes in the packed amphitheatres becomes a sexual temptation for those whose souls are weak. . . . We are not against the existence of women students, but we have to know whether a girl wearing make-up is a student or a mannequin.' Housing is onerous and crowded, with three or four students to a room in the dormitories. It is impossible to concentrate in order to memorize the mimeographed manuals. Then there is the problem of transport: people stay in their villages because housing in the city is difficult, and they are then packed into crowded buses. For all these reasons, the young are unable to play their role in society.

Prima la donna. The phenomenon of 'the return to the veil' on the part of female students, encouraged by the *jama'at*, is so prevalent that it must raise some questions about the everyday occurrences that rule the lives of Egyptian female students. In a society in which late marriage is the rule, linked as it is to the prospective groom's ability to pay 'key-money' after his return from emigration in the Gulf, and in which pre-marital sexual relations are exceptional, sexual frustration and its corollary, masturbation, have become national problems. Even were this not the case, the extreme overcrowding in all public places because of the lack of infrastructures capable of expanding to meet the rise in population would place young girls in a particularly uncomfortable situation. As it is, anything can happen in a bus carrying the young female student from her lodgings to the university.

To these critical conditions the *jama'at* responded: we will organize a minibus service for the female students in order to preserve their dignity from the assaults to which they are subjected on public transport. The first such bus-line, supervised by the student union of the medical school in Cairo, in collaboration with the *jama'at islamiyya* of this faculty, started operations in March 1977. It ran from Embaba (a poor neighbourhood) to Doqqi (a residential area) to Qasr al-'Ayni (the medical faculty) and back. Its success was immediate. But since demand exceeded supply, it was first preferable, and later compulsory, for the women to dress in 'Islamic style' — veil, long robe, gloves — if they wanted to use this means of transport.

A similar problem exists in the amphitheatres and lecture halls, filled as they are to twice their capacity. Many female students are annoyed by neighbours virtually piled on top of them. By demanding segregation of the sexes in different rows, the *jama'at islamiyya* were able to address a real problem and propose a solution that had the merit — and cleverness — of being immediate. Whether the female students were already Islamicist sympathizers or not, it was a good bet that such a measure would cause more than a few hearts to beat to the rhythm of the Koran. The indirect effect of opposition to what the most secularized students and professors called 'obscurantism, reaction, and demagogy' was to make it look as though the state's failure to provide decent infrastructures was somehow tolerable, and it was taken up only by the minority that was capable of critically analysing the tactic of the *jama'at islamiyya*; there was little chance that this opposition would be heeded in the university of crammed halls and 'large numbers'. In any event, what concrete alternative was there to the Islamicist solution to this problem?

Their tactic also had the advantage of being supported — whether explicitly or not — by more than one university official. It was characteristic of the *jama'at* to propose a slogan that seemed more or less anodyne, acceptable to the mass of Muslims convinced that this was what Islam was like at its origins, and then suddenly to proclaim, once the masses of students had come out in support of the slogan, that it represented a militant break with *jahiliyya*. One begins by declining to sit next to a classmate of the opposite sex and then finds oneself, little by little, fighting for the establishment of the Muslim state.

The Islamicists also had a solution to the distressing problem of having to revise by means of private lessons and onerous manuals: the *jama'at* organized group revision sessions at the mosques, where the assembled students murmured the texts of the manual in unison, without having to worry about distraction from radios or neighbours. More important, their control of the Student Union and the publications budget allowed them to reproduce cheap editions of the manuals, without paying any copyright fee to the professors, who thereby lost a source of income.

During 1976 and 1977, the years when the *jama'at islamiyya* were at the height of their power and operated with the regime's blessing, they exercised *de facto* control of the Union both nationally and in the major faculties. In the university elections for the 1976/77 academic year, they won strong positions, in particular the presidency of the Student Union of universities in Cairo and Minya and the most important vice-presidencies in Alexandria.

The *jama'at* claimed that their success was due to their ability to respond to the students' problems: according to an 'opinion poll' taken by *al-Da'wa* (sample undisclosed), their representatives were considered effective, well organized, serious, and favourable to democracy. They carefully cultivated their image as astute and honest administrators at a time when Sadat's 'economic opening' had made corruption and misappropriation of public funds the two udders of the Egyptian milch-cow.

This tactic had its effects: the student elections at the end of 1977 produced an Islamicist landslide. But the political conjuncture had changed. The regime, now in the midst of its peace process with Israel, no longer wanted anything to do with its erstwhile allies who, having broken the strength of the left on the campuses, were becoming cumbersome. Everything would now be done to rob them of their success.

As a movement of students, the *jama'at* aspired to become the motor force of the process of transformation of *jahiliyya* into

Muslim society. In order to do that, they had to move off campus. They chose to do so by making use of two impressive demonstrations, the public prayers of the Greater and Lesser Holidays: the *'id al-fitr*, which celebrates the end of the Ramadan month of fasting, and the *'id al-adha*, or 'festival of the sacrifice', during which Muslims slaughter sheep to commemorate Abraham's sacrifice. No matter how irregular their normal religious observance, believers experience a reinvigoration of faith during these two holidays, a result of the intense socio-religious pressure exerted in the streets, from the press, and within the family. People who go to the mosque only twice a year go on those two days.

Here too the *jama'at* gave another example of their tactical sense. They organized public prayers — at first only in Cairo and Alexandria but later, in 1980, in nearly all Egyptian cities — so that the faithful might fervently commune. The chosen site in Cairo — the broad square facing the president's 'Abidin Palace — was charged with special significance: by praying in front of the sovereign's home, his people reminded him that he must govern *bima anzala Allah* ('according to what God has revealed') and must inaugurate the reign of justice.

In 1976 the *jama'at islamiyya* assembled a considerable number of participants on both holidays. According to *al-Da'wa*, forty thousand people (the figure is very probably inflated) gathered in the university stadium in Alexandria for the Greater Holiday. In 1977 the magazine claimed one hundred thousand in Alexandria, fifty thousand in Cairo at the 'Abidin Palace, and thousands in the stadium in Zagazig. The participants, dressed in white gallabiehs and calottes, assembled in their neighbourhood mosques and then converged on the prayer sites in processions, chanting *Allahu akbar!* ('God is most great!'). The remarkably efficient defence guard of the *jama'at* then escorted them to their seats (women in a distinct area, separated from the men by an opaque screen).[1]

1. Wall posters were put up all over Egypt calling on people to come to the prayers on both holidays. The family aspect of the affair was stressed, the invitations generally being worded thus: 'The *jama' at islamiyya* invite you to the

There were collective prayers and a sermon was delivered by a preacher belonging to the Islamicist movement: stars like Muhammad al-Ghazali and Yusif al-Qardawi flew in from their sinecures in the oil kingdoms of the Arabian peninsula for the occasion. In the provinces, the speaker was usually the *amir* (leader) of the local *jama'a*, and in many cases these local leaders belonged to more radical tendencies than the two sheikhs — Najih Ibrahim, for instance, who was the commander of the Islamicist students in Asyut and was later arrested, in 1981, for having been part of the group that assassinated Sadat.

Around the tribunes were stands selling prayer rugs to suit all budgets, *siwak* (sticks of aromatic wood that are chewed in public to demonstrate that the user cleans his teeth in the traditional Islamic manner), perfume to counteract the smell of unshod feet during prayers, and the most recent Islamicist books and periodicals. In the meantime, bearded youths filed down the aisles shaking cans into which poured generous contributions.

Broadly speaking, such was the profile of the *jama'at islamiyya* in Sadat's Egypt up to 1977: the regime erected no obstacles to their freedom of expression, and the *jama'at* refrained from attacking the regime too openly. Was this a gentleman's agreement or a fool's game? The *jama'at* were well aware of the limits beyond which they could not go, but it is nonetheless clear that the infrastructure they were establishing, and the cadres they were training in the summer camps and Islamic study weeks, were well prepared for the possibility of taking on tasks other than smashing the Nasserist and Communist left for the benefit of the ruling group. As far as they were concerned, although Nasserism had been an especially execrable period of *jahiliyya*, fundamentally the Sadat era was scarcely any better. Its internal contradictions, however, had enabled the *jama'at* to grow in the regime's shadow.

---

dawn prayer for the (Greater or Lesser) Holiday, on such-and-such a day, at such-and-such a time and place; bring your children with you. Space will be set aside for women.'

How To Be a Good Muslim

Two events opened a chasm between the regime and the *jama'at islamiyya* in 1977: the *Takfir wa'l-Hijra* affair and the trial of the Society of Muslims on the one hand and Sadat's trip to Jerusalem on the other. With the arrest of Shukri Mustafa and his followers and the subsequent press campaign against them, the Islamicist students found themselves facing a stark alternative: they could either show solidarity with Shukri and his friends by denouncing the trial, as the Azhar sheikh 'Abd al-Halim Mahmud had done, or they could seek to disassociate themselves from the Shukri group as sharply as possible in order not to risk the opprobrium of the many people who had been appalled by the social practices of the Society of Muslims.

On 12 July 1977, several days after the assassination of the former minister of waqfs, Muhammad al-Dhahabi, *al-Ahram* published a series of interviews with various leaders of the *jama'at islamiyya* under the headline: 'The Young People of the *Jama'at Islamiyya* Shed Light on the Actions of the *Takfir wa'l-Hijra* Group and Declare: "We Have Opposed Them From the Beginning" '. Statements solicited and rewritten by government journalists must be read with caution, of course, but those leaders who were interviewed insisted that as far as they were concerned, 'The Islamic mission (*da'wa*) requires that one act within society and not separate oneself from it and practise *hijra*'. The neo-Muslim Brethren of the magazine *al-Da'wa* published articles on the subject by the regular editorial staff and also printed a statement by 'Isam al-Din al-'Aryan, a young physician and one of the *jama'at*'s most prominent thinkers. He argued that the excommunication of Muslims as practised by Shukri Mustafa was a sin, and that Egypt was still basically a Muslim country in which a continuous sacred combat, or *jihad*, was needed to reinvigorate Islam. To claim, as the Society of Muslims did, that Egypt belonged to the *Dar al-Harb*, or 'Domain of War', was to make the country easy prey for the enemies of Islam.

It is out of the question that Talmasani's magazine would publish an article that did not conform to the line set by the editorial board. These positions may therefore be taken as reflecting a basic division between the strategies of the Society of

Muslims and the *jama'at islamiyya*, between the sect and the mass movement, although in all probability Shukri's radicalism and the daring with which he defied the state and expressed his ideas produced more than a few admirers among the rank-and-file Islamicist student militants.

But the *Takfir wa'l-Hijra* affair aroused no apparent differences of assessment within the *jama'at*. No fissures on this question emerged in the movement, whose members were recruited on a minimalist Islamicist basis and in which indoctrination lacked the intensity to which Shukri subjected his members. The public statements of the Islamicist students gave the regime what it wanted and averted the danger of the *jama'at*'s being assimilated to the prosecuted sect (for *jama'at* members, like Shukri's, sported the characteristic Islamicist insignia of untrimmed beards and flowing gallabiehs).

This incident, which forced the *jama'at* into a preventive exculpation, was a kind of preliminary skirmish before the real battle between the Islamicist students and the state, the immediate cause of which was Sadat's trip to Jerusalem in November 1977 and the subsequent lengthy bilateral negotiations that finally led to the Egyptian-Israeli peace treaty in 1979.

There was a striking change in the tone of *al-Da'wa*'s column on 'news of the youth and the universities'. Gone were the triumphalist communiqués reporting the success of the Islamicist lists in the Student Union elections of autumn 1977. As early as January 1978 an article described the 'battles in the Student Union between puppets of the political parties and the *jama'at*'. The next month the column called attention to 'manoeuvres aimed at robbing the *jama'at* of their success in the elections', while in April statements of solidarity with 'persecuted' militants began flooding in from 'sincere Muslims'. The first of these to be printed came from a student who had been elected to the Union and who stated that although he was not a member of the *jama'at*, he was scandalized by the pressure being brought against them. Hasanain Makhluf, the retired rector of al-Azhar, proclaimed that 'the attempts to counter the *jama'at islamiyya* are stratagems against Islam'. In short, whereas 'they' were now out to get the *jama'at*, even trying to line up the *ulema* against them, the *jama'at* were appealing to all the allies they could muster to rush to their defence. 'They', whom the magazine articles failed to identify, meant the regime — at least at the national level, since individual governors and university presidents were not always quick to apply a policy that contradicted the one they had been pursuing until then.

Throughout the spring, the regime's tactic was to manipulate election results and to refuse to honour various payment orders issued by those Student Union committees that were still under Islamicist control. In the summer the Islamicist camps were suddenly shut down, as the *amn markazi,* or anti-riot brigades, barred access to them in Cairo, Alexandria, and Zagazig. The Minya camp was held, but the authorities refused to pay its expenses, despite the payment order issued by the Student Union. Far from halting the rise of the *jama'at,* however, this harassment gave them a second wind. For one thing, they now enjoyed an aura of martyrdom, which enabled them to focus opposition to the regime between 1979 and 1981. But more than that, the Islamicist students were now forced to break out of the university ghetto, access to which had been made difficult for them. The Cairo Islamicist summer camp was finally held in the Saladin mosque on the island of Manyal in the Nile, midway between the school of medicine and the Club Méditerranée; the Alexandria camp was held in a city mosque near Aboukir. The message of the *jama'at islamiyya* now began to spread beyond the world of students. Islamicist cadres and agitators went to preach among the people, making new recruits in the poor neighbourhoods. Later, in the September 1981 raids, the police had to track them down even in the villages.

The Camp David accords were signed in March 1979. When he returned from the United States, Sadat mounted the barricades against the Islamicists, hoping that his popularity as the 'peace president' would enable him to discredit those who criticized, in the name of Islam, 'the shameful peace with the Jews'. On 15 April, during a countrywide tour, he arrived in the town of Asyut, one of the cities in which the *jama'at islamiyya* had been most active (and where the support accorded them by the authorities until 1977 had been most patent). There he delivered a violent attack on those who sought to cloak their political aims in the mantle of religion, especially Communists masquerading in the white gallabieh and the untrimmed beard. Denouncing the *jama'at* by name, Sadat also called Talmasani a liar. A student member of the *jama'at islamiyya* at the University of Minya had been arrested and was found to be carrying the sum of 800 Egyptian pounds ('more than my monthly salary', said Sadat, not without a bit of demagogy); the president saw this as proof of the foreign financing of this non-national group, which was now striving to destroy the country's unity by inciting the Muslim and Christian communities against each other. Presidential ire was soon translated into specific acts. The next month's issue of *al-Da'wa* was banned. In June the *jama'at islamiyya* were targeted by decree 265/1979, which banned the General Union of Egyptian Students, froze its assets, and authorized student unions only at the faculty level, where they would be directed by eleven-member councils including six professors; the dean of the faculty now had the power of veto over all decisions. This meant, more or less, a return to the situation of 1963, when Nasser was at his most pro-Soviet, an ironic paradox for Sadat's American-flavoured regime of 1979, supposedly based on 'the sovereignty of the law'. Not for the first time, however, the measure came too late to be effective. The *jama'at* had built solid infrastructures of their own and could afford to express regret at the decree's effects on the students: it abolished the services their Union had provided — no more cheap photocopies of manuals, minibuses for the girl students, low-cost Islamic dress, cut-rate pilgrimages, and so on. Their show of force at the end of the 1979 Ramadan fast offered the regime evidence, if any were needed, that they were far from buried. In a vehement sermon, Yusif al-Qardawi reminded the president, who at the time was devoting considerable attention to the preservation of the Ramses II mummy, that 'Egypt is Muslim, not pharaonic; it is the land of 'Amr Ibn al-'As[2] and not of Ramses . . . the youth of the *jama'at islamiyya* are the true representatives of Egypt, and not the Avenue of the Pyramids,[3] the theatre performances, and the

2. 'Amr Ibn al-'As was the commander of the Muslim troops that conquered Egypt in the year 640.
3. The street is famous for posh nightclubs in which visiting Arabs from the Gulf, drunk on adulterated alcohol, stuff thick wads of money down the costumes of the belly-dancers. The demand that the cabarets along the Avenue of the

films. . . . Egypt is not naked women, but veiled women who adhere to the prescriptions of divine law. . . . Egypt is young men who let their beards grow. . . . It is the land of al-Azhar!'

Now deprived of the legal cover of the General Union of Students, the *jama'at* set out to turn the universities into inviolable bastions, while beyond the campuses they sought to penetrate various other layers of society.

The Islamicist monolith they sought to impose on the universities turned those campuses on which they were the dominant force into a kind of *terra islamica* from which they banned, clubs in hand, anything that fell foul of their norms: couples were physically attacked for violations of upright Islamic morals; films could not be shown; concerts and evening dances could not be held. One militant, for example (a medical student, judging by his metaphors), wrote that concerts were a 'pathological phenomenon that appears as a cutaneous rupture', as well as a Communist manoeuvre designed to corrupt the youth and thereby to conquer them more easily. All artistic and cinematic exhibitions were considered 'provocations against the *jama'at*' and as such were forbidden *manu militari*. Among these 'provocations' was a showing of Yusif Shahin's film *Alexandria, Why?*, 'which presents the Jews in a favourable light'. The *jama'at*, however, managed to foil that particular provocation, using iron bars for the purpose. Thus was Islamicist order imposed on the campuses, where control was now even further beyond the regime's reach than in the days when the *jama'at* had their cells in the General Union of Students.

While the Islamicists brandished sticks and clubs on the one hand, they also wrote articles seeking to protect their image as a peaceful force expressing the country's deepest sentiments and therefore unjustly persecuted by an iniquitous prince. This 'persecution', along with the defence and exposition of their cause that were its corollary, offers us an opportunity to examine the *jama'at*'s view of history and society, and to situate them intellectually.

Pyramids be closed had been an old refrain of the Egyptian Islamicist movement ever since the time of Hasan al-Banna.

Theoretical texts produced by members of the *jama'at islamiyya* are few and far between. During the period when they controlled the publications committee of the Student Union, their efforts were devoted primarily to reproducing selections from leading Islamicist authors. Their many mimeographed leaflets, on the other hand, concentrated on action slogans more than on the basic concepts that inspired their faith and its works. Moreover, it is highly likely that this organization, which aimed essentially at becoming a mass movement, deliberately shunned theoretical reflection, in an effort to ward off potential splits over points of doctrine.

Within the rather meagre corpus, two texts seem especially representative. The first was produced by a well-known figure of the *jama'at*, the young physician 'Isam al-Din al-'Aryan, whose article on the Islamic interpretation of the meaning of history was published by *al-Da'wa* to celebrate the start of Islam's fifteenth century (at the end of 1980). The second sums up the main lines of the *jama'at*'s thought and is based on the monthly bulletin distributed by the *jama'at islamiyya* of the University of Alexandria.

Contemplating the expansion of Islam in the universities during the past century of the Islamic calendar (in other words, since the 1880s), 'Isam al-Din detects a process comprising three phases: the decadence of the lands of Islam, occupation by infidels, and Islamic awakening. For the second phase to give birth to the third, however, a resolute vanguard must act as midwife. In Egypt this vanguard was unable to play its part, for it was supplanted by nationalism, which promoted independence, which in turn proved to be a new form of Westernization. The country therefore remained mired in the second phase of the process, while falsely believing that it had won emancipation. In reality, although the infidels no longer enjoyed the sort of visible presence in Egypt that they had during the days of the British, their ideas had penetrated the minds of the people: 'Westernized scholars, of whom Taha Husain is the paragon, tell the Muslims that the reason for their backwardness lies in religion and urge separation between religious sciences and new sciences.' Thus misguided, 'the Muslim peoples have experimented with

Western-style democracy and Communist socialism: the fruits have been bitter!'

We now stand, 'Isam al-Din continues, at the dawn of the phase of Islamic awakening, which will commence if the Islamicist movement will only assume its responsibilities. It must do this by relying on the two forces that stand opposed to tyrants in the Muslim world today: the ten million students packed into universities from Casablanca to Jakarta and the workers (*al-'ummal*). The cadres of the future Islamic states are studying at today's universities.

After expounding his concept of the evolution of Muslim societies, 'Isam al-Din initiates his readers into Islamicist semiology: certain signs indicate the movement's degree of development. There are four important ones. The first is the wearing of the veil: 'When the number of women students wearing the veil rises, that is a sign of resistance to Western civilization and of the beginning of *iltizam*[4] towards Islam.' The second sign is the male equivalent of the wearing of the veil: the untrimmed beard and white gallabieh, which Muhammad wore. The third sign is early marriage and the fourth is attendance at public prayers on the Greater and Lesser Holidays.

When these four signs are observable, it means that an Islamicist movement exists, the *jama'at islamiyya*, which constitute 'the vanguard of the *umma*'. Their purpose may be summed up in one slogan: to work for Good. This means that their daily energies must be devoted to the resurrection of the Muslim *umma*, including a thousand and one tasks like handing out leaflets, organizing conferences, holding Islamic camps, and so on.

But the path is littered with many obstacles. Some of these are 'external to the youth': the iniquitous regime and its non-Muslim legislation, certain teachers who combat Islam, pressure from families who fear the government and its police. Nevertheless, there must be no mistake, the greatest difficulties are those that lie 'within the youth themselves'.

4. By *iltizam* the Islamicist militants mean the accomplishment by Muslims of all the various duties prescribed by their religion. The Muslim who does this then becomes *multazim*, which means roughly 'practising' or 'pious', and his piety in turn makes him ready to receive the Islamicist message.

Among these, a distinction must be made between problems that arise from a lack of understanding of Islamicist concepts and those that arise from the erroneous implementation of those concepts. Some young people, for instance, have not yet understood that Islam is a *nizam kamil wa shamil* (a complete and perfect system), that its vocation is to encompass everything. They therefore imagine that Islam requires only private piety and the saying of prayers, failing to understand that it must also regulate government and war, the judicial system and the economy. Others have grasped the total dimension of Islam properly, but are unable to distinguish between the necessary and the contingent. Some people think, for example, that the most important thing is to throw away their toothbrushes and toothpaste and to clean their teeth only by chewing *siwak*. But here the tree of *siwak* obscures the forest of Islam. Finally, there are still others who, claiming to have read a few books on theology, feel competent to interpret the Koran and reject anyone who reads it differently, doctors of Islam included, or who believe that violence is the only way to establish the Muslim state.

Such is the road, and such are the traps along the way. In addition, it very often happens that after the exemplary *jama'at* militant has obtained his degree and left the university, social pressures turn him into a lazy Muslim who forgets that he must preach Islam if the future Muslim state is to arise. In the face of such tribulations, 'Isam al-Din al-'Aryan can do no more than call upon the aid of God.

After reading through this Islamicist panorama of the world, past and present, one wonders what were the various influences and readings that shaped its author, for his vocabulary seems almost interchangeable with that of another social utopia whose weapon is the dialectic. I do not mean to suggest that the young doctor is a camouflaged Marxist, nor that his three phases correspond to the three moments of dialectical materialism, his vanguard of the *umma* to the revolutionary party, his notion of aborted independence to that of neo-colonialism, and his 'obstacles within the youth themselves' to alienation. More simply, the author is taking up — with what degree of awareness it is impossible to say — the ideals of social justice, liberation from foreign tutelage, and the aspiration for democracy and change which are shared by Egypt's half million students and have been expressed — depending on the period, the prevalent ideological modes, and the capacity of this or that group to formulate them — in Marxist, Arab Socialist, Ba'thist, liberal, and other vocabularies. The prime significance of 'Isam al-Din al-'Aryan's adoption of these ideals is to demonstrate that the *jama'at islamiyya* were the current which, in Sadat's Egypt of the late seventies, successfully invested the terrain of social utopia and annexed to its own dissident discourse other discourses that protested against the established order, subordinating them to the fundamental project of the *jama'at*.

The intellectual descent of the *jama'at* from the author of *Signposts* is manifest throughout this text, but by the end of 1980 Talmasani's magazine was making every effort to avoid mention of Sayyid Qutb except when necessary. It was a year and a half later that Talmasani said that Sayyid Qutb never represented anyone but himself, and certainly not the Muslim Brethren.

But Qutb's name crops up repeatedly in the mimeographed leaflets and newsletters produced by the *jama'at* rank and file, and the young militants claimed allegiance to his memory, whereas the work of Hasan al-Hudaybi, the former Supreme Guide who had upheld a moderate line against Qutb's radicalism, was virtually ignored. An article entitled 'Our Thought', for example, which appeared in the fourth issue of the monthly journal of the *jama'at* of Alexandria, contains the following passage, an outright pastiche of quotations from *Signposts*. 'When we say that we have a thought of our own', the writer warns us, 'we are not, of course, putting forward an alternative to Islam. . . . But we have an understanding (*fahm*) of it, we have our own way of realizing it within ourselves (*tariq li tahqiqihi fi anfusina*) and on earth.' The *jama'at* cling particularly to certain concepts: 'There is no God but God'; '*Rububiyya* (divinity) belongs to God alone'; 'to God alone do we owe '*ubudiyya* (worship) and *ta'a* (submission)'; '*hakimiyya* (sovereignty) and the right to legislate belong to God — He has no associate'; 'divine unity (*tawhid*) in Islam signifies liberation (*tahrir*) from all that is corrupt in thought . . . and from the chains forged by the dictatorship and

the monopolists (*muhtakirin*); it is also, for the spirit, the liberation of all that is inherited or conventional, like customs and
traditions.'

For the Good of the Copts

After Sadat's anti-Islamicist speech in Asyut in the spring of 1979
and the regime's measures designed to intimidate the Islamicists, the latter sought first of all to re-establish what they considered the truth among public opinion. They had been accused of
violence; confusion had deliberately been sown between them
and Shukri's group. 'We have always denounced that group and
we disapproved of the assassination of Dhahabi', they answered.

Al-Da'wa reappeared in June 1979 after the one-month
suspension ordered by Sadat, and the regime took no further
significant measure regarding the universities after the dissolution of the General Union of Students. Did Sadat feel he had done
enough, or was he being urged to go easy on the Islamicists,
particularly the moderates of *al-Da'wa,* some of whom were
extremely well connected? Whatever the answer, the effect was a
radicalization of the movement, in particular the relative decline
of Talmasani's friends in favour of more militant elements. *Al-
Da'wa's* 'News of the Youth and the Universities' now contained
'recommendations and warnings' from Mustafa Mashhur, who
warned 'Muslim youth' against 'emotional actions, provocations
by our enemies, partial conflicts that merely waste our time'. He
exhorted them to 'let themselves be guided by those who have
preceded them on the Path, that they might begin where these
others left off, instead of starting from scratch all over again'. But
these calls to moderation went unheeded, and the atmosphere
on the campuses was extremely tense. On 24 March 1980 several
hundred members of the *jama'at* in Alexandria surrounded the
office of the dean of the science faculty. Ten of them went inside,
sequestered the dean for three hours, and presented him with a
four-point ultimatum: that there be no further festivals or film
showings in the school, that interrogations of *jama'at* members
be halted, that the faculty organize 'Islamic meetings', and that

there be no impediment to the candidacy of Islamicist students in the elections to the faculty student union.

Although the university years 1979/80 and 1980/81 saw repeated incidents and commando actions involving the *jama'at* and 'deviants', at the two universities of Middle Egypt, Asyut and Minya, tension ultimately crystallized around the confessional problem.

The Coptic community in the three governorates of Minya, Asyut, and Sohag is much larger than the national average of 6.31 per cent of the total population, reaching 19.4 per cent, 20 per cent, and 14.6 per cent respectively, according to the latest — and hotly contested — census (1976). To understand the charges of 'arrogance' (*istikbar*) made against the Copts by the Islamicists, we have to go back to the middle of the nineteenth century. The Coptic community has long been on the decline: cut off from their cultural heritage, confined to the countryside, and having few churches, the Copts have rallied round a clergy obsessed with repetition of the gestures and words of ritual. From about 1875 onwards, primarily as a result of education received in missionary schools, a Coptic elite began to assimilate modern Western culture in a way that enabled them to acquire significant weight in the public services, commerce, the liberal professions, and so on. This elite is secular-minded and has opposed the patriarch, whom it considers backward and obscurantist, in an effort to win leadership of the community. The *majlis milli*, or communal council, a creature of the Coptic notables, has always sought the support of the regime (in which bourgeois Copts were heavily represented during the thirties, through their massive participation in the Wafd Party), while the patriarch's base was traditionally among the rural masses. The Nasser regime's nationalizations, which ruined the secular Coptic bourgeoisie and forced many of them into exile, swung the balance in favour of the Church. But although the latter now enjoyed clear hegemony over the community, and although the Coptic population was rising fast, Nasser's pan-Arab ideology swamped them in a world in which they constituted a negligible quantity. Since young generations of Copts suffer the same social, cultural, economic, and political tensions as any other Egyptians, they have lately manifested a tendency to turn to the Church, just as young Muslims have turned to the mosque or to Islamic activism. The sites of newly resurgent Coptic hermitages have a symbolic value not very different from that of the *hijra* of Shukri Mustafa's Society of Muslims. The parishes of Upper Egypt have seen a rebirth of communitarian pride and Christian sentiment, while the traditional clergy has remained fairly unpolished, incapable of responding to the questions now being asked by the young: the intellectual renaissance has been confined to the monasteries, failing to reach the valley parishes.

The demand for Coptic cultural identity, however, runs directly counter to the dominant idea of the *jama'at islamiyya*, and of many other Muslims besides. In their eyes, the 'people of the Book' (Jews and Christians, that is) may peacefully enjoy their status of *dhimmi* until the inevitable day that the grace of the Islamic message penetrates their hearts and they become Muslims. They are not supposed to be too ostentatious in their rejection of this process.

According to the Islamicist view of the world, the tributary *dhimmis* enjoy an enviable happiness compared to the 'horrible' situation faced by Muslims in Christian countries. Moreover, the *jama'at* say that the Copts, if they are sincere, must also aspire to a Muslim state, for deep down they know that the government is the guarantor of justice and felicity, just as God revealed in the Koran. Unfortunately, operations are mounted from abroad as part of the world conspiracy against Islam: these are the Christian missions (*tabshir*), vanguard of the Crusade (*salibiyya*). The Crusaders — the word is used to designate both Western Christians and the Lebanese Maronites — lead the Copts astray, inciting them to reject their status as tributaries, to propagate their faith, to build new churches, and thus to provoke the Muslims. It is the duty of all good Muslims to oppose their nefarious enterprises. This is what the *jama'at* of Minya tried to do in the spring of 1980.

The incidents that erupted in Minya that spring, blossoming along with the purple flowers of the first jacarandas and opening a cycle of violence, began over the presentation to Sadat of the credentials of Eliahu ben Elissar, Israel's first ambassador to Egypt, and the asylum offered the ex-shah of Iran. In March the *jama'at* began organizing public meetings to denounce this *munkar* (absolute evil or abomination, the prosecution of which is the first commandment of Islam). It was recalled that 'in 1965 al-Azhar issued a *fatwa* forbidding peace with Israel'; retaliation was demanded against Israelis who came to Egypt and against Egyptians who collaborated with them. Concurrently, meetings were held to denounce the ex-shah's arrival. The authorities tried to ban one of these meetings, at the University of Cairo on 26 March, but another took place in Asyut and concluded with a demonstration in the town. The anti-riot police opened fire, and the demonstration ended with one dead, six seriously wounded, and about sixty arrested.

It was in this climate of unprecedented gravity that tension suddenly mounted between Sadat and the Coptic Pope, Shenouda III. On 11 April the president returned from an official visit to the United States during which American newspapers had printed full-page advertisements placed by Coptic emigrants denouncing 'the persecution suffered by Christians in Egypt'. Sadat found this press campaign an embarrassment in his meetings with American leaders, for it described him as a prisoner of what is called in the United States 'Muslim fundamentalism'. On his return to Egypt, Sadat publicly registered his displeasure with the hierarchy of the Coptic church, and especially its leader, Pope Shenouda. Relations between the two men worsened to the point that, after the inter-confessional incidents in al-Zawiyya al-Hamra in June 1981, Sadat refused to recognize Shenouda as a community spokesman, thus effectively divesting him of his office. The Coptic church had been manifesting opposition to the regime since the spring of 1980, boycotting official celebrations: no Easter ceremony had been held, and no Coptic church dignitary was present at the airport to welcome Sadat on his return from the United States.

It was around this time that incidents broke out in Middle Egypt in the city of Minya and the surrounding countryside, involving clashes between members of the Christian and Muslim communities during which several people were killed. The *jama'at islamiyya* of Middle Egypt distributed a leaflet giving their version of events:

'*Al-jama'at al-islamiyya. In the name of God, the Compassionate, the Merciful*. Is not God all-sufficient for His servant? (Koran, XXXIX, 36.)

'MINYA AND ASYUT CAUGHT BETWEEN THE NAZAREANS[5] AND THE MINISTRY OF THE INTERIOR

'Muslim Brothers,

'At a time when Shenouda has announced that the Christians will "boycott the celebration" of their holiday (Easter), when he refuses to go to the airport to greet the president of the Republic, when he sends Bishop Samuel [a member of the church hierarchy who sat beside Sadat on 6 October 1981 and died with him] to America and instructs the Nazareans living there to demonstrate and to distribute leaflets against the president, at that same moment Shenouda has ordered the Nazareans in Egypt to take up arms and attack the Muslims. So it was that a gang of Minya Nazareans stabbed two Muslims in the back while they were on their way to the mosque in the hamlet ('*izba*) of Tath-South. The families of the victims then gathered to make the criminals, who had been acting on the Church's instructions, pay the blood price. But the families never expected that the Nazareans would come out with unauthorized firearms like machine-guns and submachine-guns. They fired from the roofs of their houses, killing one Muslim and wounding others, among them women and children who now lie in the Minya general hospital.'

The police intervened, confronted the 'Nazarean militia', seized arms, and arrested the 'criminals'. The next day, the police intercepted a 'truckload of arms being sent to the Christians'. Finally, other 'Nazareans' were disarmed. And while the Muslims were undergoing this ordeal, 'the authorities tell us that all these incidents are church provocations designed to strengthen Shenouda's position abroad and to win concessions from the government. Thus did the minister of the interior ask Brother Hilmi al-Jazzar, *amir* [supreme commander] of the *jama'at islamiyya* in Egypt, to send the *jama'at* to calm the families down, in exchange for which the Ministry would release Muslims arrested by the police in the mosques, where they had taken refuge to protect themselves against the attacks of the

5. This is the polemical designation of Christians in Muslim texts.

Nazareans.' These arrested Muslims had been 'atrociously tortured': 'starved and denied water' for two days, their beards ripped out, and so on. Their families then surrounded the police station where they were being held, setting fire to the building. Calm was restored after the mediation of Hilmi al-Jazzar and the local *amir* of the *jama'at*, Muhi al-Din, and the first Muslims were released on the night of 11 April. That was the day Sadat returned from the United States, 'where we know what kind of welcome he got from the emigré Nazareans of Egypt'. 'There followed, incomprehensible events which God alone can understand': Muhi al-Din was arrested, the *jama'at* of Minya and Asyut were persecuted, university courses were suspended, and so on. 'Why all this after the return from the White House? Is it the result of pressure from the American Crusaders to strike at the Islamic movement in Egypt, as indicated in the Richard document?'

This is clearly a reference to the forgery attributed to the American orientalist Richard Mitchell by the magazine *al-Da'wa*. (The young Islamicist militants call Mitchell by his forename, in the Arab style, which makes him that much more difficult to identify.) 'How far will they go? The insolent Nazareans are on the attack, demonstrating and openly procuring arms from the Nazarean governor of Southern Sinai [the governor in question was then the sole Christian to occupy the post of provincial governor; he has since been removed], 'while for the Muslims there is only prison'.

Read in this more or less crude form, the text affords us a glimpse of how the *jama'at islamiyya* encode both interconfessional relations and their own relation to the state. It all starts when some peasants, Christians as it happens, attack some other peasants who are Muslims. The families of the victims organize a vendetta, but the better-armed Christians put the Muslims to fight. It is a thoroughly typical scene of vengeance in Upper or Middle Egypt, except that this time the Christians did not play by the rules. Instead of responding to the hunting rifles of their assailants with similar arms, thus allowing for one dead or wounded on each side, it turns out, to the great astonishment of the Muslims, that the Christians are heavily armed. The symbolism then changes. What may have been no more than a

traditional fight about boundary lines in the fields, or an argument about a she-buffalo allegedly bewitched to spoil her milk,
instead becomes a national drama of world significance. Having
come out on top in the armed clash, the Coptic peasants automatically become arrogant Nazareans attacking Islam. In all probability, this is why the *jama'at islamiyya* intervened, although the
leaflet does not say so. The police then arrive and incarcerate
members of both sides. Far from calming the situation, this
arouses fresh reactions by each community against the other,
and by both against the state. The families of the arrested
'Muslims', among whom were undoubtedly some Islamicist
militants, surround police headquarters. The emphasis on the
allegation that the police tortured the 'Muslims' by ripping out
their beards is meant to demonstrate that the victims were not
simple peasants, who are clean-shaven. The situation then gets
so badly out of hand for the police that Nabawi Isma'il, the
minister of the interior in Cairo, strikes a deal with the leader of
the *jama'at* according to which the *jama'at* troops will lift the
siege of the police station in exchange for the release of the
arrested Islamicists. The local leader of the *jama'at* carries out his
part of the bargain, and on the night of Friday, 11 April, the
prisoners are released and calm is restored.

But Sadat, upon his return from the United States, orders the
arrest of all the militants of the *jama'at* in Minya and Asyut, and
suspends classes at the two universities, thus disavowing his
own minister of the interior.

The *jama'at* leaflet does not simply present a chain of related
incidents, but also has an explanation for them — one which, at
each new turn of events, illustrates a phase of the conspiracy
against Islam executed by the Nazareans of Egypt on the orders
of the church hierarchy, which is in turn following the instructions of the Crusaders as conveyed in the 'Richard document'.

Before it is even recounted, the original incident is situated in
a context of tension between the regime and the church:
Shenouda is provoking the state and its chief, not only through
the campaign he is waging in the United States, but also through
the insurrection of Coptic peasants he has ordered. The
assaulted Muslims were stabbed 'in the back' while they were
'on their way to the mosque'. This illustrates the treachery of the

Copts and their deliberate intention to attack Muslims as such, for the victims were on their way to their place of worship. This detail is important: its purpose is to prevent the readers of the leaflet from assuming that this was nothing more than a family feud. In fact, the leaflet goes further in the very next sentence, indicating that 'the criminals were carrying out the instructions of the Church'.

There is additional evidence that a plot was afoot, for the Nazareans, according to the leaflet, had procured 'unauthorized weapons' with which they put to flight the 'families of the victims' who had come with full justification to demand the blood-money. For anyone who knows anything about the villages of the Nile Valley, the argument is hard to believe. Because of the brisk trade in contraband arms, every hamlet has its arsenal, occasionally discovered by some military expedition ordered by the provincial governor. But here again the main point is to show that the Muslims, though pursuing their vendetta, are on the side of the law, while the Copts are outlaws.

The leaflet concludes by suggesting, in the form of a purely rhetorical question, that Sadat, having received his orders from the White House, is now applying the instructions of the 'Richard document' and that a top-level functionary, the Christian governor of Southern Sinai, is providing his coreligionists with their automatic weapons.

After beginning as a violent attack on the Coptic church, the *jama'at islamiyya* leaflet turns into an indictment of the state under Sadat's presidency. Apart from being incapable even of playing its proper role in the maintenance of civil order (since according to the *jama'at*, it was they who restored calm), the state also turns out to be biased: the White House dictates Sadat's conduct, and the top administration is infiltrated by Christians whose only objective is to massacre Muslims.

This particularly revealing document merits a number of comments. To begin with, it affords us precious insights into the base of the *jama'at* in Middle Egypt. The Islamicist students of Minya are the sons of peasant 'families' and are prepared to intervene in their conflicts. They also have access to the village arms depots, and are able to turn the traditional violence of a vendetta into political violence against the state, in this case a siege of the police station. The successful neutralization of such an important state institution in a large city like Minya in the spring of 1980, with the support or complicity of part of the population, was a kind of dress rehearsal for the investing of the city of Asyut for four days by the Jihad group just after the assassination of Sadat, until elite paratroopers arrived to put down the rebellion.

Moreover — and here again it is significant that this occurred as early as the spring of 1980 — the *jama'at* did not hesitate to fan the flames of sectarian tension in order to place the state in an awkward position and to demonstrate that they were prepared to supplant the state, to step into the breach, so to speak. The same tactic was used later, in June 1981, in the Cairo neighbourhood of al-Zawiyya al-Hamra.

Finally, let us also note that there are not two but three protagonists in the scenario of sectarian confrontation: apart from the Christian and Muslim communities, the state also intervenes. The Islamicists challenge the state because, far from keeping the Christians in their rightful place as tributaries, it uses them to persecute the Muslim people and makes the Christians auxiliaries of its own arbitrary acts. Such is the setting of all these sectarian incidents, in which the characters play out their parts as in a curtain-raiser to the final conflagration between the *jama'at* and the state, which was to occur in June 1981.

June 1981: Checkmate

In November 1979 the Cairo correspondent of the Paris daily *Le Monde* concluded his account of the collective prayer organized by the *jama'at* for the Greater Holiday in these terms: 'The army is no longer what it had been since the 1952 revolution: the sole nationally organized force in Egypt. The Muslim fundamentalists, despite divisions in their ranks, now undoubtedly constitute another organized force on the Egyptian political scene.'

The sort of deal to which the minister of the interior resorted in April 1980 to settle the Minya affair perhaps illustrates the truth of this observation even more strikingly than the twice-yearly prayer assemblies of the *jama'at*. They could no longer be removed from the 'Egyptian political scene' by mere decree, for they now commanded formidable power of their own and could also rely on the sympathy and solidarity they had aroused among the Muslim masses. To attack them head on might have proved suicidal for the regime, which would be accused of attacking Islam, the *jama'at* having managed to persuade many Egyptians that they were Islam's legitimate representative.

To destroy the *jama'at*, then, it was necessary first to break the bonds of Muslim solidarity they had woven throughout the country, by accusing them of a crime so monumental that its exposure would countervail that solidarity. This crime would be the destruction of national unity, an assault on the very 'being' of Egypt as a nation by igniting the flames of confessional sedition.

The incidents in al-Zawiyya al-Hamra caricatured, and thus dramatized, this debate. Did the Egyptian nation have any meaning for Egyptian Muslims, or did they owe their allegiance only to the Muslim *umma*, as the Islamicists thought? If the state was able to defeat the *jama'at*, it was because despite their remarkable growth, they had been unable to persuade the Egyptian Muslim masses to fight alongside them for the victory of the *umma*. This was a more important factor in their downfall than the disproportion between the state's repressive forces and their ability to resist.

The *jama'at* were attacked and liquidated by the regime as centrifugal forces whose aim was the destruction of the 'Egyptian nation', based, according to an old myth reactivated by Sadat, on the harmonious coexistence of the Copts and the Muslims. When the state's attack came, there were no massive expressions of solidarity with the Islamicists on the part of Egyptian Muslims. In order to establish a confessional balance in the repression and thus to disarm any potential Muslim solidarity, the regime also dealt heavy blows to the Coptic church and hierarchy, which were cast as the Christian equivalent not of al-Azhar, which is the institutional reality, but of the *jama'at*.

Sadat's position in mid-1981 was precarious. During the past year the peace treaty with Israel had won him considerable prestige among a population weary of the uninterrupted state of war that had prevailed since Nasser's time. But the benefits the president had drawn from the treaty were being whittled down by the various insults that came from the Begin government, the most deeply resented of which was the proclamation of Jerusalem as the indivisible capital of the Jewish state. The state's inability to deal with Egypt's internal problems was also becoming more manifest day by day.

Threatened by the Islamicist movement (which capitalized on the general disenchantment), criticized by the Coptic Church, and pilloried by intellectuals in the few tolerated opposition bulletins, the president was also isolated on the Middle Eastern scene, and felt that he had been abandoned by the Reagan administration, which no longer accorded him the privileged status he had enjoyed under Carter. Sadat had also aged. The political genius who had consistently outmanoeuvred his adversaries, playing one against the other, had become a self-satisfied autocrat intoxicated by the fulsome praise heaped upon him by the Western mass media. His political advisers had been replaced by courtiers, careerists, and cops. Nabawi Isma'il, the minister of the interior, ran an army of *agents provocateurs,* thugs, and anti-riot brigades of ever-increasing size and influence. It was in this *fin de règne* atmosphere that the June 1981 incidents broke out in Cairo's al-Zawiyya al-Hamra district.

The origin of the events is not clear, and the various accounts are contradictory. Some say that it all started with an altercation between two local gossips, one Muslim and the other Christian, others that militants of the *jama'at islamiyya* had taken over a plot of land owned by a Copt to build a mosque on it. Whatever the truth, a pitched battle soon erupted between the two communities in this poor and overcrowded Cairo neighbourhood. They were egged on by mysterious *provocateurs,* and probably further inflamed by the intense summer heat and the cuts in the water supply. Atrocious crimes were committed by people who had earlier lived together peacefully: men and women were slaughtered; babies were thrown from windows, their bodies crushed on the pavement below; there was looting, killing, and arson. At the same time, leaflets were distributed elsewhere in the city urging each community to take up arms. The neighbourhood was finally sealed off by the police, who according to most witnesses intervened only after irreparable damage had already been done.

The horror aroused in the country by news of the atrocities committed by extremists on both sides created the situation the regime needed to crush the *jama'at* by severing the bonds of solidarity with the mass of Muslims: they were charged with particularly odious crimes. On 8 September a long article in *al-Ahram* presented the official version of the background to the events. The *jama'at* had just been dissolved, and their members were being sought by police throughout the country. *Al-Ahram*, its front page emblazoned with the headline 'Origin of the Leaflets That Inflamed Confessional Sedition Discovered', affirmed that a Christian faculty member 'who had studied in Moscow' had taken to sending letters insulting Islam, signed with a pseudonym, to prominent Egyptian personalities. After discovering one of these letters, the *jama'at* reproduced it in a widely distributed leaflet, accompanied by a commentary calling upon Muslims to take action against the Christians. Here, according to the 8 September 1981 edition of *al-Ahram*, is the text of a letter sent to an 'Islamic personality' by Dr Fu'ad Jirjis, the arrested Christian university professor, who was in charge of conferences at the school of agriculture of Cairo University:

'The ridiculous Islamic religion, which represses women and sexuality, is murder and destruction through and through . . . it is the cause of the Middle East's backwardness and of all the calamities that have occurred there, the cause of the terrible backwardness of the Muslim countries. It is the religion of deafening noise and forced night-time wakefulness,[6] of loud-speakers, of *tabbal*[7] . . ., the religion of theft, corruption, key-money, and violation of frozen prices. Such is Muslim society, and you demand the application of the *shari'a*! May you know that your masters the Copts view you with contempt and ridicule you every time they see a sheikh striding along in his turban, swaying from left to right, as though his head bore an unbear-able weight . . .

6. The reference is to the call to the dawn prayer, which is issued over loudspeakers every day between four and six in the morning, depending on the season.
7. The *tabbal* is a tambourine player who passes through the streets to awaken Muslims (and their neighbours) during the nights of Ramadan so that they can take their last licit meal before the start of the fast, or *imsak*, when the sun comes up.

'But will the by-products of this contemptible religion last much longer? Now that the Camp David accords have been signed, I believe that the extinction of Islam is near, as is the return of Egypt to Christianity.

'It is you, corrupt men, who have corrupted both this world and the next!'

This letter was reproduced in a leaflet by the *jama'at islamiyya* of al-Azhar University, accompanied by the following commentary (again according to *al-Ahram* of 8 September):

'Copy of a letter sent by the Crusader front to an Islamic personality.

'A word to the youth of al-Azhar!

'Their hatred is clear from what they say but more violent is the hatred which their breasts conceal (Koran, III, 118). *They will not cease to fight against you until they force you to renounce your faith — if they are able* (II, 217). *You will please neither the Jews nor the Christians unless you follow their faith* (II, 120).

'To you, my Muslim brother! You who slumber, may you awake! May the negligent pay heed! May the deserters return to the fold! May those who have gone astray all hasten back to us! This is no laughing matter: it is deadly earnest! Shall we abandon our Islam in the tempest? Shall we abandon it to conspiracies?'

Al-Ahram's article then reproduces the text of a leaflet by Majdi Rajab Warda, *amir* of one of the *jama'at islamiyya* in Alexandria:

'Muslims! Beware of the festivals of the *mushrikin* (associationists)![8] Brother in Islam, know that the true religion was founded against the associationists and that the Straight Path shuns the roads of the infidels, that it is the Jews "who have incurred Your wrath" and the Nazareans "who have gone astray".[9]

'In His book God orders us to stand against the associationists and forbids us to imitate them in anything that distinguishes

8. The Christians are called 'associationists' because of their belief in the Trinity, which 'associates' the Father, the Son, and the Holy Spirit. In Muslim eyes this amounts to polytheism.

9. The phrase is a variation on the last two verses of the *Fatiha*, the opening sura (or chapter) of the Koran: 'Guide us to the straight path/The path of those whom You have favoured/Not of those who have incurred Your wrath/Nor of those who have gone astray.'

them. Now, holidays are part of divine law and ritual. God has ordered us to stand against the weekly holiday of the Jews, Saturday, and of the Christians, Sunday, and we have preferred Friday to them. . . .

'To associate with the holidays of infidels is to violate the meaning of the *shari'a*, for they are heretical events that form part of infidel religions: they lead to their gods and are a means for the propagation of ungodliness. To be indifferent to them even to the slightest degree would have grave consequences . . . the Muslims have no right to associate with the Nazareans in their celebration known as *Shamm al-Nisim*.'

Shamm al-Nisim (which literally means 'smell the breeze') is a holiday celebrated on the Monday following Coptic Easter. It dates back to pharaonic times and is intended to mark the coming of the summer season. It features the eating of hard-boiled eggs, green onions, and *fasikh* (a small salted fish). It is also customary for well-off city families to travel out to the countryside together to 'smell the breeze'. More commonly, people crowd together on the infrequent patches of grass that grow in some Cairo squares. This holiday, which is celebrated by everyone, Muslim and Christian alike (although only Nilotic Christianity has formally placed it on the religious calendar), is a symbol of Egyptian 'national unity'.

Finally, *al-Ahram* explained that these leaflets had been widely distributed all over Egypt on the occasion of the (Christian) New Year and Shamm al-Nisim celebrations.

It is worth noting that the official version of the origin of the 'confessional sedition' as published by *al-Ahram*, while apparently careful to preserve symmetry, names on the one hand a 'Copt' who is identified as such (with the 'studied in Moscow' thrown in, although the text contains no element of Soviet ideology) and on the other hand not 'a Muslim' or even 'some Muslims' but the *jama'at*, whom the regime categorizes as 'extremists' or 'fanatics'. The responsibility of the Christian, whose letter predates the *jama'at* leaflet, is obvious to any reader, and since he is nowhere described as 'extremist', 'fanatical', or even isolated in his community, the repressive measures taken against the Coptic pope in his capacity as leader of the community are implicitly justified.

The presentation of the attitude of the *jama'at* came in two instalments. First there is their commentary on the Fu'ad Jirjis letter: relatively moderate in tone, it is cleverly designed to echo the sentiments of Muslim readers whose faith has been insulted, calling upon them to join with the *jama'at* ('May those who have gone astray all hasten back to us') before it is too late. The attempt here is to reinforce the bonds of solidarity among Muslims, under the leadership of the Islamicist movement. The second instalment is the Majdi Warda leaflet, which extols Muslim exclusivity and the sentiment of Muslim solidarity, obviously directed against the Christians, but also against the Egyptian nation, symbolized by its national holiday *par excellence,* Shamm al-Nisim.

We have no way of verifying the authenticity of these documents, the identity of their authors, or Majdi Warda's membership of the *jama'at. Al-Ahram* could provide no part of an answer to any of these questions. But the important political point is less the existence of the three documents cited by *al-Ahram* than their selection from a mass of others and their presentation in a manner intended to offer the paradigm of confessional sedition that the state wanted.

The arrests that followed the dissolution of the *jama'at islamiyya* on 3 September 1981 seem to have broken the movement. The tenor of life on Egyptian campuses changed: the beards by which the police were able to identify the Islamicist students disappeared, but the wearing of the veil, although no longer encouraged by 'Muslim Youth Weeks', is far from out of fashion, and the dramatic social and cultural problems that had offered the *jama'at* such excellent themes for agitation have not disappeared either: housing, transport, lecture halls, private lessons, and so on.

Until Sadat's death, 'extremism' and 'fanaticism' were regularly denounced, although no questions were ever raised about the conditions that had given rise to them, apart from the standard clichés about the 'alienation of youth', or worse, the search for the 'hidden hands', the 'underground ringleaders', who were naturally identified as coming from the Soviet Union, whose ambassador to Egypt was declared *persona non grata* in September. But once the president was dead, assassinated by an

Islamicist militant, and once most of those arrested in September had been released from prison, a more critical tone was adopted in regard to Sadat's policy towards the *jama'at islamiyya*. Things that had previously been said only unofficially were now printed, and evidence was published about the links between the regime and the *jama'at* in the early seventies. In a sign of the times, the *jama'at*'s godfather, Muhammad 'Uthman Isma'il, was removed from his post as governor of Asyut.

The Sermons of Sheikh Kishk

Each component of the Islamicist movement that we have discussed so far occupies some definite field of activity. Shukri and his group had withdrawn from the everyday world to take refuge in a land of their own; the neo-Muslim Brethren put out a magazine and brought pressure to bear on the members of the People's Assembly; the *jama'at islamiyya* had their roots on the campuses, which they sought to turn into fortresses of Islam.

Sheikh Kishk, on the other hand, is omnipresent. In the last years of Sadat's presidency, it was impossible to walk the streets of Cairo without hearing his stentorian voice. Climb into a collective service-taxi and the driver is listening to one of Sheikh Kishk's recorded sermons on his cassette player. Stop for a fruit juice at a street-corner stand, and while the palate savours mango or cane sugar, the ear is bombarded by the sermon delivered by Sheikh Kishk the previous Friday: the juice peddler has it blaring from his scratchy recorder, between two tracks by Umm Kulthum, the nightingale of the East, and a hit by some other popular singer. Go back to your flat and you hear a voice rising from the street hammering out phrases in Koranic Arabic: the doorman, sitting on his bench day in, day out, is listening to Kishk.

They listen to Kishk in Cairo, in Casablanca, and in the North African district of Marseilles. A Saudi-funded magazine has dubbed him 'the star of Islamic preaching'. He has his imitators, of course, but none commands his incomparable vocal cords, his panoramic Muslim culture, his phenomenal capacity for improvisation, and his acerbic humour in criticizing infidel regimes, military dictatorship, the peace treaty with Israel, or the complicity of al-Azhar. For Kishk, the great tenor of the Islamicist movement, is an oppositionist.

In the countries of the Third World, where much of the population is still unable to gain access to written culture, audiovisual equipment is the prime medium. Governments understood this early on: they normally make inordinate use of radio and television in consolidating their power, in telling and showing people how to think, even in the most remote areas. But the spread of the cassette player during the seventies — and every emigrant brings back several for his family when he returns from the Arabian peninsula — changed the flow of this discourse. People can now choose the cassettes they want, and can use them as antidotes to official discourse. The cassettes recorded by the ayatollah Khomeini, for instance, were a powerful factor in the overthrow of the shah of Iran.

Official Islam has made abundant use of the media in Egypt. Radio and television stations first began broadcasting readings and commentaries of the Koran, recited according to the rules of *tajwid,* which codify the proper pronunciation and intonation. Next the *ulema* took to the airwaves to explain to the people that the latest government measures were in perfect accordance with the prescriptions of the Book. With Sadat's conquest of power, religious television programmes acquired such enormous importance that a preacher like Sheikh Sha'rawi appeared on television even more often than the president himself. His sermons, clever and much appreciated, generally dealt quite openly and unashamedly with the problems of everyday life, indicating the relevant Islamic solutions. But his televised speeches never suggested any challenge to the regime's legitimacy, and he even served as minister of waqfs.

Sheikh Kishk, on the other hand, was a sensation in contemporary Egyptian Islam. His popular, down-market eloquence won him considerable success. But since he had tasted the Nasserist concentration camps early in life, he never placed his talent at the government's disposal, and cast himself instead as the censor of mores and attitudes which, whether in morals or social and political life, ran counter to Islam as he understood it. The sweep of Kishk's reprobation is vast, and he fears nothing and no one, or so his admirers believe. He thus came to be seen as a sort of Muslim Robin Hood for whom 'commanding the Good and forbidding Evil' was not just a matter of style, but a law of life itself. This brought him even greater success, as his popularity swept the entire Arab world, making him untouchable except in periods of the sharpest crisis, as in the month that preceded Sadat's death.

A Sheikh's Childhood

'Abd al-Hamid Kishk was born in 1933 in Shabrakhayt, a village in the province of Buhayra in the western part of the Nile Delta, not far from Alexandria. His family was of rural origin, and his father was a very modest merchant, 'a simple man who always kept smiling, whatever life's difficulties'. 'Abd al-Hamid had three brothers and two sisters when his father died, leaving his thirty-year-old widow responsible for six children, the youngest of whom was not yet of school age. Although a simple peasant woman, his mother had a grandiose idea of her responsibilities, for her own father had been careful to give her a good Muslim education, that she might set an example to other women. Her six children were all she had, but she knew the verse of the Koran that says: *Those who would be anxious should they leave behind them helpless offspring should be mindful of their obligation to God in respect of orphans. Let them fear God and speak for justice* (IV, 9).

Armed with this principle, she made sure that her boys would acquire a good education: the oldest would study law; 'Abd al-Hamid, whose eyesight was bad, would study religion; the younger ones would learn a trade. So it was that 'Abd al-Hamid, who knew the Koran by heart at the age of twelve, was enrolled in a religious primary school in Alexandria. There he was heavily influenced by his grammar teacher, Sheikh Muhammad Jad, who acted as 'a father who taught us the rudiments of social life, helped the poor . . . and got angry when he caught a pupil smoking'.

By the time 'Abd al-Hamid had obtained his certificate of primary religious studies, he was completely blind, probably a victim of trachoma, which ravages the children of poor peasants in Egypt. He sought treatment for two years, but finally realized, according to his official biography, that 'God had granted him the gift of blindness; he pressed on with his studies seriously and assiduously, and praised God who had taken his sight but given him vision'.

This admirable perseverence brought him to Cairo's Azharist secondary school, where he was always first in his class. Here again his grammar teacher, Kamal Shahin — who always chose 'Abd al-Hamid to summarize the course aloud at the end of each lesson, so prodigious was his memory — exercised a great influence on him. His Azhar baccalaureate, attained with honours, won him enty into the *usul al-din* (principles of religion) faculty of al-Azhar University, which he attended before the Nasserist reform. In 1961, at the age of twenty-eight, he represented al-Azhar at the Science Festival, and then became a leader of prayer, or *imam*, in the *hukumi* (government) mosques — in other words, an employee of the Ministry of Waqfs. In 1964 he became a preacher at Cairo's 'Ayn al-Hayat (Source of Life) mosque, but he was arrested in 1966 during the 'ordeal' Nasser inflicted on all those suspected of being Muslim Brethren, or, as Kishk put it, when 'the men of the revolution . . . opened prisons and concentration camps and erected gallows for those who had the idea that there is no god but God' (*la ilah illa-llah*).[1]

Incarcerated first in the Citadelle prison and later in the Tura camp, Kishk was not released until 1968, although no definite charge was ever brought against him. He suffered various forms of torture, of which he still bears the marks. Despite sporadic prison terms in subsequent years, he retained his post as preacher at the Source of Life mosque. Distribution of his recorded sermons seems to have begun in 1972. So great was his fame that the Ministry of Waqfs had to build several annexes to the mosque to accommodate the Friday crowds. In 1981, however, even these were insufficient to shelter the approximately ten thousand people who regularly attended. In addition to the weekly sermon, Kishk gave his disciples daily courses (also recorded) between the sunset and night-time prayers, and he

1. This expression is the credo of all Muslims. In the context of the years 1965–66, however, it was the rallying cry of the disciples of Qutb, who had used the phrase as the title of one of the most striking chapters of *Signposts*.

held 'consultations' four afternoons a week: anyone could come to see him to explain a problem or simply to talk.

The group of bearded youth around Kishk, who also see to the distribution of his message, is sufficiently structured to provide a squad of ushers to control crowds effectively during sermons and to make sure that any provocation is averted. The recordings are available on the spot as soon as Kishk has finished speaking, and within a few days they travel the length and breadth of the Arab world, carried by enthusiastic young converts who distribute them by plane.

In July 1976 Kishk was among a group of Islamic personalities who drafted an article for the first issue of the new series of the magazine *al-Da'wa*, organ of the neo-Muslim Brethren. Ignored by the official and semi-official press but known to all Egyptians, who adulated or damned him depending on their intellectual, social, or confessional affiliation, the sheikh was among the victims of the final confrontation between Sadat and the Islamicist movement. He was arrested at the beginning of September 1981 and interrogated on the twenty-third by a socialist public prosecutor in the course of the inquiry into 'confessional sedition'. Some of his tapes were banned. The conditions of his imprisonment were eased considerably after the assassination of the president on 6 October, and he was allowed to receive newspapers. On 27 January 1982 he was released. Since then, the new regime has given him access to the media. He now has a regular column in the mass-circulation Islamic weekly *al-Liwa' al-Islami*. In the many interviews he granted the press after his release from prison, he denounced extremism.

Kishk was not the only sheikh arrested in September 1981: his Alexandrian colleagues Mahmud 'Id and Mahallawi, closely linked to the *jama'at islamiyya*, and a throng of professional and amateur preachers suffered a similar fate, for 'having turned the pulpit into a rostrum for anti-government meetings', according to the official phraseology of the time. But none of the others had his breadth, and none was as famous.

The Friday Sermon

The Source of Life mosque, better known as Sheikh Kishk mosque, lies at the edge of Cairo's Qubba Gardens district, not far from the poor neighbourhoods of Zaytun and 'Abbasiyya. It is this proximity to two of the city's teeming districts that seems to provide the bulk of the mass attendance at Kishk's Friday sermons, as groups of the faithful arrive on foot, some of them dressed in the white gallabieh, but most in Western clothes of mediocre cut and quality. But many people also travel from one end of the city to the other to listen to the sheikh; most come by bus, a few in their private Mercedes. Judging by their style of dress, however, most listeners belong to the poor urban masses that form the bulk of Cairo's population, and not to the better-off classes. The mosque itself stands in the midst of a decrepit housing project dating from the sixties.

In Islam the mosque is a matter more of flesh than of stone, if we may use a Christian metaphor. Its lay-out and architectural design matter little: the important thing is that it offers a place to pray and to gather on Friday to listen to the sermon. Hence the sometimes surprising forms of spatial extension of contemporary mosques in Egypt, and hence also their proliferation, which is encouraged by law.[2]

Sheikh Kishk's mosque is a prototype of this sort of spatial expansion. The Friday crowds pack not only the original mosque and the additional prayer halls built by the Ministry of Waqfs, but also the alleyways of the adjacent housing estate. The ground is covered with mats on which the faithful sit to listen and prostrate themselves for the prayers. Powerful loudspeakers are attached to the walls of nearby buildings to relay the sheikh's voice.

The crowd begins arriving in compact groups about an hour before the midday prayer on Friday. While waiting for the sermon, they pass the time at the stands of the temple merchants.

---

2. In principle, any site consecrated as a mosque retains its function eternally and becomes inviolable. Moreover, if the owner of a building consecrates a room as a mosque, he is exempt from certain property taxes. There is no impediment to the installation outside the holy area of loudspeakers to call the faithful to the five daily prayers, from three in the morning to eight in the evening.

Photographs of Kishk are snatched up, as are cassettes by the hundreds, and dozens of pamphlets published by the 'Sheikh Kishk Library'. But all varieties of Muslim and Islamicist literature are on sale at bargain prices, along with the paraphernalia of the pious Muslim: prayer rugs, worry beads, *siwak*, perfume. More mundane peddlers also do a roaring trade in everything from food and drink to automobile accessories.

Everyone takes his place. The muted chanting of the Koran fades from the loudspeakers. Silence reigns. Then suddenly, like a thunder clap, the phrase rings out: *al-hamdu li-llah rabb al-'alamin* ('Praise be to God, Lord of Creation'). Sheikh Kishk's sermon begins. Lasting for about an hour and a half, some three times as long as an ordinary sermon, it will take up both sides of a ninety-minute Maxell cassette. The faithful will be able to buy their tapes of the sermon on the spot.

The sermon that is summarized below was delivered on 10 April 1981. Its inspiration was fairly general, for nothing out of the ordinary had occurred during the first week of April that year. It was read out like a long, continuous speech, in which a few chanted passages stand out. Kishk can speak so-called classical Arabic without the slightest difficulty, as any al-Azhar graduate must in theory be able to do. But he ventures occasional stylistic flourishes to great effect. Although these shock purists, they delight his audience. As his listeners see it, the sheikh speaks the prestigious language of the Koran with assurance, but he also brings it within their grasp. Only in the last ten minutes of the sermon does the sheikh lapse into the Cairo dialect, as though after having submerged the faithful in the flood of his classical rhetoric, he suddenly captivates them by switching to everyday colloquial.

Kishk's address is structured into three movements of different rhythm and content: an exordium that lasts some twenty minutes; a Koranic commentary of about half an hour; and finally the sermon proper, which deals with recent events and the state of the world.

THE EXORDIUM

'Praised be the lord of the worlds, O Lord! O Lord who has made the Holy Koran, springtime of our heart, light of our breast [various invocations of God, protector of men], I affirm that there is no god but God! Through His thought the heart is soothed, sin is pardoned. . . .

'Listen with me to what our Lord says in the holy *hadith*: "My worshipper! Remember Me when you are angry, and I will remember you when I am angry!" . . . If you suffer from anger, think of God! Anger comes from Satan, who has insinuated it into the race of Adam! If one of you is angry, let him make his ablutions. Ablutions are done with water, anger is fire, and only water extinguishes fire. . . . If you are angry, say: "There is no god but God." . . .

[Chanted.] 'O you believers in Oneness, who is the One? [The faithful: 'God!'] Who is the Discoverer? [Again: 'God!' Similar phrases and responses then follow, thirty-three times.] . . . The Prophet said to the son of Adam: "Do not be quick-tempered and you will go to Paradise." . . . Why? Because anger irritates and thereby unleashes a chemical process: there is something in the blood called adrenalin, and when a man gets angry, particles of adrenalin are released into the blood, which cause a rise in blood pressure, and blood is pumped from the heart to the brain, and that is why the son of Adam's face and eyes become so red; thus he angers God, he decides to divorce, though the Beloved [God] has said: "Marry and do not divorce." . . .

'The blood rises to the brain, whose arteries explode, and this causes thrombosis, paralysis, and that is why (*wa-lidhalika*) Christ, when he saw his mother sad, told her: *"Do not despair! Your lord has provided a brook that runs at your feet,*[3] a sparkling brook, *and if you shake the trunk of this palm-tree it will drop fresh ripe dates in your lap. Therefore rejoice.* Eat the ripe dates *and drink* the flowing water, and *look upon* the pure boy." But, O Christ, do eating and drinking soothe anger? The angry man will find the manna and quail that are placed before him tasteless! And Christ, blessings be upon him, said to her: "Are you sad because you conceived me without a father? When *you meet any mortal say to him: 'I have vowed a fast to the Merciful and will not speak with any man today.'* " Who, then, will speak? He said to her:

3. All quotations from the Koran are in italics in this and subsequent passages of Kishk's sermon. In this case they come from verses 24–26 and 29–33 of the Sura Mary (XIX).

"Point in my direction and I will plead your case eloquently before the court of divine justice." And so it was that *she made a sign to them, pointing to the child. But they replied: "How can we speak with a babe in the cradle?"* Then Christ took out his family registration booklet. Name: *"I am the servant of God."* He did not say "I am God", nor "I am the son of God", nor "I am a member of a triumvirate that rules the world", but "I am the servant of God." Level of education: *"He has given me the Gospel."* Profession: *"And ordained me as a prophet."* Degree of divinity: *"His blessing is upon me."* Commandments: *"He has commanded me to be steadfast in prayer and to give alms to the poor as long as I shall live."* Munificence: *"He has exhorted me to honour my mother."* Elevation: *"He has purged me of vanity and wickedness. I was blessed on the day I was born, and blessed I shall be on the day of my death; and may peace be upon me on the day when I shall be raised to life."* Were I the one to whom prayers are addressed, to whom would I pray? Thus, I am not God! Does God pray to God? No! . . . I emerged from a narrow vagina! Does the god whose seat is as great as the earth and the heavens live in a narrow vagina seven centimetres long, five centimetres wide, and two and a half centimetres thick? God has resolved the problem of Christ in one word: *Jesus is like Adam in the sight of God. He created him of dust and then said to him: "Be", and he was* [III, 59] . . .'

KORANIC COMMENTARY

'O Muhammad, guardian of the faith, where are we headed today? To court. Which court is that? The court of the revolution, the people's court, the court of fraud, the court of state security, the military tribunal, the ethics court, the more-or-less court, or the court of the socialist prosecutor?[4] Neither the one, nor the other, nor any of these! We repair instead to a court on whose doors are inscribed the words: "God judges by the Truth!" Those

4. The list includes, apart from the names of various courts established first by Nasser and then by Sadat, two fake courts ('of fraud' and 'more-or-less') that are meant to discredit the others humorously. The Court of the Revolution was established to try 'counter-revolutionaries', notably the Muslim Brethren in 1954. The Court of State Security is the one that sentenced Qutb to death in 1965. The Ethics Court and the socialist prosecutor are creations of Sadat and try infractions of the 'values' or ethics of the regime.

who invoke any other principle of judgement judge by nothing
at all! *God hears and observes all men!* [XL, 20]. My brothers, who is
it that we will summon before this divine tribunal? With this
four-hundred-and-eleventh lesson, I lead you to the tribunal of
the Koran. I do not tell you that the president of the court is
general so-and-so, that the first assessor is colonel such-and-
such, its second assessor this or that lieutenant-colonel . . . and
the court clerk major so-and-so![5] . . . And who is it that is summoned? Iblis [the devil]! And what are the charges? What crime
has he committed? . . . Today we shall judge him, and I ask you,
gentlemen, to be patient during the reading of these divine
words, for what I tell you now are prophetic narratives. They
have nothing to do with any lewd American television series that
encourages sin, or any licentious film or trivial play. . . .

'[God said to the angels:] *"prostrate yourselves before him"*
[Adam]. *The angels all prostrated themselves except Iblis, who was
too proud.* Question: *"Why do you not bow down to him whom My
own hands have made?"* [XXXVIII, 72, 73, 75]. The court is in
session. Response no. 1: *"I am nobler than he. You created me from
fire, but him from clay"* [XXXVIII, 76]. . . . [Abu Bakr] al-Siddiq[6]
sent to Khosroes, sovereign of the Persians, a messenger without
fear in his eyes and said to him: "Khosroes, are you so proud as
to take yourself for a god? How can this be, when you are doubly
issued from the urinary tract? Once during the paternal erection,
for whence comes the sperm? — from whence flows the piss!
. . . And a second time when you came out of your mother
through the hole she pisses out of. . . . Do not forget your origin,
for he who forgets his origin is lost, plunges into the fire, and
swells with pride to equal the One, the Victorious." . . .

'[God said to the devil] *"Rouse with your voice whomever you
are able"* [XVII, 64], by singing, in other words. Song is the
devil's pipe, the courier of fornication! . . .

'[The devil is found guilty of premeditated crimes by virtue

5. This list repeats the set formula with which newspaper accounts of the
sessions of the military court usually begin (in particular when Shukri Mustafa's
Society of Muslims was on trial, but also during the 1954 and 1965 trials of the
Muslim Brethren).

6. Abu Bakr al-Siddiq (570–634) was the friend and father-in-law of
Muhammad and also the first caliph, or 'successor', of the Prophet.

of 'articles' 77, 78, 84, and 85 of the Sura *Sad*,[7] and other similar texts.]

'We are in danger! Iblis was the more knowing . . . but he was morally evil. . . . Knowledge is like the rain that waters, and morals like the earth; if the land is bad, the rain has no effect. . . . [The devil had said to God:] *"I will seduce all men, except your faithful servants!"* [XXXVIII, 82]. I ask God to make us His faithful! One day, the *imam* Hasan al-Basri[8] saw Iblis in a dream. He said to him: "O Iblis, how goes it today with the servants?" and Iblis replied: "O Hasan, yesterday I showed men the path of error, but today it is I who learn it from them!" The master has become the pupil and the pupil the master! Thus it is that we conclude the judgement of Iblis the enemy of God, so that I may say to you that we live in times in which conspiracies are woven against Islam, concocted to lead the Muslims astray, to incite doubt among them, and to wage war against God and His messenger!'

THE SERMON

'Listen to the news I read in the magazine *al-Da'wa* this month: "In the Cairo suburb of Ma'di a group has been arrested whose members prayed facing Jerusalem (*bait al-maqdiss*)." Here we have a new sect (*firqa*) of those who have been led astray! A group that prays without facing the *qibla*, but Jerusalem instead! God said: *Many a time We have seen you turn your eyes towards heaven. We will make you turn towards a qibla that will please you. Turn towards the Holy Mosque [of Mecca]; wherever you be face towards it* [II, 144]. This sect sought to damage Islam by turning towards Jerusalem! I tell you in all frankness — and pain lies heavy on my soul — that since Israel entered Egypt and set up an embassy in Cairo, I am absolutely certain that there is a suspicious sect that receives its instructions from a hidden hand, to spread rumours and doubts about God and His messenger.[9] . . .

7. The verses are from Sura XXXVIII, as follows. *'Begone, you are accursed!' said He* (77). *'My curse shall remain on you until the day of reckoning'* (78). *God replied: 'Learn the truth then (and I speak nothing but the truth)'* (84). *'I shall fill Hell with your offspring and the men who follow you'* (85).

8. Hasan al-Basri: a preacher of the Umayyad period (eighth century).

9. Kishk himself had been a victim of these 'rumours' (*sha'i'at*), as he explained in *al-Muslimun*, no. 23, p. 13: '. . . the last was that Jesus — peace be upon

'All sorts of sects have arisen in recent times: they claim to be linked to God, affiliated to His messenger, and meanwhile al-Azhar slumbers the deepest sleep, in unparalleled dishonour! . . . When the revolution occurred in Egypt — or rather the military coup [of 23 July 1952] — orders were given to liquidate Islam. The first step taken by the men of the revolution (*rijal al-thawra*) was to exterminate the magistrates of the *shari'a* courts [the Muslim religious courts], who ruled in accordance with God's orders![10]

'One way or another, they fabricated an indictment against two sheikhs, two holy men, Sayf and Fil, whom they accused of drinking wine and fornicating. . . . But later a medical examination of the two sheikhs established that they were impotent and were therefore as innocent as the wolf was of Jacob's blood, but Egypt excels in fabricating charges against the innocent! Then [in 1954] they built prisons and concentration camps and erected scaffolds, for all those who thought that there is no god but God! In 1961 a terrible blow was dealt al-Azhar in the name of a "reform" that was in fact its destruction! Tell me, Azharists, after you get your degree, what proportion of the Koran do you know by heart, how many suras can you recite? There are Azhar graduates today who cannot even read the Koran with the text in front of them! . . . Al-Azhar was hit so hard that the sheikh of al-Azhar was an expert in philosophy! Since when is the sheikh of al-Azhar supposed to specialize in philosophy? One sheikh had obtained a *dukturah* [doctorate] in Germany, the one before him in France.[11] Are the Muslims so sterile that they have to go to France for a *dukturah*? I do not know who the next sheikh will be! Maybe an army general will take over al-Azhar? Who knows? But in any event, ever since the reform, the leadership of al-Azhar has ceased to render any service to Islam! In 1965 they built

---

him! — appeared to me in a dream and told me that if I abandoned Islam — may God forbid! — and became a Christian, he would restore my sight!. . .' Eliahu ben Elissar, Israel's first ambassador to Egypt, arrived in Cairo in 1980.

10. The religious courts of other denominations were abolished as well, however.

11. The references are to 'Abd al-Halim Mahmud (d. 1978), who had obtained a doctorate in France, and 'Abd al-Rahman Bisar (d. 1982), who earned a state doctorate in West Germany.

gallows yet again for those who said: "There is no god but God."
After which they abolished personal status,[12] and then they
present the *shari'a* to the People's Assembly![13]

'Are you going to accept it or reject it, O People's Assembly?
God's *shari'a* is submitted to a handful of His worshippers that
they might approve or reject God! What sort of comedy is this?
And al-Azhar continues to slumber, while preachers are imprisoned. . . . We are now seeing the advent of all kinds of sects
that arrogate the divine religion to themselves. . . . "These
mosques belong to the waqfs", "these are Sunni", "those are
part of the *ansar al-sunna*",[14] "those of the *jama'at al-tabligh*",[15]
"those are *takfir wa'l-hijra*'s", "those are waqfist",[16] and indeed

12. Kishk is alluding to law 44/1979 on personal status (*al-ahwal al-shakhsiyya*),
promulgated at the insistence of Jihan Sadat, the president's wife. Previously,
the personal status of Muslims was regulated by the Sunna (the Tradition of the
Prophet) and permitted men, for example, to take one or more wives without
informing any of them of the others' existence. The new law required that the
man inform his wife, through a court order, that he wanted to take another wife.
If the first wife objected, she could immediately obtain a divorce and would
preserve the right to live in the husband's home until their children attained the
age of majority. This law, drafted by the office of the Ministry of Social Affairs
and a commission of Azharists, aroused the fury of the sheikhs, who held that it
contravened the *shari'a*. They pilloried their 'collaborationist' colleagues.

13. The application of the *shari'a* has long been one of the grand designs of the
People's Assembly, especially since 1977, when Dr Sufi Abu Talib, himself a
French-educated jurist, became the Assembly's president. The 1971 constitution
states that the *shari'a* is the principal source of legislation. But it was only in
December 1978 that the Assembly formed a commission — composed of the
sheikh of al-Azhar, the minister of waqfs, the mufti of the republic, and various
university professors and jurists expert in Muslim law — to review all laws
passed prior to 1971, abrogate those that contradict the *shari'a,* and supply the
relevant Koranic references for the others.

14. The *jama'iyyat ansar al-sunna al-muhammadiyya* is a Muslim charitable
association that teaches its members the Koran and gives them a social education
with a strong Wahhabi bent. Because of its orientation and the source of its
financing, it has been nicknamed 'the religious embassy of Saudi Arabia'.

15. The *jama'at al-tabligh* are of Pakistani origin; their spiritual leader is Abu'l-
Hasan al-Nadawi.

16. Here again, as in his list of courts, Kishk has slipped in an invented name:
there is no such thing as the *jama'at al-tawaqquf* (which I have translated as
'waqfist'). His target is the Ministry of Waqfs, symbol of the regime's version of
Islam and reduced by Kishk's epithet to the level of one sect among others. The
joke is followed by a pun on the root *w-q-f*, which means 'to bequeath property',
but also, originally, 'to stop', 'not to progress'. The association of ideas suggests
that the role of the Ministry of Waqfs is to prevent the spread of Islam. For a
Muslim, it is scandalous to hear someone say that a mosque 'belongs' to human
beings, since the Koran teaches that mosques are the property of God.

Islam has come to a halt (*waqafa*) in the midst of all these sects.
. . . Muslims, what has happened? . . . All this comes to us from
the American, Israeli, Soviet, or British embassy.

'. . . The new fashion among pubescent thinkers is to acquire
knowledge without professor or sheikh: they go directly to
books, but they understand nothing! . . . These days, a great
seventy-year-old Muslim preacher is liable to be interpellated by
a pubescent boy who has read three words or a few pages of Ibn
Taimiyya or Ibn 'Abd al-Wahhab and can pose as a guardian of
the faith! What a farce, O Azhar sheikh, and all you who slumber
and who have left Islam out to pasture with anyone who happens
by!

'[One of the *ulema* informed Kishk that at the end of a lecture
he was giving in Minya one day, someone had asked him: "Is
vinegar licit or forbidden in Islam?" He had also been asked the
same question in Abu Dhabi.] This question was asked by one of
the embassies! The Israeli, American, Russian, or British embassy, with the aim of sowing confusion in Islam! Who knows?
Maybe tomorrow a *fatwa* will be issued prohibiting lentils or
basara[17] because they distract one from the thought of God! Why
not? There is no god but God! Those who act in this way have
taken from Islam only its appearance while abandoning its
truths; they mix up ideas and divide the ranks of Muslims. And
what is Israel doing all this time? In the land of the Muslims it is
digging a canal that will link the Mediterranean and the Dead
Sea, and if that happens, the Gaza Strip and the West Bank[18] will
be cut off from Arab land! And how do the Muslims react?
"Wearing glasses is forbidden", "vinegar is forbidden", "so-
and-so is the *amir* of one sect and so-and-so of another", and all
are as lost sheep in the blackest of nights! . . .

'[After once again incriminating al-Azhar, Kishk cites the
examples of education as it was practised by the Prophet and of
old-fashioned piety: parents whose only child had died did not

17. *Basara* is a popular Egyptian dish made of beans and boiled lentils.
18. There were violent polemics in Egypt about Israel's irrigation problems and
the plans to dig canals to resolve them. In late 1980 the weekly magazine *al-Sha'b*
launched a furious campaign around the theme 'the water of the Nile is not for
sale', against plans to dig a canal across Sinai to carry water from the Nile to Israel.
On 10 March 1981 the same weekly virulently attacked the project to which Kishk
is referring here.

cease to pray on that account.] But today, if someone's kid comes second — second mind you! — in an examination, he says: "To hell with the mosque! No more prayers! What the hell for? The kid screwed up[19] . . ."′

However disconcerting it may seem on first reading, this sermon is an extraordinary texture of meanings that attract listeners and point them in the direction Kishk desires. Translation and transcription, given the cultural gap between the reader of these lines and the believer who stands listening to the sheikh, can convey no more than a pale reflection of his rhetorical art.

The preacher's problem is to take the meanings of a text that is held to be divine, and therefore shrouded in holiness, and get them across to listeners who, while they know the text in whole or in part (or at least have memories of it, having attended either one of the *kuttab* or compulsory courses in religion), usually hear it only as dogma. The audience is aware of the prescriptions of the Koran, limited to a few traditional taboos (abstention from wine and pork, and so on), but rarely finds in it the solution to all the problems of contemporary life.

The preacher's art is to repeat his exegesis of the Book relentlessly, and to discover within it the answers to all the questions troubling his audience. All Egyptian Islamicists insist that Islam is a total and complete system (*al-islam nizam kamil wa shamil*); their problem is to get this across to Muslims whose conduct is now motivated by considerations drawn from other systems of thought (whether the socialistic or liberal jargon of successive governments or more simply the hustles of day-to-day survival).

If he is to saturate his audience with the Book and its meanings, then the preacher must try to reach his listeners at their own level: he has to talk their language. Kishk is good at this, perhaps so good that he stoops to what his censors call demagogy. He has a strong bent towards frequent mention of the sexual organs. Islam, as it happens, lacks the modesty of Western Victorianism, for although *zina'* (fornication) is denounced so thunderously as to impose an apparent desexualization of

19. This colloquially translated passage was delivered in the Cairo dialect, unlike the rest of the sermon, which was in so-called classical Arabic.

society in public, licit sexuality (within the confines of marriage) is considered excellent, not only because it perpetuates the species, but also because it is a source of pleasure (for the man, in any event).

Whatever our assessment of Kishk's sermons, we must understand above all that their extraordinary success is a result of his ability to speak to his audience, to the hundreds of thousands of Muslim Arabs who listen to him again and again, playing his cassettes day after day, from Morocco to Iraq. He speaks their language and gives expression to their latent discourse. This is itself testimony to the failure of the 'modern' educational system supposedly borrowed from the liberal or socialist varieties of the Western system, the sort of system that Nasserism sought to institute on a mass scale. The tedious parroting of mimeographed manuals has not equipped the masses of 'educated people' to view the world in accordance with the categories that were supposed to have been transmitted by secular knowledge. They are therefore ripe for Sheikh Kishk's sermons.

Two kinds of rhetorical figures are especially revealing: medical metaphors and the transposition of the Koran into contemporary categories.

The medical metaphors are striking. The passage in the exordium about adrenalin is a typical instance. Kishk gives a medical description of the chemical changes in the blood brought about, according to him, by anger, and he then extends it to the apocalyptic vision of an 'explosion of the brain's arteries'. Several different meanings are interlaced here. The most explicit is the perfect concordance between faith and science: God forbids anger, which is especially ill-advised since medicine comes to exactly the same conclusion.

The selection of medicine rather than some other scientific or technical discipline is no accident, for Kishk could just as well have taken his metaphors from engineering, electronics, physics, or whatever. But in the popular mind, medicine is *the* science on the hit parade of faculties in Egypt, the subject the most brilliant students are supposed to graduate in, according to the selection process. By mining the medical textbooks for his figures of speech, Kishk places himself on the level of the Egyptian intellectual elite in the eyes of his audience. But the practice of medicine — the elite discipline that stirs in every Egyptian the dream that one day his own son will recite the Hippocratic oath — arouses another image too: the exorbitantly priced consultations and the practitioner's utter contempt for the patients, who are given incomprehensible prescriptions written in English (just as Molière's doctors used Latin, the better to overawe their patients) and who leave the consultations, for which they have waited long hours, without the slightest understanding of either the diseases from which they suffer or their causes. Kishk, on the other hand, describes the pathological process in terms that might well bring a smile to the lips of practitioners of the art but which reveal the mysteries of the 'chemical process' to the faithful just as the mysteries of the Koran are revealed. At the end of the digression about Christ, the 'medical' argument becomes the key to Kishk's proof: the mention of Mary's vaginal measurements suffices to annihilate Jesus's pretensions to divinity, in a manner quite similar to the message Abu Bakr's envoy addresses to Khosroes, recalling the latter's origin in terms not unlike Saint Augustine's *inter feces et urinam nascimur*.

By using these arguments, all of which claim an agreement between medicine, the supreme 'science' in Egypt, and faith, Kishk subordinates modern knowledge to Koranic knowledge. But this Islamicization of science, far from making science seem more remote from his listeners, brings it closer to them by demystifying it. What the doctor writes in English, Kishk explains (in his own way) in Arabic; and he is understood.

The sermon's second rhetorical procedure, another important element in the preacher's success, is his fragmentation of the Koranic passages into small units linked by comments or simplified arguments couched in contemporary terms. During the digression about Christ, for instance, Kishk breaks up verses 30 and 31 of Sura Mary, using familiar terms designed to encourage his audience to 'get into' the text. Where the Koran actually says: *Whereupon he spoke and said: 'I am the servant of God. He has given me the Gospel and ordained me a prophet'*, Kishk's sermon has: 'Then Christ took out his family registration booklet. Name: *I am the servant of God.'*

This procedure is used most effectively during the exegesis proper, when Iblis (the devil) is condemned in accordance with 'articles' 77, 78, and so on of Sura *Sad:* the articles, of course, are actually verses. These rhetorical flourishes establish the reign of the *shari'a* in the discourse itself, in opposition to human justice, which, as later passages of the sermon make clear, is nothing but a tissue of injustice, of 'trickery' and 'more-or-less' courts. The verse *God will judge men with fairness* (XL, 20) is introduced at the end of a grotesque list of Egyptian courts, as the motto emblazoned on the pediment of a tribunal. Here again, the discourse establishes the applicability of the Koran quite naturally, with no necessity for proof. Kishk's biting irony about the well-known dependence of the legislative and judicial branches on the executive, nowhere more strikingly evident than in the military or 'socialist' courts, delegitimates the current Egyptian legal system, which is inspired by French law. Here it is portrayed as no more than the juridical machinery of the despot: only the *shari'a*, directly inspired by God, is immune to manipulation by the prince and therefore guarantees, according to Kishk, that people 'will be judged with fairness'.

Kishk's themes are the familiar ones of the Islamicist movement, which have often been expounded by individuals who never followed the curriculum of traditional Azharist studies: al-Banna, Qutb, and still less the youth of the *jama'at islamiyya* or Shukri Mustafa. But his originality and impact within the Islamicist movement arise from his denial of the regime's Islamic legitimacy in his capacity as a sheikh, as a member of the corps of *ulema*. Himself an Azharist, he could never adopt the positions of a Shukri or a Faraj, the theoretician of the group that assassinated Sadat. In fact, they are targets of his lampoon, 'pubescent thinkers' the sum total of whose reading amounts to 'three pages of Ibn Taimiyya'. Nevertheless, they express, however maladroitly, the profound disarray for which the prime responsibility, in Kishk's view, lies with al-Azhar itself. This supreme institution of Islam has failed in its task, which is to educate the youth. This observation of failure recalls the remarks of the military prosecutor during Shukri Mustafa's trial. But where the officer saw the root of the evil in the *ulema*'s inability to understand the problems of the modern world, Kishk holds that it is al-Azhar's dependence on the political and military regime itself ('I do not know who the next sheikh will be! Maybe an army general will take over al-Azhar?') that prevents the religious institution from performing its function. To remedy the situation, Kishk proposed the following measures in an interview:

'1. The sheikh of al-Azhar must be designated by election.

'2. The salary of the Azhar sheikh must be raised from the *waqfs* of the Muslims.

'3. Al-Azhar must return to its pre-1961 status [before the Nasser reform], especially as concerns the curriculum.

'4. The "modern" faculties at al-Azhar must be eliminated so that all that remains are the two departments of *usul al-din* (origins of religion) and the Arabic language.'

Here the entire 'modernization' sought by the Nasserist state is challenged by someone who has the status required to speak in the name of Islam.

Nevertheless, while the 'star of Islamic preaching' offers a merciless analysis of the independent state, stigmatizing it in terms of great violence, he is less than eloquent when it comes to any plan of action to overthrow that state and to establish the Muslim society in its place. But it is toward just such a prospect that his sermons lead, even though he himself merely warns his audience against the vagaries of 'pubescent thinkers' without indicating his own recommended road. At the same time, his discourse in no way endorses the 'reformist' practice of the neo-Muslim Brethren grouped around Talmasani and *al-Da'wa*, as is evident in the biting irony with which Kishk notes, 'Here they are submitting God's *shari'a* to a handful of His worshippers, that they might approve or reject God!', just at the moment when *al-Da'wa* was heavily involved in bringing pressure to bear on the People's Assembly to apply the *shari'a*.

Kishk, like Qutb, stakes out a path without charting it through to its destination. In October 1981 other forces turned to tyrannicide in an attempt to bring down the state.

To Assassinate Pharaoh

On the sixth of October 1981 Anwar Sadat, resplendent in a ceremonial uniform, stood in the reviewing stand to watch a military parade marking the eighth anniversary of the launching of the October war against Israel. This commemoration was always celebrated with special pomp, for it was in October 1973, when the Egyptian army crossed the Suez Canal and broke through Israel's Bar-Lev Line in Sinai, that the president really cemented his authority. The crossing of the canal was for Sadat what its nationalization had been for Nasser: a prestigious achievement which, invoked *a posteriori*, afforded the regime its supreme legitimacy. In both cases, that legitimacy was in turn used to silence, or to try to silence, any criticism of the negligence and corruption of the bureaucracy, the monopolization of power by a clique, and the perpetuation of poverty and underdevelopment.

The members of the Islamicist group called al-Jihad (Sacred Combat) chose that symbolic date to act against the Egyptian state in the most spectacular way possible: by assassinating the president.

The personnel of the entire Egyptian political apparatus were assembled in the reviewing stand that day, in dress uniforms. They looked unreal, like cardboard cut-outs frozen in ceremonial poses, and no one in Egypt had the slightest doubt that the pomp of the celebration was in part designed to obfuscate the subsequent victorious counter-offensive of the Israeli army in 1973 and its rapid drive towards Cairo.

Suddenly, in full view of the television cameras, a military truck ground to a halt and discharged four men, who opened fire on the reviewing stand with automatic weapons. The masquerade became a massacre: the president's bodyguards scattered, and Sadat was killed in the midst of indescribable panic. Had the grenades hurled by one of the assailants hit their target, nearly everyone in the official stand that day would have died with the president.

When the moment of shock and stupefaction had passed, all Egypt came to know of Lieutenant Khalid al-Islambuli, the leader of the group of assassins, and the sentence he had shouted just after opening fire was repeated everywhere: 'I am Khalid al-Islambuli, I have killed Pharaoh, and I do not fear death.'

Among the wealthier classes, the videotape of the events, which fetched astronomical prices on the black market, was played and replayed. No assassin had ever been more fashionable, while the funeral of his victim, attended by the world's leaders, met with an openly sullen reaction from the Egyptian people. Khalid killed Sadat at the peak of the president's unpopularity, after a year marked by the Zawiyya al-Hamra troubles in June and September's sweeping repression against the religious and secular opposition, with more than fifteen hundred people arrested. In the eyes of Egyptian public opinion, Khalid therefore appeared as a sort of 'right arm' of the popular will, and not merely as a militant exponent of an Islamicist group.

It was a spectacular success for the movement, coming after two decades of abortive confrontations with the state and triumphant repression. But after 6 October and the brief alarm aroused by Islamicist sedition in the city of Asyut on 8 October, that success proved to be no more than spectacle. Sadat was replaced by his vice-president, and there was no structural modification of the state likely to satisfy the Islamicist movement. Repression against the movement intensified, and it was condemned to languish. To employ the terminology inspired by Sayyid Qutb, the movement entered a new 'phase of weakness'.

The group to which Islambuli belonged is somewhat more widely known than the other tendencies of the Islamicist movement that have been described so far. A pamphlet by the group's main thinker, an electrician named 'Abd al-Salam Faraj, is even available. Its title, *al-Farida al-Gha'iba* ('The Hidden Imperative'), is a reference to *jihad*, the holy combat which it is imperative to wage against the iniquitous prince but which the *ulema* have striven to obscure or hide. Moreover, an Egyptian daily newspaper published a detailed list of those accused of membership of the group. Finally, one of the lawyers sold the transcripts of the interrogations of the major defendants to a Lebanese newspaper.

The ideology and actions of the Jihad group mark a shift in the line followed by the Islamicist movement since the publication of *Signposts. The Hidden Imperative* presents the group's theory and practice in the form of a negative assessment of the various components of the movement. Jihad, Faraj explains, is seeking to overcome the record of failure.

In Faraj's view, all the varieties of transitional strategy conceived by Shukri Mustafa, the *jama'at islamiyya*, the neo-Muslim Brethren, and everyone else — each designed to avoid harsh state repression while simultaneously training militants — had ultimately failed. Despite all his precautions, Shukri Mustafa died on the gallows in 1978. On the other hand, the anti-Islamic nature of the state had not changed since the inauguration of the Islamicist movement, and that was in itself evidence of failure.

The reader of *The Hidden Imperative* is struck by the author's lack of concern for the process of resocialization undertaken by groups like the Society of Muslims or the *jama'at islamiyya*, and by his refusal to acknowledge the creeping re-Islamicization of Egyptian society during Sadat's presidency. Mosques were being constructed everywhere, the codification of the *shari'a* was under discussion in the People's Assembly, and veiled women and bearded young men had become common features of the Egyptian landscape — but as far as Faraj was concerned, all this was of no importance so long as power was held by rulers he characterized as apostates from Islam.

This ideologue therefore devoted his short book to the question of power and the state, ignoring any analysis of society. In examining what had been the weak point of Islamicist thought ever since the time of Hasan al-Banna — namely the strategy for the seizure of power — he ascribed absolute priority to *jihad* against the iniquitous prince, to holy combat in the form of an uprising against the regime and the assassination of the head of state. In this Faraj broke with the strategy of *Signposts* and its successive versions through the seventies.

The Modern Tartars

'Abd al-Salam Faraj's tract presents an action programme for the establishment of the Islamic state. It has an undeniable originality, although within the Jihad group, divided into one branch in Cairo and another in Middle Egypt, the leaders of the latter section seem not to have held the Cairene Faraj's text in high esteem. Karam Zuhdi, head of activists in the Minya and Asyut section, declared during his pre-trial hearing that *The Hidden Imperative* contained nothing really new and amounted to no more than a collection of quotations from various *ulema*.

The inattentive reader could well come away with such an impression of the pamphlet. Unlike a Shukri Mustafa, who rejected the Tradition as a whole, Faraj mined it for a point of anchorage for his own ideas. His central reference is a brief text by the great medieval thinker Ibn Taimiyya, Faraj's interpretation of which (or his distortion of it, according to his detractors) enabled him to argue that although the mass of the people are now Muslims, their rulers only invoke the name of God the better to govern in contravention of the principles revealed in the Koran. The model followed by today's iniquitous princes, Faraj wrote, is that of the Tartars — or Mongols — who conquered Muslim countries and then applied a non-Islamic system of law, *yasa*. And just as Ibn Taimiyya issued a *fatwa* — a juridical ruling based on the Book — that commanded *jihad* against the prince who governed according to the principles of the Mongols, so Faraj ordered a holy war against a regime that did not govern according to the *shari'a* alone but instead applied a legal system adulterated by Western legislation.

After the customary preliminary eulogies, Faraj's text begins this way:

'In spite of its gravity and its extreme importance for the future of Islam, the sacred combat in the path of God (*jihad*) has been neglected by contemporary *ulema*, who claim to know nothing about it, although actually they know very well that if the great-ness of this religion is to be re-established there is only one path to follow: each and every Muslim must adopt exclusively the ideas and system of thought that God has inspired in him, for His greatest power.

'Now, there is no doubt whatever that the false gods (*tawaghit*) of this earth will disappear only at sword-point. That is why the prophet said: *I was sent sword in hand, that they might worship only God — He has no associate.* . . . The Prophet proclaimed the con-struction of the Islamic state and the re-establishment of the caliphate. This was God's order, and it is the duty of every Muslim to spare no effort to execute that order. . . . Neverthe-less, certain Muslims claim to know nothing of this, although God's Book offers striking proof of it: *Govern them according to what God has revealed. . . . Those who do not govern according to what God has revealed are wrongdoers*[1] . . .

'Today a question must be asked: do we live in an Islamic state? This would be true only if the laws of Islam held sway. . . .

'In his collection of *fatwa* (fourth part, the book of *jihad*), the sheikh of Islam Ibn Taimiyya issued a *fatwa* in response to a question about the status of a city called Mardin.[2] That town had been ruled by the laws of Islam, but later fell into the hands of people who established an infidel government there. He was asked, "Is Mardin part of *Dar al-Islam* or is it part of the Domain of War?". This was his answer: "It is a composite that has elements of both; it is neither the land of peace — where the laws of Islam hold sway — nor the land of war — whose popula-tion are infidels — but lies in a third zone. The Muslims have

1. Koran, V, 48 and V, 44.
2. The city of Mardin, which lies in a well-fortified position at a crossroads of trade routes in Upper Mesopotamia, was conquered by the Muslims in the year 640. In 1261 the Mongol Hülegü Khan demanded the obeissance of the prince of Mardin, Najim al-Din Ghazi Sa'id, who sent Hülegü his son Muzaffar as a hostage but nevertheless maintained a neutral stance. The following year the city was besieged, and Muzaffar killed his own father in order to put an end to the sufferings of the populace. He was then crowned by the Mongols, who be-queathed the crown and the parasol, symbols of royalty, to his descendants. Muzaffar, then, was a sovereign who was Muslim by descent, but whose throne was guaranteed by the infidels whose hostage he was, so much so that the emblems of power (crown and parasol) had meaning in Mongol symbolism but not in Islam.

relations with those of its inhabitants who are worthy of it and
they combat, as they deserve, those who place themselves outside the *shari'a*." . . .

'Peace, then, for he who is worthy of it, and war on he who
merits war. The state is governed by infidel laws, even though
the majority of its population is Muslim.

'The laws that rule the Muslims today have been infidel laws
. . . since the definitive disappearance of the caliphate in 1924,
the eradication of all the laws of Islam and their replacement by
laws imposed by the infidels. . . . What was true during the time
of the Tartars is true today as well, as is established in Ibn
Kathir's commentary[3] on divine verse 50 in the Sura 'The Table':
*Do they then seek to be governed by ignorance? Who then better than
God can govern a people that believes?* Ibn Kathir writes: "God
rejects all that lies outside His law; He is the Universal Arbiter of
all good, and He who prohibits all evil. He has done away with
all private opinions, with whim, with arbitrariness, with all that
is characteristic of men who base themselves not on the *shari'a*
but, like the people of *jahiliyya*, govern according to their pleasure, in ignorance, or rather, in the manner of the Tartars,
according to the 'policy of the prince' (*al-siyasa al-malikiyya*).
This expression refers to their prince, Genghis Khan, for he gave
them the *yasa*,[4] which is a code assembling laws borrowed from
the Jews, Christians, Muslims, and others, apart from many
other laws issued directly of his own concepts and his own
whim.

' "It is impiety to allege that such a system of law is the basis of
a government founded on the Koran and the Sunna of the
Prophet; it is imperative to combat the infidel until he is brought

3. Ibn Kathir (1300–1373) was a Muslim Traditionist strongly influenced by Ibn
Taimiyya.
4. The *yasa* (also called *yasaq* or *jasaq*) was Genghis Khan's codification of
Mongol traditional law and popular laws and customs. Its promoter held that it
would be a collection of eternal and immutable precepts that could inspire both
his contemporaries and his successors. Very little is known of the *yasa*, except for
some fragments reported by rather unreliable Muslim authors. Maqrizi (1364–
1441) devoted a few famous passages to it, in the course of which he coined the
Arabic word that now means 'politics' (*siyasa*); its etymology is actually derived
from *yasa*. See my article 'L'Egypte d'aujourd'hui: mouvement islamiste et Tradition savante', in *Annales* ESC, no. 4, 1984.

to govern in accordance with the injunctions of God and His Prophet, from which one must not depart even in the slightest" (Ibn Kathir, Second Part, p. 67). . . .

'Today's rulers are apostates from Islam, nourished at the table of colonialism, be it Crusader, Communist, or Zionist. All they have preserved of Islam is its name.'

Holy War Against the Infidels

It would be tedious to wade through the many quotations from Ibn Taimiyya presented by Faraj. They form the clearest section of the first part of the text, and the pamphlet's author does no more than slip in occasional transitional paragraphs meant to bring them up to date so as to apply them to contemporary Egypt.

Nearly all Egyptian observers rejected the legitimacy of Faraj's use of the authority of the great Traditionist. Their argument was that Faraj, whom Sheikh Kishk would call a 'pubescent thinker', understood nothing of the texts he quoted and that in any event these texts lack any validity in describing society or the state in contemporary Egypt.

Why did Faraj decide to base his argument on Ibn Taimiyya's Tradition? And why did he choose a text that is not only not one of the author's most famous works, but is no more than a collection of *fatwas* dealing with conjunctural questions?

Ibn Taimiyya (1263–1328) was born to a family of jurists and was brought up at the height of the Mamluk era, in a cultural milieu in which non-resistance to injustice was the rule and in which 'the canonical act *par excellence* was originally the *jihad,* which demanded the greatest energy from each and the greatest cohesion of all. It became an act of social contrition and of individual retreat through prayer, fasting, and withdrawal' [23]. Political circles — dominated by the emirs, partially Arabized Turkish ex-slaves whose training was purely military — sought Islamic legitimation from the *ulema,* whose 'docile spirit made them strictly dependent on the class of emirs; they never took part in the various popular revolts, which always remained social movements devoid of cohesion and ideology' [23].

Although 'the authority of the *ulema* was essential in ensuring the domination of a foreign oligarchy's military dictatorship over deeply Islamicized masses' [23], 'the juridical doctrine of the Mamluk state was not the *shari'a*', and 'legal secularization . . . was further accelerated by the unworthiness of certain sovereigns, by the purely personal circumstances in which sultans were inclined to act under the competing solicitations of individual caprice and outside pressures, and perhaps even more by the venality and corruption of an administrative staff that seems to have been more intent on using the law than on serving it' [23].

Such was the world of Ibn Taimiyya. There seems little doubt that but for the foreign character of the military class, this description of Mamluk Egypt invites comparison with contemporary Egyptian society as seen by the Islamicist movement.

Faced with a society whose pathology he acutely perceived, one in which injustice, now a supreme principle, offended his Muslim conscience, Ibn Taimiyya devoted both his work and his life to a struggle to replace 'the regime of social exploitation founded on the rule of a military minority . . . with an ideal of communal cooperation for the greater glory of Islam' [23].

This struggle is the *jihad* for which Ibn Taimiyya's entire doctrine was, in the words of Henri Laoust, a long and continuous plea.

One chapter of Ibn Taimiyya's master work, *al-Siyasa al-Shar'iyya* [24], is devoted to *jihad*, 'the best of the forms of voluntary service man can devote to God. The *ulema* agree in proclaiming it superior to pilgrimage and to the *'umra*, as well as to prayer and supererogatory fasts, as is shown in the Book and in the Sunna.'

One's true quality as a Muslim is manifested neither in maceration nor in withdrawal into individual piety, but in *jihad*: 'There are people', Ibn Taimiyya writes, 'who insist on striving to accomplish the most taxing acts for their religion, acts prejudicial to their material prosperity, despite the minimal advantage they can draw from them, whereas *jihad* is far more profitable and useful than any other arduous action' [24]. Although the Damascene rebel aimed these words primarily at those who had taken refuge in mysticism, it is understandable that a man like

Faraj, reading this text, would apply them to those of his coreligionists who, in his view, had been wasting their time seeking to practise an Islam that was not entirely devoted to *jihad*. In fact, as we shall soon see, this was the major criticism the author of *The Hidden Imperative* made of the other Muslim and Islamicist groupings.

Ibn Taimiyya legitimated what has been called '*jihad* within the community', stating: 'It is established by the Koran, the Sunna, and the *ijma'* that one must combat whosoever departs from the law of Islam, even if he pronounces the two professions of faith' [24]. But *al-Siyasa al-Shar'iyya* does not make it clear whether this injunction is directed primarily to the prince or to the rebel. Faraj therefore had to resort to a lesser-known text, one that clearly identifies the infidel sovereigns of Mardin and the Tartars as targets of *jihad*. He then identifies these historical figures with today's rulers.

Such are some of the elements of the work and struggle of Ibn Taimiyya that the Islamicist militants of the Jihad group were able to use to establish the justice of their action in Muslim Tradition. Whether or not they distorted the texts is a question disputed by the various protagonists of the contemporary Egyptian scene, each of which claims a monopoly on the canonical or 'progressive' interpretation of the great Traditionist. For our purposes what is important is only that Faraj felt it necessary to resort to Ibn Taimiyya's authority to legitimate his own *jihad*, the assassination of Sadat.

Carrying Out God's Orders

If Faraj considered *jihad* part of a hidden Muslim tradition whose restoration was his task, he also held that it was the only effective way to fight for the establishment of an Islamic state, since all the other possibilities, no matter how 'prejudicial to the material prosperity' of their practitioners, had ended in failure.

In his effort to marshal the evidence of this failure, Faraj drew up a sort of catalogue of the various tendencies of the Islamicist movement as representatives of Muslim forms of resocialization in contemporary Egypt. First he criticizes the *jama'at khayriyya*,

Muslim charitable associations which some Egyptian Muslims founded in order to organize their daily lives cooperatively. These associations function under close surveillance by the Ministry of Social Affairs, but their initiatives (local services, readings and commentaries of the Koran, and so on) are organized by their own members and not by the administrative authorities [6]. During Sadat's presidency, some of them became breeding-grounds from which radical Islamicist groups recruited members. Faraj held that these charitable associations made no contribution whatever to the fight for Islam:

'Some say that by creating associations under state control they can encourage people to say their prayers, give alms, and undertake works of charity . . . of course, that is one of God's orders, which we must not neglect, but one may well wonder whether these acts of charity and this devotion will establish the Islamic state. The immediate answer, without the slightest hesitation, must be negative. Not to mention the fact that these associations are subject to state control, registered and directed by it.'

After also criticizing those who seek the Way through self-improvement, *The Hidden Imperative* continues:

'There are people who say that we must create an Islamic party in the image of the existing political parties. . . . But this would only achieve the opposite of its objective, namely the destruction of the infidel state, for it would lend comfort to the state by participating in political life, by sitting in the legislative assemblies that legislate without God. Others say that the Muslims must seek to gain control of posts of responsibility and fill the decision-making centres with "Muslim doctors", "Muslim engineers", and so on, so that the infidel regime will collapse automatically and effortlessly and will give way to a Muslim sovereign. . . . One need only hear this argument once to realize that it is pure fantasy. . . .

'Still others say that the Islamic state will be built through *da'wa* [preaching] alone, and on the basis of very broad [recruitment] . . . . For some, this serves as a diversion from *jihad*, although in truth it is a small faithful minority that will build the Islamic state. . . . In any event, how can *da'wa* score any great success when all the media are controlled by the infidel regime, which makes war on the religion of God? . . .

'Some say that to establish the Muslim state one must practise *hijra* to some other country, construct the state there, and then return as conquerors; to economize on their efforts, let them begin by building the Islamic state in their own country, and then leave it as conquerors. . . .

'Now, those who say that they will perform their *hijra* in the mountains, and then come down and match strength with Pharaoh as Moses did, wind up fearing Pharaoh and his earthly soldiers. . . .This is only an evasion that forsakes the sole authentic and legitimate means of building the Muslim state. . . .

'Finally, there are those who say that what must be done now is to apply ourselves to study, for how can we wage the sacred struggle if we are not educated? . . . Now, to wage the sacred struggle, it is enough to be aware of the imperative of *jihad*, and let he who is ignorant of its rules . . . be aware that they may be learned easily and in very little time! . . . To delay the *jihad* on the pretext of lack of education is sorry reasoning. . . . Since the dawn of Islam, there have been combatants of *jihad* . . . who were not scholars.'

Reading these lines, we recognize the now-familiar features of the various tendencies of the Egyptian Islamicist movement. Faraj reminds the neo-Muslim Brethren, who in 1976 and 1977 loudly demanded the creation of an Islamic party, that one cannot participate with impunity in a system controlled and manipulated by infidels. To those, like Kishk, who rely on *da'wa* alone, Faraj retorts that the regime will always be able to drown out the voice of the preacher whenever it deems the moment opportune. To the *jama'at islamiyya*, who were unable to move beyond the campuses and some of whose members dreamt of infiltrating the state apparatus in an effort to undermine it from within, he replies that knowledge must not enfeeble determination and that participation in the state strengthens the state. Finally, Faraj tells those who followed Shukri Mustafa in his *hijra* that this was merely a pretext for avoiding unyielding commitment to *jihad*.

It must be acknowledged that in drawing up this sweeping catalogue of failure, Faraj perceived with remarkable acuity the common factor in his predecessors' lack of success: their inability to pose the problem of the seizure of power.

Not that the significance of *jihad* was underestimated by people like al-Banna, Mawdudi, and Qutb, whose most important texts dealing with the sacred struggle in the Path of God were widely distributed in pamphlet form by Islamicist students in the late seventies. But until Faraj, the Egyptian Islamicist movement was still afflicted with the trauma of repression: the memory of the massacres of 1954 and 1965 was still bright. The dialectic of the phase of weakness and the phase of power (*marhalat al-istid'af, marhalat al-tamakkun*), however, was now alien to the Jihad group. Since ultimately it all led to the gallows and the concentration camps, what was needed was the most rapid possible attack on the infidel state, the seizure of power above all else.

Faraj's decision was irrevocable. He preached *jihad* as immediate armed struggle against the iniquitous prince. This, he said, was the duty of all Muslims, and the first target had to be the enemy at home, the attack on external enemies coming later:

'In the Islamic countries, the enemy is at home; indeed, it is he who is in command. He is represented by those governments that have seized power over the Muslims, and that is why *jihad* is an imperative for every individual (*fard 'ayn*).'

This assertion shows just how concerned Faraj was to situate his action within the framework of Muslim Tradition. The imperative of *jihad* can be of two types. When it consists in a war of expansion out of the territory of Islam, it 'constitutes a duty of collective obligation (*fard kifaya*): some Muslims assure its execution, while the others are excused from it'. On the other hand, 'when the Muslims are attacked, the war becomes a defensive conflict; it then constitutes a duty of individual obligation (*fard 'ayn*) for all the faithful, even those who have not been personally attacked' [24]. Here the enemy is within the land of Islam itself. The ruling despot must be fought just as Crusaders who invade the country are fought: through a mobilization that is not merely general, but universal. That is the difference between the fight against the enemy at home and the enemy abroad:

'There are people who say that the goal of *jihad* today is the liberation of Jerusalem, the holy land. Of course, this is a legal obligation and a duty for all Muslims . . . but:

'First: the fight against the enemy at home takes priority over the fight against the enemy abroad.

'Second: since the blood of the Muslims flows until victory, one may well ask who benefited from this victory. Was it the Islamic state, or the infidel regime, whose foundations were only consolidated by this victory? . . . The entire fight must be waged exclusively under Muslim command.[5]

'Third, the responsibility for the existence of colonialism or imperialism (*isti'mar*) in our Muslim countries lies with these infidel governments. To launch a struggle against imperialism is therefore useless and inglorious, a waste of time; we must concentrate on our Islamic problem, namely the establishment of God's law in our own countries.'

These lines are reminiscent of Shukri Mustafa's answer to the judge's question about the attitude his group would have taken had 'Jewish forces' invaded Egypt: 'We would flee to a secure place as rapidly as possible.' Apart from the radical difference between the tactic of *'uzla* (or withdrawal) preached by Shukri Mustafa and the *jihad* urged by Faraj, there had also been an evolution in the character of discourse about Israel, November 1977 marking the watershed. Before that date, it was the state that sounded the belligerent tone, whereas subsequently the various opposition groupings took up the call, the left in the name of a fight against 'the beach-head of imperialism in the Middle East', the neo-Muslim Brethren and a part of the Islamicist movement in the name of the 'liberation of the holy places of Islam'. Faraj was addressing the opposition, whereas Shukri Mustafa had been talking to the state.

The author of *The Hidden Imperative* harbours no illusion in the state, which is itself in sharp contrast to the politically naive

5. Here Faraj is criticizing those Islamicists who hailed the fact that the 'victorious' war of October 1973 was waged in the name of the Koran.

attitude of the Society of Muslims. He also heaps scorn on those who blame imperialism for all Egypt's problems. He holds that anything other than immediate combat against the despot is at best mere verbiage and at worst actually helps to consolidate the regime by diverting into futile rhetoric or towards evanescent objectives energy that could be more judiciously expended. In fact, even if the enterprise of *jihad* fails, it must be attempted none the less:

'To carry out God's order is to build the Islamic state. We do not insist on this or that result; . . . the mere fall of the infidel regime will bring everything within the reach of the Muslims!'

Finally, it ought to be noted that the organization the Egyptian press called 'the Jihad group' actually lacked the degree of cohesion that might have been expected of a group that managed to assassinate the head of state. Not only were there two distinct branches — one in Cairo and one in Sa'id (Middle Egypt) — which in the best of cases merely collaborated without either dominating the other, but even the assassination itself was decided only about ten days before it was carried out. The prime mover in this was Khalid al-Islambuli, who had it approved by the organization's 'consultative council' (*majlis al-shura*), which was actually confronted with a *fait accompli*.

Killing Christians

Just as Faraj's pamphlet was the product of critical reflection about the Islamicist movement, so the militants of the Jihad group were by no means babes-in-the-woods. Reference has already been made to the phenomenon of defections from one *jama'a* to another, in particular in connection with Shukri Mustafa's threats to punish as apostates those who left his group. The Islamicist movement, which Faraj called 'the field of those who work for Islam', is best seen as a sort of nebula of small groups whose ideology hovers between that of a Shukri or a Faraj at the one pole and that of a Talmasani at the other. The moment any star burns especially brightly within that nebula, it attracts a halo of wandering militants of the Islamicist movement.

After Sadat's trip to Jerusalem, the *jama'at islamiyya* stepped up their verbal assault on the regime, but no real action was proposed to the troops: *jama'at* violence took the form of physical action against morals offences by couples, musical recitals, film shows, and so on. These acts turned the campuses into *terra islamica*, but there was nevertheless a chasm between word and deed of which those who later became Jihad militants were well aware.

That the Jihad group arose out of splits from the *jama'at islamiyya* is particularly evident in Middle Egypt. The *amir* of the *jama'at* in Asyut, Najih Ibrahim 'Abdallah Sayyid — a man known throughout the Nile Valley simply as Najih, a gifted speaker of great eloquence, which he demonstrated especially in the sermons he delivered in the university stadium during the two holidays[6] — became one of the leaders of Jihad, the fourth on the list of defendants. The leader of the Sa'id branch, Karam Zuhdi, who lived in Minya, was put in touch with Faraj by an Islamicist student he encountered regularly at *jama'at* meetings. Finally, Lieutenant Khalid al-Islambuli's brother, Muhammad al-Islambuli, was the leader of the *jama'at* at the department of commerce at Asyut University. In fact, much as Lenin was prodded into action after the execution of his brother by the Tsarist state, Khalid decided to kill Sadat when he learned of the conditions under which his brother had been arrested, for Muhammad was one of the 1,536 people imprisoned at the beginning of September 1981 after the incidents of 'confessional sedition'.

Khalid's mother later said in an interview with a weekly magazine: 'When he heard the news, Khalid burst out crying and said to me, ''Why have they arrested my brother, who committed no crime?'' He cried so much that he had convulsions. When he finally calmed down, he said to me, ''Be patient, mother, it is the will of God . . . every tyrant has his end.'' '

It was the thirst for more radical action on the part of *jama'at islamiyya* militants disillusioned by the *jama'at*'s hesitancy and lack of national strategy that encouraged some of them to join together in the Jihad group, which offered the prospect of rapid

6. See chapter 5.

and violent action. This phenomenon is especially perceptible in Middle Egypt, where 64 per cent of Jihad's membership were students (while only 36 per cent had off-campus jobs). In Cairo, on the other hand, students were a minority within the group. This was probably due to the influence of Faraj, who did his recruiting mainly among the youth who attended Cairo's 'militant' mosques and in the Bulaq al-Dakrur district on the western outskirts of the capital.

In this belt of substandard housing, where thousands of rural migrants live packed together and less than 30 per cent of dwellings have running water or toilets, Faraj used to deliver the Friday sermon in a private (*ahli*) mosque that had been built by his in-laws. During discussions with his listeners, he spoke of the necessity of waging an armed *jihad* to establish the Muslim state, and after exchanges of visits, he managed to convince many of them. They in turn introduced him to friends and relatives of theirs, additional potential recruits. The Cairo organization was composed of five or six groups (*majmu'at*), each of which had its own *amir*. The *amirs* met weekly to work out general strategy. Each *amir* seems to have retained some degree of autonomy, and Faraj, whether through lack of will or lack of ability, appears not to have exercised over the members, and still less over the *amirs*, the sort of absolute power that Shukri Mustafa commanded within the Society of Muslims.

Faraj and Karam Zuhdi, who was then the head of a group of Islamicist activists in Middle Egypt, first met in 1980. According to the author of *The Hidden Imperative*, it was Faraj who convinced Karam Zuhdi that an armed *jihad* against the iniquitous prince — which in the circumstances meant the assassination of Sadat — was the necessary and sufficient condition for the establishment of an Islamic state. According to Zuhdi, who did not hold Faraj in the highest esteem, he learned nothing from this meeting that he did not already know. In his view, *jihad* was an imperative upheld by all consistent preachers, but he also felt that it had to be waged first of all against the Copts, and only later against the president, whom he considered their hostage.

Despite the apparent lack of sympathy between the leaders in Cairo and Middle Egypt, regular meetings were held, alternately on their respective turf. In June 1980 they decided to coordinate their activities, each retaining freedom of action within his own region. To seal their agreement, they asked Sheikh 'Umar 'Abd al-Rahman, a blind professor at the Azhar faculty in Asyut, to become their mufti.

The sheikh had had links with Karam Zuhdi since 1974, when the latter was a member of the *jama'at islamiyya*, which regularly invited the sheikh to hold meetings in Minya and Asyut. Deeply attached to the *sunans*, the blind professor forbad his female students to ask him any questions, insisting that their male classmates read out their questions for them. Although his blindness protected him from the crime of *zina'* (fornication) of the eye, he did not want to risk committing fornication by the ear, by hearing the voice of a woman who did not belong to him.

In the spring of 1981 the sheikh agreed to act as mufti for the group. While Faraj and Zuhdi represented the executive, or caliphal power, their 'mufti' issued *fatwas* legitimating all their actions. He was their Azhar. When they heard the *fatwas*, the young militants were assured of their entry to paradise when they joined the armed *jihad* or when they killed Coptic gold-smiths during the robberies committed to finance the organization.

But the militants of Middle Egypt and Cairo did not view the Christians in the same way. The Cairo group held that the prime objective of *jihad* was the destruction of the infidel state. The problem of the Christians would be dealt with somehow in the process, and no further details about their fate in the future 'Islamic state' were given. Zuhdi and his friends, on the other hand, considered Christian proselytism the major obstacle to the propagation of Islam.

'The way I see it', Zuhdi later told the examining magistrate, 'the Christians are concentrated in Minya and Asyut and they take advantage of their numbers to hold demonstrations of strength and superiority. They have arms, and this is what encourages the Muslim youth to react forcibly against mission-ary proselytism in order to put an end to the Crusaders' manifes-tations of superiority. . . . These operations consist in the distri-bution of Nazarean pamphlets, proclamations, and cassettes that attack Islamic dogma and incite the youth to take refuge in the Church; in provocatively setting up *naqus*[7] where they do not belong; in ringing bells during the call of the muezzin; in organizing parades of scouts and Christian associations to demonstrate their strength; and even in distributing copies of the New Testament in the buses and coffee houses, as they do in Minya. That is how Crusader proselytism manifests itself. . . . The Christians have a lot of money . . . and they use it to buy arms, which they stockpile, as far as we know, in their houses and in churches, waiting for the day they will take them out, as in Lebanon, so they can turn Egypt into a Coptic country whose capital would be Asyut, as the late President Sadat recalled.'

Question. 'Do your previous answers mean that the mode of propagation of Islam has been transformed from peaceful *da'wa* [preaching] to *jihad?*'

Answer. 'By the nature of things, and in the wake of these repeated events, *da'wa* has had to include everything. We have called upon the youth to prepare to wage the sacred struggle (*jihad*), up to and including taking care not to yield to the obvious plot hatched by the Nazareans without the Muslim youth being ready for it.'

The desire to get at the Christians became especially vehement after the 'inter-confessional incidents' in al-Zawiyya al-Hamra in the summer of 1981. Sheikh 'Umar 'Abd al-Rahman responded to this desire with a well-timed *fatwa*:

'At the time of the events of al-Zawiyya al-Hamra', Karam Zuhdi said, 'he issued a *fatwa* on the Nazareans of Egypt, who had taken up arms, fired on the Muslims, and taken control of a mosque. He declared that if a Christian aids the Church financially with the aim of causing injury to the Muslims and takes up arms against them, then it is licit to deprive him of his life and property. If he only takes up arms, then it is licit to take only his life, and if he only aids the Church financially, it is enough to take his property. . . . The consultative council [of the organization's Middle Egypt branch] then met in Asyut and decided to launch a vendetta against the Christians. 'Ali al-Sharif proposed that this take place in Naj' Hammadi, a city in which there are

7. Wooden bars struck to call Christians to assembly.

fanatical Christian goldsmiths who have taken up arms against the Muslims and have given considerable financial aid to the Church, money with which they buy arms. We could go and attack them, kill them, and take booty (*ghanima*) with which to buy arms for the organization. . . . We killed six Christians and came away with booty consisting of about five kilos of gold and 3,000 Egyptian pounds.'[8]

The extreme violence of these words stunned the officers who had been interrogating Zuhdi. They asked him whether he was aware that the Koran declared that the Christians (and the Jews) were 'people of the Book' who in this capacity could enjoy the status of *dhimmis,* or tributaries, in the land of Islam. Zuhdi replied to this question with a highly original exegesis of the Koran:

'In law the Christians and Jews are called "those people of the Book who are infidels" (*al-ladhin kafaru min ahl al-kitab*). And God said: *Those who say that God is Jesus, son of Mary, are infidels,* and also: *Combat those of the people of the Book and the associationists who are infidels.* Which means, according to the commentaries, the Jews and the Christians. What is meant by the expression "those of the people of the Book who are infidels" is the people of the Book, since they have not believed in this Book.'

For Zuhdi the activist of Middle Egypt, the Christians are infidels, and therefore proper targets of *jihad,* of the sacred combat in the Path of God, even before the despot. For the Cairo branch of the organization, on the other hand, the struggle against Sadat took priority. This difference between the two regional branches was the product of a number of factors, not the least of which was the heterogeneity of recruitment. The militants of Middle Egypt, former members of the *jama'at,* like the Islamicist students of Minya who wrote the leaflet distributed in April 1980,[9] were closely linked to the social milieu of the rural hinterland and shared traditional reflexes like the vendetta. The Copts, whose numerical weight in Middle Egypt exceeds the Islamicist 'threshold of tolerance', were far more urgent targets of the violence of the militants than the despot, who seemed far

8. The Cairo group was likewise financed by robbing a Christian goldsmith during Ramadan at the time of the end of the fast, although no one was killed.

9. See chapter 5.

away and inaccessible. Zuhdi and his comrades had formed a group with deep roots in the regional Muslim clans; if their traditional ties inclined them to adulterate the category of sacred combat as Faraj had defined it, these same ties enabled them to take advantage of the hidden bonds of solidarity that proved so valuable on 8 October 1981, when the group seized control of Asyut. Conversely, the federated Cairo groups were determined to act against the despot in the first place, and attached no great importance to the Copts. But they enjoyed no networks of complicity or sustenance, and their isolated act — the assassination of Sadat — was not followed by the uprising of the Muslim population of Cairo so ardently sought by Faraj and his friends.

To Assassinate Pharaoh

It was Khalid al-Islambuli who made the decision to assassinate Sadat. Twenty-four years old at the time of the assassination, he was born to a family of notables in Mallawi, not far from Minya, in Middle Egypt. His father had been trained as a lawyer and held the post of legal adviser at the large nationalized sugar refinery in Naj' Hammadi. Khalid did well in secondary school, and although his baccalaureate marks entitled him to enter the school of medicine, he chose instead to attend the Military Academy in an effort to fulfil his childhood dream: to become a pilot. He was refused that position, however, and was assigned instead to the artillery corps, with the rank of lieutenant. A bachelor, he lived in the barracks; like many students, he would go home to his family every Friday to get his laundry done.

On 3 September 1981 he arrived at his parents' home for a family get-together. It was then that he learned that his brother Muhammad, leader of the *jama'at* at the Asyut faculty of commerce, had been arrested the previous evening in the round-up of more than fifteen hundred oppositionists ordered by Sadat. Muhammad had been dragged out of bed in his pyjamas and 'taken away'. When Khalid heard the story, he was seized with a burning feeling of revolt. He told his mother that he would seek vengeance, and that 'every tyrant has his end'.

Nine days before the 6 October military parade, Khalid, who

was a member of Faraj's group, explained his plan to his leader: he would kill Sadat during the parade. Khalid had been placed in command of an armoured transport vehicle and had managed to replace the three soliders assigned to ride with him by three accomplices. When the vehicle passed the official reviewing stand, Khalid explained to Faraj, he would stop it with the hand-brake (the driver was not among the conspirators) and the four men would spill out, hurl their hand-grenades, and then open fire on the president's position with machine guns. All they had to do was to find the grenades and ammunition.

According to statements made by Khalid during his trial, the assassination of Sadat was the logical consequence of Faraj's and his reasoning about the Tartars. Insofar as any of this is certain, it appears that the theoretical framework for the assassination had been established by the sort of thinking exhibited in Faraj's pamphlet, that it was triggered by Khalid's desire for revenge after the arrest of his brother, and that the opportunity was furnished by this young lieutenant's participation in a parade at which the head of state would be present.

Faraj took charge of finding the grenades and ammunition. In the end, they were purchased from rings of arms smugglers by intermediaries who were ex-militants of the Islamicist movement (and paid for with money raised by selling the booty that had been taken from the Copts), all of which demonstrates the links the dissidents had managed to forge with the traditional underworld.

On 26 September a meeting was held in Saft al-Laban, a poverty-stricken district in Cairo's suburbs. The participants included the *amirs* of the Cairo groups and the leaders from Middle Egypt, who had been specially summoned for the occasion. After the plan was presented, a heated argument broke out between Karam Zuhdi and 'Abbud al-Zumur about whether or not the organization was capable of moving directly from the assassination of Sadat to the 'popular revolution' (*thawra sha'biyya*) that was supposed to bring about the Islamic state. While Zuhdi declared that he could take control of Asyut, 'Abbud had the greatest doubts about the ability of the Cairo branch to paralyse the nerve centres of the capital. 'Abbud was a 35-year-old air force officer trained in problems of military security. In the transcript of the interrogations, he comes across as a strong personality, more mature than his co-defendants. Where Faraj endlessly expounds the works of Ibn Taimiyya, Zuhdi delights in violence, and Islambuli seems impetuously to have decided to engage in an act of great physical courage with scant thought to the consequences, 'Abbud, by contrast, evinces a methodical mind capable of coldly evaluating a plan in terms of its risks and results. His military training and command experience were undoubtedly important factors in this, and he was apparently well aware of his superiority in this domain. During the pre-trial hearing he stated that he had been in charge of the 'execution' of the group's operations. In all probability, he did not relish seeing his territory invaded by Lieutenant Khalid al-Islambuli, eleven years his junior.

'Abbud, in fact, seems much like a Free Officer thirty years on, though with an ardent religious consciousness that had no equivalent among the putschists of 1952. Issued of a family of rural notables, declassed from them, and assuming a modern 'trade', he took up arms against the state in the name of the values of Islam. The danger of the presence of a military-security officer among the leaders of an Islamicist plot was not lost on the examining magistrate, who was quite curious to know how many army officers and police officials belonged to the organization. Although he was an officer, 'Abbud had not forgotten that the infidel rulers against whom he and his friends had revolted had originally come out of the army, and he therefore satisfied the magistrate's curiosity:

Q. 'Which officers of the armed forces and police are members of your organization?'

A. 'A very small number of reservists. We did not seek to recruit army officers, but it did happen sometimes. We would meet someone at the mosque and then find out by chance that the person we were talking to was an officer.'

Q. 'Why didn't you try to gain recruits in the armed forces?'

A. 'Our plan was based on popular revolution, and the preparation of the rank-and-file towards that aim. . . . I think that popular revolution will solve the problem of the armed forces and the police, because it is impossible for them to turn their guns on the people.'

Q. 'Continue and explain . . .'

A. 'The Iranian experience shows that in the event of popular revolution, it is very difficult for the armed forces and the police to combat the popular masses (*al-jamahir al-sha'biyya*) who want the application of God's *shari'a*. So there will be splits in the armed forces, sections of which will come over to the popular revolution arms in hand, without any need to prepare them for this; that way, the revolution will gain strength.'

'Abbud's insistence on establishing a link between the assassination of the prince and the preparations for 'popular revolution' inclined him to oppose Khalid al-Islambuli's plan at first. He argued that it would be at least two years before the organization would be capable not merely of killing the president but also of using the assassination as a springboard for the process of building the Muslim state. But 'Abbud was ignored, and on the night of 26 September the Cairo group decided to set plans for the assassination in motion, while Karam Zuhdi and his followers returned to Middle Egypt to get ready for the seizure of Asyut.

'Abbud's predictions of the Cairo branch's lack of preparation were confirmed sooner than expected. When he left the meeting, he found that he could not go home, for he realized that the police had set a trap for him there. Faraj and his friends were thus under close surveillance just ten days before the assassination, and they found it more than difficult to prepare 'to take over the vital nerve centres'. Only Khalid al-Islambuli seems not to have been the target of any surveillance, and he began setting his plan in motion. He issued leaves for the three soldiers who had been assigned to share his vehicle on the day of the parade, and on the night of 5 October he had his three confederates slip into the barracks. Khalid was carrying the grenades and ammunition in his duffel bag, and officers are not searched. The four men took their places in the vehicle, and when it passed the reviewing stand they surged out and made those few gestures that were immortalized by American television cameras. Sadat collapsed and Khalid shouted, 'I have killed Pharaoh!'

Cairo remained calm, apart from a few isolated explosions for which responsibility has never been clearly established. As 'Abbud had predicted, the organization was incapable of paralysing the city's nerve centres in order to touch off 'popular revolution'.

In Asyut, Zuhdi's friends launched their attack not on the sixth, but at dawn on the eighth of October, the first day of the Greater Holiday, *'Id al-Adha,* during which it is traditional for people to stay at home with their families. The element of surprise was therefore complete: determined groups of assailants set off for the security headquarters, where only a skeleton crew was on duty, under the command of a Christian officer. He was beheaded, while a large number of *shawish,* poor policemen paid miserable salaries, were massacred, Muslims and Copts slaughtered indiscriminately. Completely overwhelmed, the security forces of Middle Egypt were unable to regain control of the city, and the rebellion was crushed the following day by paratroopers flown in from Cairo, who descended on the university stadium where the *jama'at islamiyya* had held their mass prayer assembly.

Massive arrests swelled the already large number of prisoners incarcerated in September, and Egyptian prisons faced a serious overcrowding problem. Vice-President Husni Mubarak succeeded Sadat after a routine plebiscite. The people who had been arrested in September were gradually released, while those suspected of membership in the Jihad group were tried in two separate trials.

The first dealt with the assassination of Sadat. There were twenty-four defendants, five of whom were sentenced to death. Khalid and his three accomplices, along with Faraj, were put to death on 15 April 1982. Faraj had also been accused of having written *The Hidden Imperative.*

The second trial, not yet ended at the time of writing (September 1983), had 302 defendants, some of whom had fled and were being tried *in absentia.* The prosecutor demanded the death penalty for all the accused.[10] Earlier, a list of the defendants had been published in a Cairo daily newspaper.

This list, which appeared in the 9 May 1982 issue of *al-Jumhuriyya,* constitutes the broadest and most complete sample

---

10. Since then, the trial has ended. Generally lenient sentences were handed down against the defendants, and no one was given the death penalty.

yet available for studying the recruitment patterns of the Islamicist movement in Sadat's Egypt. It must be treated with caution, of course: we cannot be absolutely sure that all the people accused by the Egyptian prosecutors were actually militants of the Jihad group. But with that reservation, the list does provide information about the ages, professions, and addresses of the defendants, and thus offers a profile of the Islamicist militants which seems highly significant and tends to confirm the impression I have formed in studying the movement's ideology and social practices.

There are quite a few doubtful points. A defendant identified as a 'merchant', for example, may be anything from a poverty-stricken newspaper seller to a successful shop-owner. Similarly, although exact addresses are mentioned in most cases, no detailed map of Cairo's streets exists on which they could be accurately plotted. In charting the homes of the defendants listed as living in greater Cairo, it was therefore necessary to rely on the *qism* (borough) or *markaz* (district).

In addition, we have two other samples of Islamicist militants. The first is a list of those accused in the 'Military Academy case' of 1974, published in *al-Ahram*. It indicates the age and profession of each defendant. The second additional sample, the population of which is small, appeared in an article written by the Egyptian-American sociologist Sa'd Eddin Ibrahim after an investigation of imprisoned members of the 1974 group and the Society of Muslims.[11] The table, figures, and map printed at the end of this chapter codify the available information about all these defendants.

The classification by province given in the table indicates two distinct groups, one in greater Cairo, including a few small towns in the Delta, the other in Upper Egypt, concentrated in the three provinces of Minya, Asyut, and Sohag. The group is thus fairly evenly distributed throughout the country, with the notable exception of Alexandria. This is probably purely accidental, for that city had not been spared Islamicist dissidence,

11. 'An Anatomy of Egypt's Militant Islamic Groups', *International Journal of Middle East Studies*, 1981.

since half of the defendants in the Military Academy trial were from Alexandria and the *jama'at islamiyya* had a strong base there. The explanation seems to be simply that Faraj had had no opportunity to forge links in Alexandria as he did with the militants from Asyut.

Fig. 1 indicates that the great majority of defendants from Upper Egypt were students, whereas in greater Cairo and the Delta students were a minority of the accused. The three provinces of Minya, Asyut, and Sohag have the country's highest proportion of Copts, and their capitals are university towns. The geographic sweep of these universities is extremely broad (the University of Asyut has two major locations: Asyut itself for the scientific, law, and commercial faculties, Sohag for the faculties of literature and the humanities), and their students therefore tend to live outside the family context more often than is the case elsewhere, grouped into dormitories or student neighbourhoods like al-Hamra in Asyut. This is probably the reason for the greater cohesion of the Upper Egypt group compared to the branch in the capital.

Fig. 2 shows that the overall proportion between students and non-students is about even, students having a slight edge. The comparison with the Military Academy group is instructive: in the absence of fresh information to the contrary, we can only assume that the Islamicist movement, or at least its Jihad component, did manage to break out of the campus ghetto, as 'Isam al-Din al-'Aryan had hoped. If true, this new characteristic could be a source of strength for the Egyptian Islamicist movement in the future. A similar trend is shown in fig. 5: although most of the defendants in both trials were between twenty and twenty-five years old, the proportion of people between twenty-six and thirty among the Jihad defendants was more or less the same as the percentage of under-twenties in the Military Academy group.

The information on the social composition of the groups is summarized in figs. 3 and 4 and the map. Fig. 3 shows that slightly less than a third of the Jihad defendants were students in the elite faculties of medicine and engineering, a proportion far higher than the national average, although below the record levels of the Military Academy group. The virtual absence of defendants attending military faculties, who constituted more than a quarter of the 1974 defendants, is complemented by the feeble representation of officers and policemen among the employed defendants (fig. 4) and corroborates 'Abbud al-Zumur's statements on this subject. Jihad is proportionally less student-based than the Military Academy group, and its students are also more representative of the masses of students. Once again, if the apparent trend is real, this is a potential source of revolutionary strength.

Fig. 4 must be interpreted with great caution. The classification by profession made in order to simplify the data was only approximate. Does the large number of artisans and merchants — which incidentally tends to reinforce the impression one gets in the streets of Cairo, where large numbers of grocery-store owners sport beards and white calottes — mean that these social layers, which in appearance have benefited from the economic opening, have a deeper reason for challenging the regime? We cannot be at all certain of the answer.

The map, which is designed to relate the addresses of the defendants to a typology of the neighbourhoods of Cairo, is far more eloquent.[12] The concentration of defendants in those areas of the poverty belt west of Giza, where most housing units are sub-standard, is striking. On the other hand, both the middle-class residential neighbourhoods and the central sections of the old city, where buildings are well structured but very dense, are virtually devoid of Jihad members. Part of this distribution, of course, is purely contingent, the simple result of Faraj's movements. Nevertheless, the portrait of recruitment by the Cairo branch as suggested by the map fairly closely corroborates the hypotheses I have proposed on the basis of documents from the Society of Muslims trial and my study of the *jama'at islamiyya*. The milieu that is the most fertile source of Islamicist militants is the 20-25 age-group in the sprawling neighbourhoods on the outskirts of the big cities. These people are marginal in every sense of the word, to begin with in their physical location in a middle ground that is no longer the countryside from which they

12. This map was made possible by the great competence and kindness of Robert Ilbert, to whom I am most grateful.

came but not yet the city, whose heartland they do not penetrate. Their cultural complexion, too, is marginal: the traditional village structures no longer work for them, and can no longer provide them with the resources of material life or with any real social integration. They are the children of the rural exodus, and they arrive in the suburbs with outdated customs. Contrary to their expectations, however, education (even higher education) fails to provide them with the keys to modernity. It is from these circles that the heavy battalions of the Islamicist movement are drawn. They are the living symbols, and their numbers are massive, of the failure of the independent state's modernization projects.

Table

BREAKDOWN OF DEFENDANTS BY GOVERNORATE

1. Greater Cairo and Delta		*2. Upper Egypt*	
Gharbiyya	1	Fayum	9
Qaliubiyya	1	Beni Suef	9
Ismailiyya	1	Minya	25
Sharqiyya	11	Asyut	31
Daqahliyya	5	Sohag	27
Buhayra	4	Qena	11
Cairo and Giza	137	Aswan	1
		New Valley	1

(The table includes only those defendants whose residence is known.)

FIGURE 1

Regional Breakdown of Jihad Defendants: Students and Non-Students

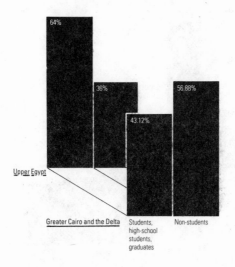

FIGURE 2

Breakdown of Defendants, Students/Non-Students, Jihad Group and Military Academy Group

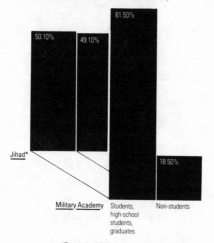

*The missing 0.80% are not identifiable from the sample

FIGURE 3

Breakdown of Student Defendants by Faculty

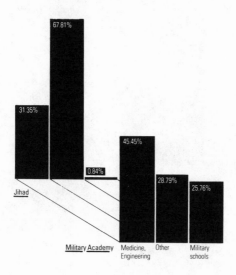

FIGURE 4
Breakdown of Working Defendants of Jihad Group by Profession

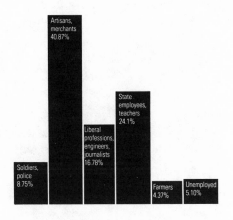

FIGURE 5
Breakdown of Defendants by Age

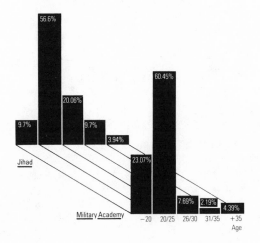

222

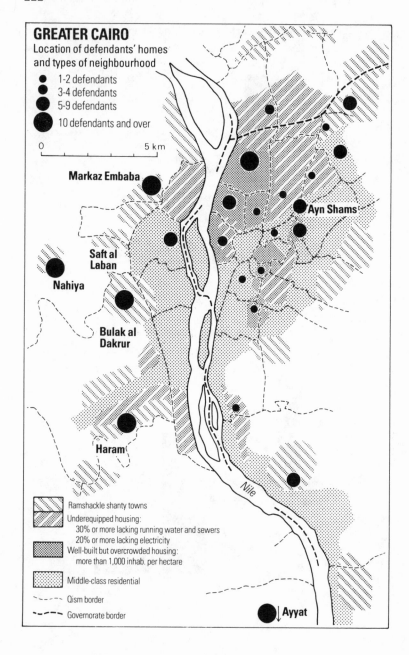

GREATER CAIRO
Location of defendants' homes
and types of neighbourhood

● 1-2 defendants
● 3-4 defendants
● 5-9 defendants
● 10 defendants and over

0 ——————— 5 km

Markaz Embaba

Ayn Shams

Saft al
Laban

Nahiya

Bulak al
Dakrur

Haram

Nile

Ramshackle shanty towns
Underequipped housing:
30% or more lacking running water and sewers
20% or more lacking electricity
Well-built but overcrowded housing:
more than 1,000 inhab. per hectare

Middle-class residential

Qism border
Governorate border

Ayyat

Conclusion

> When a new order of phenomena becomes the object of scientific study, these are already represented in the mind's eye not only by definite images, but by crudely formed concepts as well. . . . How often are [these concepts] as dangerous as they are inadequate! It is therefore not by developing them, in whatever manner, that we will ever succeed in discovering the laws of reality.
>
> DURKHEIM

Until now, I have presented the discourse and practice of the Islamicist movement in a more or less raw form. I say 'more or less' because the selection of sources and the translation and organization of the material, inevitable in studying any real object, was meant to offer the broadest possible view of the subject. My intention has been to present the sometimes antagonistic varieties of the movement, to reveal its contradictions and not to conceal this or that action because it might have invalidated some pre-established schema.

Readers may well have found this disconcerting. But they should instead be gratified, for it is essential to find the Orient disorienting when pondering the Islamicist movement. Surprise and astonishment have a heuristic value, as an antidote to the spontaneous tendency to reduce unfamiliar objects to known categories, in other words, to deny the unfamiliarity. One must allow oneself to be disoriented if one is to apprehend the full richness of the Islamicist movement.

It is not mere caprice to recall these elementary epistemological precautions, for few contemporary phenomena have been so superficially observed and hastily judged as this movement. This is evident even in the terms used to designate it: *intégrisme musulman* in France or 'Muslim fundamentalism' in the English-speaking world. These two expressions transpose to the Muslim world intellectual tools forged to interpret particular moments in the history of Catholicism and Protestantism respectively. There is no justification for such a transposition.

Apart from the terms used, two different approaches to the movement may be discerned. The most common is inspired by a polemical stance that considers the Islamicist militants no more than atavistically backward fanatical terrorists. Those who share this approach will remember only the anti-Semitism of *al-Da'wa* and Karam Zuhdi's thirst for Christian blood; they will have sneered at Sheikh Kishk's observations about the Virgin Mary's vagina. They will have ignored anything that might conflict with their iron-clad certainties, held Qutb's work to be worthless, and Shukri Mustafa's attempts at resocialization without interest.

The second approach stands opposite to the first, but is likewise satisfied with a merely partial understanding of the Islamicist movement. It studies only the theoretical texts and seeks to ignore the risks of their implementation, especially when they are violent. It jettisons any contradictions and deliberately obfuscates anything that might disturb its idealized view, in an effort to present a 'generally positive balance-sheet'.

Rejecting all these value judgements and this intellectual laziness, we must accept the challenge the Islamicist movement represents to the traditional categories of social science and to orientalism.

Although the social sciences distinguish politics from religion, the proximity, even outright intermingling, of the two has been noted since the nineteenth century, in particular by thinkers committed to revolutionary movements. Their attention has been drawn to many phenomena, from Late Antiquity to the modern epoch, that have appeared to be religious but whose social or polital dimension they have sought to uncover.

This attitude was epitomized by Engels and has had a remarkable posterity. He argued, for example, that 'what are called the religious wars of the sixteenth century . . . were class struggles'. And even when 'these class struggles had a religious character . . . that changes nothing in the matter and is easily explained by the conditions of the epoch' [46].

But the perspective opened by Engels — which has since engulfed a significant portion of 'progressive' critical thought —

has been used so effectively to bring out the social dimension of religious phenomena that it has obscured the real significance of religious expression itself, dropping it through the trap-door of ideology ('in the popular insurrections of the Christian West, the religious guise serves only as banner and mask for attacks on a decaying economic order; ultimately, this order is overthrown, a new order arises, there is progress, the world advances' [46]). All that remains of religion here is the 'mask', which the analyst unhesitatingly tears away in his effort to reduce the popular insurrections to the categories of historical materialism.

Unfortunately, Islam had already proven resistant to this elegant dialectic: 'The uprisings of the Mohammedan world', Engels again explains, '. . . are movements born of economic causes although they bear a religious disguise. But even when they succeed, they leave economic conditions intact. Nothing changes, and collisions become periodic' [46]. Whether the world is seen as marching ever onward toward the radiant future or on the contrary spinning endlessly in place, the analytic approach is the same: the religious dimension of the phenomenon is a disguise of little intrinsic importance; only the supposed effects of the movement really count.

These effects are then viewed in normative terms. This is due notably to the conditions of the workers movement in the nineteenth century: religious utopias were sprouting aplenty in the vicinity of the young shoot of communism, and Marx and Engels were determined to nip them in the bud. As an example, consider their *Circular Against Kriege*, who 'seeks . . . under the banner of communism, a clientele for all the abominations of Christianity' [46].

A century later, the 'Mohammedan world' is challenging the treatment of religious phenomena as purely ideological. The doubt acknowledged by Engels has become a central difficulty, not only for Marxists concerned with the Orient (who have suffered a train of disappointments), but also for all those who are interested in the intersection of the religious and the political. The problem must be posed anew, the hypotheses inverted, for in this domain 'ideology' is but another name for ignorance: the religious expression of a social phenomenon is not its disguise, but its unveiling.

The Religious and the Political

'Are there not instances', Miguel Abensour asks, 'of utopias in which the prominence of the religious question discomforts a variety of social thought that would seem all too prepared to turn in on itself? Does the typological understanding of a spiritual movement afford us the key to its foundations? At the point of intersection of the religious and the utopian, what becomes of the prophetic call, the demand for justice, ethical aspiration, the eschatological objectives?' [41]. Seeking the answers to these questions suggested by the Islamicist movement will allow us to understand how and why its rejection of the present leads it to develop an eschatological perspective based on a past model.

All the varieties of the movement that we have examined evoke this past model, but each recalls or relives the lost epoch in its own way: the 'sole Koranic generation' that *Signposts* urges its readers to imitate; the Prophet and his companions successively experiencing the phase of weakness and the phase of power that Shukri Mustafa wanted his Society of Muslims to re-enact; the 'pure Muslim life' as it was lived in the summer camps of the *jama'at islamiyya*.

To understand the elaboration of this model, we may begin by looking at how the various currents of the Islamicist movement view present-day Egyptian society. Each draws its own portrait, emphasizing this or that contrast or shading. Shukri and Faraj were combating the same society and the same state, but the former condemned society as a whole as *jahiliyya* and withdrew from it, while the latter concentrated on challenging the state and denied that 'the political' had any place as an autonomous category in a genuine Muslim society.

After first establishing a vision of contemporary Egyptian society's relation to the state, the Islamicists then transform that vision into an archetype, and gaze upon it in the light of the past.

It is this second procedure that is problematic, and that makes the Islamicist movement unique among other movements for social demands, expressions of utopias, or revolutionary theories. Its view of the past, of history, is polarized by a 'golden age': the period from the hegira in the year 622 to the seizure of power by the Umayyad caliph Mu'awiya in 660. The subsequent fourteen centuries are considered less important, or even objectionable. These thirty-eight years saw the advent of the ideal Muslim society and the territorial expansion of Islam, under the command of the Prophet and the four 'rightly guided caliphs' who succeeded him.

In itself, this sort of reference to an originating myth is not unusual; Periclean Athens has been the ideal of Western democrats at a distance of two millennia. This did not induce them to try to copy all the features of Athenian society, the institution of slavery in the first place. The important question, then, is why this particular archetype was selected. To choose Mecca is to reject Athens, the Western archetype. Moreover, the two reference points are different in character. The ancient city is closed, both territorially and transcendentally; its metaphoric appropriation by contemporary democrats jettisons its religious dimension, following Aristotle in this respect. In his description of the principles (*archai*) of the Athenian constitution — the six elements necessary for the constitution of a city — Aristotle places service to the gods in fifth position, and religious institutions play no decisive role in the functioning of the *polis* [42]. The golden age of Islam, on the other hand, is open-ended. Spatially, it expanded relentlessly, from the Hijaz in Arabia to Syria, Iraq, Persia, Egypt, and so on. Transcendentally, it was explicitly founded on God, or, to repeat Guyau's phrase, 'sociability, seen as one of the features of human nature, extended up to and beyond the stars'. This ontological difference between archetypes corresponds to a difference between those who employ them: the political class that governs the Western societies encourages the originating myth of Athens because it provides legitimation for the system. In contemporary Muslim societies, however, it is those layers that contest the established order who refer to the golden age of Islam, in order to delegitimate the existing order. As far as the most radical tendencies of the Islamicist movement are concerned, time stops in the year 660 when Mu'awiya seized the caliphate and introduced the dynastic principle. They do not recognize subsequent history, which nevertheless continues up to the present day. Shukri Mustafa said as much when he told the military tribunal that once the doors of *ijtihad* were closed, the history of Islam was no more than the story of the *ulema*'s complicity with the princes. He regards this history, as well as the present-day states in which it is embodied, as alien. His allegiance, like that of Faraj, is not to nations in their present frontiers. They are not Egyptians, but first and foremost Muslims.

What distinguishes the extremist Islamicist movement from the bulk of Muslims as far as reference to the golden age is concerned is that the former blot out history in favour of the reactivation of the founding myth, while the latter accommodate themselves to the history of Muslim societies. They may consider this history an adulteration of the archetype, but they do not regard the fourteen centuries that have elapsed since then (contemporary life included) as alien. For most Muslims, reference to the epoch of the Prophet and the first four caliphs does not necessarily entail a negative appreciation of the established order.

In the cultural tradition of Western Europe, Periclean Athens came to be seen as a political model only very belatedly, as a seal of the autonomy of the temporal from the spiritual. This separation was possible because from its very origin, Western thought has borrowed from two sources: Christian doctrine on the one hand and secular Roman law on the other. These two principles have been articulated throughout all the centuries of Christianity; there has been a relation between them, but never an identification.

Islam, on the contrary, is marked by *tawhid*, or fundamental unity. The distinction between *din* and *dawla*, the spiritual and the temporal, is meaningless in Muslim doctrine, since one and the same text, the Koran, revealed by God to the Prophet Muhammad, contains both the rules regulating relations between man and God and the principles governing social life. No system of secular law was ever articulated with Islam as Roman law was with Christian doctrine, and the attempt to graft Greek philosophy onto Islam during the time of the Abbasid caliphs (who ordered translations of it) perished. If *tawhid* is to be realized, the commander of the faithful, the caliph, must see to the application of the Koranic imperatives. In particular, he must permit the smooth functioning of justice and must safeguard Muslim ethics. He therefore plays a fundamental social role, and according to the Islamicist militants, only Muhammad and the first four caliphs properly acquitted themselves of this task.

Nevertheless, Muslim societies have lasted down to the present day, even though the holder of power has been successively transformed, from 'rightly guided caliph' to caliph issued of a *coup de force* or dynastic succession, to sultan, emir, Mamluk, king, or president. What the most rigorous Islamicist militants object to about all these princes, whom they call iniquitous (*al-hakim al-zalim*), is that their claim to be serving Islam is purely an attempt to lend their system legitimacy, to conceal the reality of a regime that obeys only their own whim. 'The rulers of our time', Faraj writes, 'are apostates of Islam, nurtured at the table of colonization. Of Islam they have preserved no more than the name.'

Faraj is not the first Muslim to suspect or accuse the prince of infractions of the law of Islam. And long before the advent of the Islamicist movement, questions were raised about the problem posed by Mu'awiya's accession to power through a *coup de force* — a procedure which, with rare exceptions, has continued to the present time.

This kind of accession to power posed two sorts of problems — and indeed still does. The prince who employs the *coup de force* feels an imperative need for a *post facto* legitimacy that will afford his regime a stability that coercion alone cannot procure. Only the *ulema* can confer this legitimacy, for they hold the monopoly on interpretation of the Book of God, and they alone are entitled to declare that the prince, whatever the modalities of his rise to power, is governing according to the injunction of God (*bima anzala allah*).

If the ideal 'good government' is that of the golden age, then under actual 'good government' the whim of the prince is tempered by the wise advice of the *ulema*, the jurisconsults, *de facto* mediators between the populace and their sovereign. Thus it was that the great medieval Muslim thinker al-Ghazali (1058–1111) wrote that 'the jurisconsult serves as master and director of conscience for political authority in administrating and disciplining men that order and justice may reign in this world' [40].

The *ulema* therefore assume what Bourdieu called the two 'polar positions' of the religious task, namely 'justifying the existence of the ruling classes as rulers' and 'imposing recognition of the legitimacy of domination on the ruled' [9].

In agreeing to play this role, the autonomous corps of 'managers of the means of salvation' acquire substantial advantages in social status. Nevertheless, they must achieve a balance between the prince and the ruled: if they grant the sovereign too much legitimacy without bridling his caprice, the *ulema* lose their credibility in the eyes of their flock, who then dispense with their services and turn instead to independent, sectarian forms of religious practice. The prince then holds the clerics to be ineffective, and they suffer his wrath. This is what happened during Shukri Mustafa's trial when the military prosecutor claimed that the incompetence of the religious dignitaries was responsible for the existence of the Society of Muslims. Nevertheless, in this the state merely reaps the fruit of its policy of domestication of the *ulema*, the epitome of which came with the reform of al-Azhar during the Nasser epoch.

Sheikh Kishk asks ironically whether the next sheikh of al-Azhar will be an army general. But although both the preacher and the people he calls 'pubescent thinkers' (Shukri and Faraj, in the event) challenge the role of the *ulema* in contemporary Egypt, they disagree sharply about the solution to the problem.

For Kishk, the *ulema* must be reformed so that they can play their classical role of advising the prince, as Ghazali recommended. This is the meaning of his proposals that Azharist education consist strictly of meditation of the Book of God, that the sheikh of al-Azhar be elected and no longer named by the prince, and consequently that his salary be paid from the revenue generated by Muslim property, the *waqfs*, and not from the state budget.

For Shukri, on the other hand, the *ulema* are no more than lackeys of the iniquitous prince, 'preaching parrots of the pulpit', and they have no place in the Society of Muslims.

For Faraj, finally, the *ulema* have failed in their task by concealing the imperative of *jihad* against the prince; they have failed to proclaim that he is alien to Islam, as Ibn Taimiyya did in his *fatwa* about the sovereign of Mardin enthroned by the Mongols.

The three approaches therefore differ, but at the root of each lies the aspiration to justice as they see it, justice which the prince does not apply but the Book of God guarantees.

It may seem surprising that an understanding of the contemporary Islamicist movement requires a view so far into the past of Muslim societies. Why is the aspiration for justice formulated in religious terms in today's Egypt, whose legal system is largely inspired by French legislation?

Is the Islamicist Movement Inevitable?

Although the roots of the Islamicist movement lie deep in the history of Muslim societies, the varieties of the movement that we have been considering here nevertheless arose in the seventh decade of the twentieth century. It would be a strange analysis indeed that followed the spokesmen of official Islam in reducing the movement to a variation of the Kharijite sect. Throughout this book, I have tried to situate the movement in its context, Egyptian society of the seventies, so that the context might reveal the object of study and the object of study illuminate the context in a constant give and take.

In observing the development of the *jama'at islamiyya* in the universities, I remarked that they took over the campuses after silencing the competitive dissident discourse of Marxism and left-Nasserism, which had been predominant at the beginning of the Sadat era. And in discussing a text drafted by the young doctor 'Isam al-Din al-'Aryan, one of the ideologues of the Islamicist students, I pointed to a surprising relationship between his view of history and the vulgar dialectical conception of Marxism. This analogy is paralleled by another striking phenomenon, which has been noted by French anthropologists and political scientists working in North Africa: in Tunisia and Morocco, many young Islamicist preachers, disciples or emulators of Kishk, are ex-Marxist-Leninists who studied at universities in France.

As I indicated earlier, these and other similar facts must not automatically be interpreted as evidence of 'Communist manipulation' of the Islamicist movement, which is thereby seen as a pawn of the Soviet secret services. It is by no means impossible that militants belonging to antagonistic schools of thought may have infiltrated the movement here and there, either to spy on it from within or for other reasons. Nevertheless, the scope of this phenomenon has never seemed significant, and in any event it neither negates nor even modifies the specific character of the Islamicist movement. It seems to me, on the contrary, that this movement has succeeded, at a particular moment in history, in exercising a remarkable power of attraction on an entire section of the dominated layers of society, and in making its discourse the crucible in which all dissident demands are forged.

In Egypt, as elsewhere, this sort of dissent has flourished in a welter of forms of expression ranging from what Michel de Certeau has called 'ways of getting by' to elaborate forms of communalism like the Sufi brotherhoods. They represent what Dr Sayyid 'Uways, the most subtle of Egyptian sociologists, calls 'popular forms of resistance to oppression and tribulation' [48] and constitute the fabric of everyday political life in contemporary Egypt, over which the institutions of legal political life — whether civil, religious, or military — have little control.

Michel de Certeau writes that 'although it is true that the grid of "surveillance" penetrates every corner of life, it is equally important to discover why society as a whole is never completely dominated by it. What sort of popular procedures (themselves also "minuscule" and ordinary) toy with the mechanisms of discipline and conform to them only the better to distort them? What "ways of getting by" serve as the counterpart, among consumers (or "the ruled"?), of the mute procedures through which sociopolitical order is maintained?' [44].

Dr 'Uways, approaching the problem in a manner quite different from de Certeau's, has sought to develop a provisional typology of these popular procedures, listing ten 'outlets or modes by which the members of Egyptian society manage to confront misfortune and the various sorts of oppression'. These outlets range from 'indifference', 'hypocrisy', and 'raillery' to 'emigration' and 'rebellion and revolt'. The 'minuscule' outlets, like the first three cited, are familiar to anyone who lives or has lived in Egypt: the humiliated and insulted strata resort to them day by day in their relations with the powerful. There is no Arab country in which language and attitudes have been more arduously and ludicrously coded: the lowliest functionary is addressed as 'bey' or 'pasha'; people snap to attention with a muttered *hadir* ('at your service') every time a superior asks for something, and after executing this machine-like gesture, after playing the good soldier Schweik, they compete in lampooning these same functionaries, calling them names like 'Abd al-Rutin ('slave to routine'). All the pharaohs, great and small, who have similarly scorned and exploited the people for five millennia regularly become the targets of ridicule.

This sort of popular release preserves a kind of social equilibrium: although he grows rich, the exploiter gains no prestige, but only ridicule and derisive nicknames. Meanwhile, everything the dominated layers do, they do badly. The underpaid *bawwab* (porter) who sleeps on a mat in the building's entranceway deliberately scratches the bodywork of the tenants' automobiles, which it is his job to polish. The miserably paid teacher comes to class late and teaches the pupils nothing. The only students who pass their examinations are those who have paid for private lessons, the fees for which enable the teacher to survive. The whole dialectic is expressed in two famous words in the Cairo dialect: *ma'alesh* ('that's all right', 'it doesn't matter') and *bakshish*, which needs no translation. *Ma'alesh*, the car is scratched; *ma'alesh*, the child is ignorant; *ma'alesh*, the machine is broken; *ma'alesh*, there is a three-day — or three-month — delay. *'Ma'alesh*, monsieur', an official in the Egyptian consulate in Italy told Ungaretti after forgetting to issue his visa and thus making him miss the boat for Alexandria. The mumbled *ma'alesh* represents the indifference commensurate with the gap between price and cost, between wages and effort: starvation wages yield *ma'alesh* efforts. The compensation for this gap is called *bakshish*, or corruption.

Although the *ma'alesh* form of individual resistance affords its practitioner a small but undeniable slice of freedom, the annulment of its effects by the *bakshish*, on the contrary, has invidious consequences for the socio-economic system, since it favours the individual holder of money, who regulates the *bakshish* to the detriment of the mass of have-nots. The dialectic of *ma'alesh* and *bakshish*, while it lampoons and expresses contempt for the social order, acts to preserve the system in the final analysis.

That is why people whose existence remains intolerable despite these everyday, 'minuscule' outlets of discontent turn towards other, more elaborate modes of resistance to oppression and tribulation, towards those that Sayyid 'Uways groups at the end of his list: emigration (*hijra*) and rebellion.

These traditional outlets may well constitute no more than partial and temporary tactics that do not lead to a strategy for the overthrow of the state and the seizure of power. Emigration to the Gulf, followed by a return to the country several years later, would be an example. Another would be the sort of crime or vendetta practised in the rural areas. But once they are taken up by the Islamicist movement — like the Society of Muslims, the *jama'at islamiyya*, or the Upper Egypt branch of the Jihad group — they are transformed into a counter-strategy envisaging the overthrow of the regime. This counter-strategy may acquire some degree of sophistication, like Shukri Mustafa's theory of the phase of weakness and the phase of power.

The state has always been well aware of the danger represented by these traditional forms of resistance, for they constitute an obstacle not only to the established order but to all 'Jacobin' attempts to modify the social system from above. Saad Zaghloul, the founder of the great nationalist Wafd Party and a leading figure in many Egyptian governments, wrote in his memoirs: 'The people have always regarded the government as a bird regards a hunter. . . . We must replace this attitude with one of confidence in the government and must persuade the people that the latter is an integral part of the nation.' Likewise for the prestigious inter-war Egyptian intellectual Lutfi al-Sayyid: 'None of us is astonished that most villagers do their utmost to protect anyone accused of a crime and to prevent the case from coming to trial. The government and its agents do not work for the good of the nation, and the people therefore obstruct their decisions, even when it is clear that they are just!' [45].

When the Free Officers seized power in July 1952, they intended to change history by making the revolution by means of the state. Although they explicitly claimed to be acting on behalf of Egypt's oppressed strata, and although they abolished political parties, which they considered symbols of institutional life under the *ancien régime*, they soon reconstituted new institutions that the population came to regard as equally oppressive, if not more so. Confronted with the realities of daily administration, Nasserism's great enthusiasm for Arab nationalism turned into a bureaucratic machine generating routinism and inefficiency in all domains and building concentration camps for those who manifested opposition. In this the Egyptian independent state acted much like its predecessors.

Nevertheless, during the three decades between the July 1952 coup and the assassination of Sadat in October 1981, the state did apply an unprecedented educational policy, one that enabled a broad socio-cultural category to gain access to the written word. Maurice Martin, an acute observer who spent more than a half century travelling around Egypt, termed this category of people the 'cultivated' [27]. It comprises all those — and the population explosion has meant that there are large numbers of them — who come from social layers that have traditionally been illiterate, until today's young generation. They have now been thrust into an educational system whose upper reaches were described in chapter 5. Education has taught them the mannerisms of modern life but not its techniques or spirit, and they regard the state's talk of modernization as deceit. Among them, resistance to oppression and tribulation has taken the form of emigration or rebellion. They provide the prime audience for the Islamicist movement, which has been able to address itself directly to their ideals of justice, heavily stamped by memories of the Islam of yesteryear, and by their yearning for a native village which — in the context of the crowded neighbourhoods on the outskirts of the great cities — has become almost as mythical as the golden age of Islam. The bearded militants in their flowing gallabiehs have been able to speak the language of plausible utopia to these young people. This new generation feels cheated. The youth have been the guinea-pigs in the maladroit experiments of the independent state, and there is every reason to believe that, once profoundly reshaped by Islamicist ideology, they will no longer be satisfied, as their elders were, with the dialectic of the *ma'alesh* and the *bakshish*.

Facets of a Utopia

From that obscure day in the late fifties when Sayyid Qutb, lying in the infirmary of the Tura concentration camp, wrote the passage in *Signposts* stating that the Muslim state would be established by the 'movement' (*haraka*) and not just by propaganda (*da'wa*) to October 1981, when Anwar Sadat was cut down by a reader of *The Hidden Imperative*, the radical Islamicist view had always been that only revolutionary violence could bring down *jahiliyya*, the barbarism that had forsaken the ethics of Islam. Against that background, however, many different theories had been woven.

Qutb's notion of the *haraka*, originally conceived to remedy a defect in the strategy of the Muslim Brotherhood, was meant to preserve the concept of *jihad*, of sacred combat, within the Islamicist movement by defining it as an actual struggle against the independent state established by Nasser. The state, however, effectively defeated all the various attempts of Islamicist militants to confront the regime directly. Except in October 1981, the repressive institutions were always able to strike at the movement at times when it had attained a degree of organization sufficient to provide material evidence of 'conspiracy' but was not yet prepared for confrontation, since the exact modalities of a tactic for the seizure of power had not been determined. The '1965 conspiracy', which enabled Nasser to hang Sayyid Qutb, the Military Academy case of 1974, the confrontation with the Society of Muslims in 1977 (the year of Sadat's trip to Jerusalem), and the June 1981 conflagration in the Zawiyya al-Hamra district of Cairo were all instances.

In this sense, it may be argued that the limits of *Signposts* as a manifesto have been reached. The annihilation of Shukri Mustafa's Society of Muslims marked the failure of a strategy based on imitation of the prophetic model, with its expected succession of phases of weakness and phases of power, in the image of Muhammad, who was weak in Mecca before the hegira and powerful after his withdrawal to Medina.

Sayyid Qutb profoundly underestimated both the state's capacity to respond and the tenacity of the ideology it propagates, of all the various 'obstacles external to the youth' listed by the young doctor 'Isam al-Din al-'Aryan, leader of the *jama'at islamiyya*, when he surveyed the tasks of the Islamicist student movement at the dawn of the fifteenth century of the hegira. Indeed, although the masses of the 'cultivated' were convinced by the movement's mobilizing theories, the movement was unable to split the other social layers away from the regime. Qutb and his emulators were very likely taken in by their own rhetoric: although the model of the concentration camp afforded a metonymic approach to the Nasserist state that spoke louder than any number of long-winded theoretical analyses, the image was nevertheless quite inadequate in providing combat-ready militants with any real understanding of the mechanisms through which the state maintains its grip on society. Shukri Mustafa and the *jama'at islamiyya* underestimated the skill with which the secret police egged them on only to strike them down with greater ease. The *jama'at* believed in June 1981 that Muslim solidarity would work in their favour against both the Copts and the state, failing to grasp that the Egyptian masses did not feel allegiance to the *umma* in the mythical form resuscitated by the Islamicist movement, and that this population had not radically broken with the values of the Egyptian nation as such, values of which Islam is the most important, but not the sole, component.

The difficulties encountered in waging Islamicist violence against the state apparatus and the need to give militants something to do partially explain why the aggressiveness of the *jama'at* students or of the members of the Jihad group was focused on targets other than the state. I have already mentioned the effect this had on the campuses, where bearded students established their notion of moral order, iron bars in hand, attacking couples, forbidding film shows and singing concerts, and organizing bonfires of Darwinist, Marxist, and other satanic books.

But the most spectacular instance came during the Islamicist movement's participation in inter-confessional incidents. The anti-Christian violence attracted the attention of foreign observers and tended to obscure the other dimensions of the movement, the forest being hidden by the trees.

These incidents, in which the Islamicists were either participants or instigators, have generally been analysed in one of two ways. The first is simply to claim that Muslims are tainted by a fanaticism that is satisfied only by the shedding of Christian blood, and that Islamicist militants did no more than extend this attitude to the point of paroxysm. The second is to compare what was done to the Copts during these inter-confessional incidents with the fate of other minorities during periods of economic or social tension: the Jews of Europe, the Syro-Lebanese of West Africa, the Indians of East Africa, the Armenians of Turkey, or the Bahais of Iran, all of whom became the scapegoats of a frustrated population, targeted by governments in search of legitimacy. Neither schema, however, allows us to understand the specificity of the phenomenon. At the end of my description of the incidents in Minya in the spring of 1980, I remarked that the inter-confessional tension involved not two protagonists, Muslims and Christians, but three, for the state intervened too. It is not surprising to find all three protagonists prominently featured in the commentary on al-Zawiyya al-Hamra presented by Sheikh Kishk in his sermon of 6 June 1981:

'There were riots in the depths of a dark night. Yes, it was tragic to see Christians open fire, taking aim at the hearts of the Muslims. Since when have the Christians had such audacity? . . . Since 'Amr Ibn al-'As conquered Egypt, the Christians have lived together with the Muslims without ever having the slightest reason for complaint. . . . Nowhere on earth is there any minority that has been accorded the rights enjoyed by the Christians of Egypt, who occupy so many important posts: ministers, chairmen of the boards of directors of banks, generals, and their pope, who sits on the throne of the Church with all its authority. . . . As for me, I whisper to him, "Amba Shenouda, drive from your mind this desire for predominance, do not think that one day you will be head of state. . . . If you think you can be saved by America, know that we will be saved by God, who is eternal." . . .Who is responsible for this tragedy? The prime responsibility lies with al-Azhar! If the youth had found real leaders to guide them, this would not have happened! . . . The Christians know very well that since the beginning of the revolution, courts have been established to try Muslims; has a single Christian ever been brought before the "People's Court" presided over by Jamal Salim? No, all the accused have been Muslims! And the

"supreme court of state security" condemned Sayyid Qutb to the gallows in 1965, at a time when there was neither state nor security! The prisons were filled, I myself was incarcerated, but I never encountered a single priest. . . . Look at them, these Copts, so sure of their strength and so honoured! . . . Young Muslims,
. . . Amba Shenouda wants to incite you so that he can appeal to America, Britain, and France to send their fleets to Egypt's shores, on the pretext that the minority is persecuted!'

In this brief passage, the Muslims are depicted as victims of state persecution, while the Christians are supposedly laden with honours and occupy high posts. According to Kishk, they are favoured by the Muslim prince, although they are not Muslims, to the detriment of the Muslims.

A year before the 'star of Islamic preaching' delivered this sermon, an Egyptian document dating from the fourteenth century was published and translated by a young French orientalist. It recounts an anti-Christian riot in the city of Qus, in Upper Egypt, as told by a sheikh who accused the Copts of 'taking advantage of their position with the emirs to gain privileges for their own people and to harass the Muslims'. He described these same emirs as 'tepid and sophisticated Muslims who put their own interests above those of Islam', preferring 'power and money to the justice it is their task to impose' [13].

While it is true that throughout the long history of Muslim Egypt, the Copts have provided many state officials, especially tax-collectors, it is equally obvious that they can by no means reasonably be characterized as such, nor described as 'generals, ministers, and chairmen of the boards of directors of banks'. The vast majority of the Copts are peasants, just like their Muslim compatriots. But the Islamicist argumentation, echoing the pious medieval polemic, is aimed, through the Christians, at the state that allegedly favours them. In Islamicist thought, the Copts are ignorant of Muslim ethics and justice as revealed in the Koran, which are the only true ethics and justice. They are therefore willing, in exchange for honours and riches, to offer themselves as tools of the iniquitous prince, to execute his whims and his nefarious policy. For the *jama'at islamiyya*, a Christian provincial governor like the governor of Southern Sinai in 1980 cannot be similar to his Muslim colleagues: in their mind he seeks to abuse his functions, to favour his coreligionists, to harass Muslims, and to cater to the sovereign's whims.

For the Islamicist movement, to assault the Copts is to assault the state. It matters little to the victims, of course, whether they are clubbed and assassinated because they believe that Christ is the son of God or because their attackers consider them the executors of the whims of an iniquitous sovereign. But it is nevertheless the case that inter-confessional incidents of the sort that occurred in the late seventies were the Islamicist movement's substitute for its inability to strike directly at the state.

With Sadat's assassination on 6 October 1981 by a member of the Jihad group, we may try to draw up a provisional balance-sheet of the movement's activities. To begin with, by successfully striking down the president himself, Islamicist violence demonstrated both its effectiveness (perpetrating tyrannicide) and its futility, for not only did the state founded by Nasser survive, but so did the regime of Sadat, whose leading associates continue to occupy the key posts in the economic and political apparatus.

There are too many unknown factors to predict whether Faraj's *Hidden Imperative* will enjoy the posterity of *Signposts* or whether it will instead sink into oblivion like the now-unobtainable writings of Shukri Mustafa. But the text of this young electrician does, I think, at least begin to go beyond Sayyid Qutb, if not to inaugurate a new era in Islamicist thought. *Signposts* came after the setbacks suffered by the Society of Muslim Brethren between 1948 and 1954, and indicated the road of struggle against *jahiliyya*, the barbarism of the twentieth century, just as *The Hidden Imperative* attempted to assess the Islamicist movement's failure in the fight against this same *jahiliyya* since 1965. To the strategies of withdrawal and resocialization upheld by the Society of Muslims and the student *jama'at islamiyya* it counterposed a simpler and more effective concept involving the foreclosure of politics. The prime objective of *jihad,* Faraj argued, was to cut down Pharaoh.

In the Middle East of the 1980s, largely alien to Western political categories, the message of Muhammad the Prophet threatens to become ever more insistent the greater is the execration of Pharaoh.

Afterword:
Ebb and Flow, 1981–1985

Mubarak's Egypt offers a choice setting for an inquiry into the present capability of Islamicist groups to inflame the populace of a Muslim country. Although one of these groups, al-Jihad, succeeded in assassinating Anwar Sadat and holding for several days the nerve centres of Asyut, a city in Middle Egypt, nonetheless it must be said, four years later, that these events have had no significant follow-up along the course set by the conspirators. In other words, the power structure on the shores of the Nile remained substantially the same before and after October 1981, with no changes approaching the scale of those Iran experienced after the fall of the shah and the declaration of the Islamic Republic. And although Islamicist groups remain active, they seem, at this conjuncture, at least, to have lost their ability to constitute a movement that might serve as the mouthpiece of civil society in its confrontation with the state. The brief period considered here (autumn 1981–summer 1985) of course prohibits drawing definitive conclusions that further eventualities may quickly counter. But it does allow us to advance certain hypotheses that facilitate comparison with the situation prevailing in other contemporary Muslim countries.

One hypothesis is that the Islamicist movement functions as a surrogate for the direct political expression which the regime suppresses in all other social debate. In their monopolistic claim on the transcendental order, the Islamicists implicitly criticize the established order and devise actions that aim to transform and overturn it. The movement's surrogate function is not intrin-

Afterword translated by Rose Vekony.

242

sic, but it has the marginal potential of giving the Islamicist movement a power that could swiftly turn it into a revolutionary force. The regime, however, can deprive the Islamicists of that function by privileging the expression of critical or oppositional debate based outside the transcendental order. The regime thereby attacks not the causes that gave rise to this type of movement—for such a policy would be social suicide for the dominant strata—but only its impact for mobilization.

Thus, in Mubarak's Egypt in 1985, Islamicist groups still exist —legal, semi-legal, or underground—but they are in a less powerful position than in the years preceding the assassination of Sadat: they must compete, both on the level of actuality and on the level of symbolic values, with other political currents that question their legitimacy or strive to recoup it for their own ends. In either case, the Islamicists must defend their claim as an intellectual force for Egyptian civil society; yet they find themselves much less able, because of their rudimentary training, to fend off the arguments of their rivals than previously, when the stamp of repression automatically conferred the legitimacy of martyrdom on their discourse.

At the same time, their ambition for Islamic militancy as an eventual challenge to the state is weakened, for it can be fuelled only as long as the prospect seems ripe and the objective clear. That objective, however, has been muddled by the plurality of dissident discourses, and it has lost its immediacy now that the state no longer offers a personalized image that invites regicide (as Sadat did before his death, by crystallizing in his very person the hatred of the people). Islamicist groups have experienced a certain disaffection, for their only specific proposals retreat into utopia, whereas the numerous charitable, devotional, or congregational Muslim groups compete with them in the area of social change, in mores and religious matters. Moreover, political parties of the opposition now offer credible alternatives to the project of transforming the social order.

These few hypotheses are based, on the one hand, on the way the Egyptian regime after 6 October 1981 has managed its relations with Islamicist groups and other components of the opposition and, on the other hand, on the Egyptian press's reflections of social debates that stemmed from religion during the first four years of Mubarak's presidency.

The Carrot and the Stick

Numerous arrests of Egyptian citizens preceded and followed the assassination of Sadat. Prior to 6 October, the 1,536 people deprived of their liberty were equably distributed among all possible categories of the regime's actual or merely imagined opponents—from the Islamicists to the Copts, along with the communists, ex-Wafdists, and Nasserists of every leaning, including Heikal. But the extensive police raids following the assassination focussed more or less exclusively on the Islamicist movement, all of whose militants or known sympathizers were summoned before the police services.

As soon as the results of the October 1981 plebiscite were declared, bringing Mubarak to the head of the country with 98.46 per cent of the vote, the new president inaugurated a style of leadership that, from the aspect of his public manner, offered a striking contrast with that of his predecessor. Rejecting the toadyism that had been solely acceptable in dealing with Sadat at the end of his presidency, his successor displayed a relaxed, even ironic, attitude in his relations. Reports from Cairo tell of how, in Mubarak's first days in office, he was accosted by a courtier who loudly sang his praises. The new president interrupted with the reply, *'Al gayb farigh, al gayb fadi!'* ('My pockets are empty', I have nothing to give you). The portraits of Sadat that had covered the city quickly disappeared, except the one in front of his ex-residence at Giza, where the image of the former pharaoh was left to face the inevitable ravages of wind and dust. And, whereas Sadat had been depicted with wide eyes fixed on the horizon, as a seer leading his people towards a destiny that only he knows, the few portraits of the new president showed him in three-quarter view with a huge ear in the foreground, as a leader who listens to his citizens.

On 25 November 1981, thirty-one oppositionists were freed by order of the president and were immediately led to the residence of the chief of state, where they conversed with him before the press. This spectacular operation was clarified by Mubarak himself, who proclaimed that 'the era of arrests of leaders of the opposition and of their alienation from political life is now behind us', and appealed for unity 'in order to confront the danger of religious fanaticism that has imperilled Egypt'. But these releases were selective, and for more than three years the government used its discretionary power to keep any member of the opposition it deemed unrepentant in a prison or penal colony. The thirty-one persons who on 25 November were led from their cells to the presidential salon included, aside from Hasanain Heikal and the old Wafdist leader Fuad Siraj al-Din, eleven members of the Progressive Unionist Rally, the Nasserist current led by Khaled Muhieddin. Key members of that current's Marxist faction remained in prison until, three weeks later, the Marxist economist Isma'il Sabri 'Abdallah was released. The leader of the neo-Muslim Brethren, 'Umar Talmasani, left prison only at the end of December, along with the owner of the magazine *al-Da'wa*, Salih Ashmawi. Sheikh Kishk, however, was not freed until 28 January 1982, as was the polemicist Jabir Rizq.

As in this policy of cautious and completely selective releases, the regime maintained its pressure on certain oppositional currents. On 8 February, thirty-one figures from the left were arrested for 'reconstitution of the underground Communist Party', and on 6 March, the court trying Sadat's assassination case pronounced five death sentences: the four assassins and the author of *The Hidden Imperative*, 'Abd al-Salam Faraj, were executed on 15 April.

The regime's policy thereby isolated three forces that it hoped to marginalize: in addition to the communists, who represented no very urgent danger and were repressed chiefly as a warning to the public, it is the extremist tendency of the Islamicist movement and the hierarchy of the Coptic church led by Pope Shenouda III that remained under attack. Only on 1 January 1985 did a presidential decree annul the decrees made in September 1981 against the head of the church, and the Coptic leader finally broke his retreat at Wadi Natrun to return to Cairo on 4 January, so that he could celebrate Coptic Christmas Mass on the night of the sixth. As regards the Islamicist extremists, all conspirators charged in the murder of sixty-eight members of the armed forces and police at Asyut on 8 October 1981 were rather leniently sentenced on 30 September 1984, in spite of the prosecutor's requests, on 11 May 1982, for the death of 299 defendants. Only fifty-eight sentences of prison under high security or hard labour were pronounced.

The legislative elections of 27 May fell between the indictment and the verdict. By outlawing the Islamicist extremists and keeping the Coptic pope in retreat, the regime was able, during the electoral campaign, to hold these two forces outside the political debate. It thereby set the limits of a freedom that nonetheless was without equal along the shores of the Nile since the beginning of the Nasser period. The elections, even if their results were considered deceptive or perhaps suspect by the opposition, served the function of political catharsis and so lent a new legitimacy to the regime. By virtue of its renewed foundations, the regime could now demonstrate lenience towards the Islamicists or a Coptic pope whose return to society no longer seemed threatening.

As is evident, the political tactic of the Egyptian regime towards Islamicist groups was the complete opposite of the one employed during the early years of Sadat's presidency: whereas the 'believer president' had muzzled all political expression while giving full rein to Islamicist groups—especially at the universities, in order to confront the Nasserist left on campus and elsewhere and force it into silence—his successor encouraged political debate, authorizing opposition parties and press. The culmination was reached in an election campaign lasting three weeks, during which the party in power was accused of having been the cause of every ill the country suffered. This of course did not prevent the party from winning an overwhelming majority of seats. It is remarkable, however, that in setting the critics loose on his National Democratic Party, the president, for his part, was never taken to task in the debates, even though he was also the Party's head. Thus, by changes that affected more the style and manner of the regime than its operations, Mubarak's advisers robbed the Islamicist movement of its surrogate function. Even if the preachers continued to denounce the state and its policies in their Friday sermons (at least until the measures of

246

summer 1985; see below), their impact was very greatly attenuated in comparison with the period when Sheikh Kishk's sermons constituted the only effective public antidote to the powerful, totally acritical media soporifics.

Having set Islamicist discourse in the midst of a pluralistic oppositional debate, the regime further strove to divide Islamicist ranks by isolating the extremist from the moderate wing and by encouraging the expression of certain of its leaders in various organs of the press. Those leaders were given full freedom to expound on any subject, so long as they did not explicitly question the president and his policies. Thus Sheikh Kishk enlightened the readers of *al-Liwa al-Islami* in his regular reports; *al-Mukhtar al-Islami* and *al-I'tisam*, banned since summer 1981, reappeared (but the ban on *al-Da'wa* was not lifted); and the magazine *al-Nur* became the virulent champion of the Islamisation of practices and mores.

Depoliticizing Islam

The isolation of the extremist wing was implemented by a campaign of repentance, widely broadcast over Egyptian television and retranscribed in the newspapers. Committees of professors, *ulema* of al-Azhar, and other 'Muslim intellectuals' were portrayed entering the prisons where the young militants arrested before and after 6 October 1981 were incarcerated.[1] Before the television and newspaper cameras, the committee sat at a table facing a room filled with calm and attentive young bearded men, some of whom were scrupulously taking notes. Following a scenario that never failed to be enacted, the president of the committee delivered a long exposé to explain that, although it was perfectly proper to assert that Islam should provide the norms of life in society, the use of violence in the contemporary Egyptian context could in no way be justified to achieve such ends. After this a discussion was opened, in the course of which a number of young militants admitted their error and declared themselves ready to pursue the fight for the Islamisation of society, but

1. Note the contrast between the *ulema*'s attitude here and previously, during the trial of Shukri Mustafa (see chapter 3).

without shows of violence. They therefore agreed to withdraw their activities from the immediate political arena.

In the press and on television, moderate or repentant Islamicists have had every latitude to preach the radical re-Islamisation of social life, morals, and customs. But the workings of the political system have remained out of bounds, and even the judicial system has been shielded from the constraining logic of the watchwords demanding the immediate application of the *shari'a*. In this latter issue, the regime developed its strategy with caution. In Sadat's period, the president of the People's Assembly, Sufi Abu Talib, had endlessly explained that the *shari'a* was going to be applied once the long and detailed job of codification was completed. But Abu Talib was cordially dismissed on 5 November 1983 and replaced by Kamal Laila. Then, after the legislative elections of May 1984, Rif'at al-Mahjub was appointed president of parliament on 22 June. On 4 May 1985, Mahjub fought down, by an overwhelming majority of the House, a motion presented by an Islamicist member of the People's Assembly, Salah Abu Isma'il, calling for the complete application of the *shari'a*. Without any major reaction arising in the populace, the project of application was laid to rest. The public was certainly prepared for this event by rather harsh newspaper coverage of the effects of the decision to immediately apply the *shari'a* in Sudan, which was linked with Egypt by a 'treaty of complementarity'. The decision of Sudan's President Nimeiri drew a profusion of reports of thieves' hands being severed and bottles of alcohol destroyed. Further, it resulted in the renewal of guerrilla activity in the south of Sudan, which is animist and Christian, and work stoppage on the Jonglei Canal, situated in the rebel zone. The digging of this canal is essential for Egypt, for its reserves from the Aswan dam drop year after year, and the canal would prevent a considerable amount of water from evaporating from the Nile. But, besides revealing the effects of the bad press in Cairo on Khartoum's decision, the Egyptian parliament's rejection of the project of immediate application of the *shari'a* surely demonstrates the limits beyond which the debate on Islamicism cannot go. It is out of the question for Mubarak to let his policy or the administration of the economy be subject to constraints or pressures from partisans of absolute Islamisation. They must restrict their influence to cultural or social domains. This distinction accounts for the court order, seventeen days after the measure's defeat in parliament, to confiscate the newly published complete Arabic edition of *The Thousand and One Nights* because it offended the values of Islam.

In the cultural and social sphere, the regime has intervened only intermittently, allowing controversies to grow and thereby generating a need for the partisans of Islamisation to develop a defensive argument in the face of the many who rise up against their claims. And whereas in coming to grips with despotism the Islamicist polemic has achieved a measure of success, it has proved much less effective and convincing in the contradictory debate on social phenomena. The confiscation of *The Thousand and One Nights* provoked numerous scandalized reactions in the press. Likewise, Egypt Air's decision on 22 March 1984 to forbid the consumption of alcoholic beverages on all its flights was held up to ridicule in the regime's favoured weekly, *al-Musawwar*. Moreover, the intellectuals Tawfiq al-Hakim, Yusuf Idris, and Zaki Nagib Mahmud did not hesitate to attack the wearing of the veil or raise other issues considered taboo by the partisans of Islamisation, drawing retorts from that group.

In this way, a forum to debate the Islamisation of society was opened; it was relatively free and allowed the expression of a large variety of opposing views, but the controversial nature of the question argued for the regime to keep the organization of the political system out of reach. As I have endeavoured to show throughout the preceding chapters, in Sadat's Egypt, Islamicist militancy set out to rectify everyday affairs—for example, to end the harassment of female students on packed buses—but soon evolved into a revolt against the iniquitous prince who rules in contravention of divine injunctions. The regime has focussed on this very process and, after October 1981, fought to subvert its logic, not without success.

The Islamicist groups clearly perceived this danger but lacked the means to incite a new activist movement within civil society along the lines of the one that had coalesced by the end of Sadat's presidency. The repression of autumn 1981 essentially destroyed the infrastructure of the movement. By outlawing those who envisioned subverting the political system for religious ends, the

regime cut off most of the connections the Islamicists had cultivated with institutional Islam and the Islamic masses. Thus the
automatic solidarity manifested around the 'unjustly persecuted
young Muslims', with various dignitaries of al-Azhar defending
the militants of the *jama'at islamiyya* in the columns of *al-Da'wa* in
the late seventies, no longer surfaced after 'the autumn of fury'.
Instead, the *ulema* fully played out their role as prison counsellors, preaching to bring the lost sheep back into the fold.

Even within the Islamicist sphere, roles were redistributed
and new actors moved into the spotlight. Formerly the regime
had taken aim at every public or mass movement that, by appealing to the transcendental order, could relate the problems of
everyday life to a challenge of the social order. The most notable
successes in this territory were Sheikh Kishk's sermons and the
jama'at islamiyya's agitation on the campuses. But after October
1981, Kishk participated in the social debate run in the columns
of *al-Liwa al-Islami*, and the two sheikhs who tried to take up his
former role, Ahmad al-Mahallawi and Hafiz Salama, have not—
at least not yet—managed to revive the public movement rallied
by 'the star of Islamic preaching'.

Electoral Strategies

The neo-Muslim Brethren, for their part, attempted to break the
vicious circle of social debate as the sole outlet for their free expression. They turned instead to party politics and the electoral
contest of May 1984. In order to run, they formed an electoral
alliance with the Wafd Party. This unexpected move did not fail
to raise controversy among the general public as well as in the
regime, which for a time felt the alliance to be a threat.

Ever since the Sadat era, the neo-Muslim Brethren kept up
their ties with the People's Assembly, and through their partisan
in parliament, Salah Abu Isma'il, as well as through their connections in various business milieus and religious or political
circles, they strove to exert pressure to speed the codification
and application of the *shari'a*. The prospect of free elections
offered them the possibility of renewing this tactic, but certain
provisions of the electoral law threatened to eliminate any hope

250

of gaining a seat if they did not form an alliance with some other current. In fact, law 114 of 1983, which provides for the parliamentary election by the list system and by proportional representation within each district, stipulates in article 17 that 'any party whose slate has not won a minimum of 8 per cent of the valid votes at the national level cannot be represented at the People's Assembly'. This restrictive measure put Ibrahim Shukri's Socialist Worker Party, which fell short of the required percentage by less than fifty thousand votes, out of the running, and likewise Khaled Muhieddin's Nasserist party, the Progressive Unionist Rally, which garnered 4.2 per cent of the vote.[2]

The alliance between Talmasani's friends and the neo-Wafd Party, announced in March 1984, facilitated the latter's access to parliamentary representation, giving it 58 members (versus the 390 of the ruling party, the National Democrats). Nonetheless, this 'alliance contrary to nature' between the partisans of the application of the *shari'a* and a force that, to many Egyptians, embodied the secular tradition at first provoked splits within the Wafd. Later, Sheikh Abu Isma'il, taking note of the differences between him and his colleagues, withdrew from the Wafdist parliamentary group in 1985.

Thus, the alliance did not, properly speaking, yield very tangible results, nor enable a Wafdist landslide in the elections. In the ranks of that party, many had felt that the Muslim orientation of the Egyptian populace might translate into votes on the ballot paper bearing a palm tree, the Wafd insignia. That did not prove to be true, and it is probably the very weak voter turn-out that explains this failure most plausibly. Although the mean rate of abstention was 59 per cent, it exceeded 70 per cent in Alexandria and 75 per cent in Cairo, and neared 80 per cent in Suez.[3] In the previous decade, Islamic dissidence had been voiced in the great urban centres. In rural areas, however, the prominent local figures more easily mobilized the votes of the *fellah*s in favour of the party in power, which controlled the channels of

2. Some candidates from these two slates were later to 'win' seats in parliament; they were among the ten members appointed by the president of the Republic in June 1984.
3. For an analysis of the election results, see A. Buccianti, 'Les Elections législatives en Egypte', *Maghreb-Machrek* 106, 4 (1984), and the *Revue de la presse égyptienne*, no. 3.

redistribution (such as cooperatives and irrigation)—something the urban politicos could not claim to do. The oppositional parties did best in the cities and the NDP fared poorest there; but the bulk of the urban populace did not go to the polls. In the absence of surveys, one can only wonder whether the Islamicists' promising first steps towards mobilizing civil society before autumn 1981 had any chance of yielding votes for the alliance of the neo-Muslim Brethren and the Wafd. The arguments against this hypothesis are several. The Wafd Party of 1984 seemed to express more the aspirations of the well-to-do strata than those of the impoverished masses in the suburbs, where the radical tendencies of the Islamicist movement recruited their great battalions. One might further deduce that the Egyptians who had been caught up by the Islamicist uproar now focussed on the debate around the Islamisation of society and mores; and the electoral stakes, although ratified by Talmasani, to them seemed more part of 'hack politics' and only very distantly related to the problems of their daily life.

Modes of Preaching

One other Islamicist tendency strove to resist the regime's efforts to divorce Islamisation from politics. Indeed, after the slight impact of the neo-Muslim Brethren on the electoral arena, a number of preachers worked to unite Islamic opinion against the indefinite postponement of the application of the *shari'a*, voted in parliament on 4 May 1985. It is worth noting that the two most visible figures of this current have in no way identified themselves with the genealogy of the Muslim Brethren.

Sheikh Ahmad al-Mahallawi, of humble origins, was born in the thirties in a village in the province of Kafr al-Sheikh [50]. Very early in his life he learned the Koran by heart. His immersion in that book, as his biographer explains, led him to decide, while still a child, to cast his lot with the lowly and to fight injustice. A graduate from the faculty of Arabic at al-Azhar, he rejected the teaching profession and chose instead the path of preaching, although it was even less remunerative. As imam in a rural area in his native province, he was firmly dedicated to the needs of the poverty-stricken peasants. He then moved to Alexandria, where he officiated in the great mosque Qa'id Ibrahim, not far from the university campus. His influence on the students who came to listen to his sermons and lectures was great, and he did all he could to facilitate their reviews for exams. He even installed microscopes in the annexes of the mosque to help those enrolled in scientific disciplines, thereby also implying that Islam and science were compatible. As the unwearying voice of the underprivileged, Mahallawi continually demanded higher wages and lower prices. In 1979, he ran in the legislative elections on a 'Muslim' slate, with the lawyer Mahmud 'Id and Sheikh 'Adil 'Id. However, because the elections were rigged, he was not elected. Denouncing the housing and transport conditions in his Friday sermons, Mahallawi invited his listeners to 'carry on the struggle against the Jews' and insisted that no one, be he the president of the Republic, is above the laws of God. His considerable renown attracted financial offers from the Arabian peninsula; but he and his family continued to live among the underprivileged in a two-room hut atop the roof of an Alexandrian building. 'He refused every inducement to work in the oil-producing countries and rejected the comfortable Islam that brings riyals and a peaceful sleep; and he opted instead for the perilous Islam that leads to prison, as well as for an ascetic life for his children and himself'. For the sheikh, 'the proper field of Islamic action is the Islamic political struggle of the masses, action by the people and through them—and not merely in their stead'.

It is no surprise that Mahallawi incurred the ire of Sadat: summoned on 18 July 1981 before the socialist prosecutor, who wanted to prohibit his preaching, he would not give in and ended up being arrested on 4 September, after having galvanized 'the Muslim masses' against the regime in the summer. Following his release, the sheikh was ripe for becoming a successor of Kishk; but although he retained a certain notoriety, with the magazine *al-Mukhtar al-Islami* having made him their hero, he could not quite recreate the collective movement that the blind preacher had aroused. Under close observation by the police, Mahallawi exercised greater caution than his colleague Sheikh Salama, but he nonetheless remained, in the regime's eyes, the exemplar of the subversive—one committed to leading the faithful from an awareness of their unacceptable conditions of existence to an indictment of the political system, and this in the name of the injunctions of Allah. It remains to be seen whether this proselytizer who is so preoccupied with the socio-political dimension of Islam manages to catch a second wind in the eighties. If not, future studies must determine which obstacles repression laid in his path and which could simply be inherent in the historical depletion of this kind of message.

It is Sheikh Hafiz Salama who, in the first half of 1985, embodied the Islamicist confrontation with the regime. Here again, it is impossible in the wake of the events themselves to ascertain whether they denote a rear-guard action that is lost from the start or whether they presage new eruptions. The story of the sheikh, by the same biographer who wrote of his Alexandrian colleague, is nonetheless enlightening, for it helps us understand the Islamicist force that is seeking out the vanguard to wage a war of skirmishes against the regime. If Ahmad al-Mahallawi's great distinction rests on the social dimension of his preaching, 'God willed that Hafiz Salama come to grips first of all with Zionism, which constitutes the central challenge to the Islamicist movement' [49]. Hafiz Salama began his life of struggle in the forties, at the age of twenty. He was a member of the Youth of Our Lord Muhammad (*Shabab Sayyidina Muhammad*), a group that broke off from the Muslim Brethren in 1939 to denounce Banna's compromises with the regime. He began conducting raids in Palestine in 1944, then, in 1948, joined the paramilitary units fighting the Jews. Next he battled the English. He specialized in handling and fabricating explosives, and decided to settle in Suez.

After 1952, Hafiz Salama and his friends declined any collaboration with the Free Officers; in their view, Nasser had ensnared the Islamicist movement. The Youth of Our Lord Muhammad were instantly repressed, and the Muslim Brethren refused to defend them, arguing: 'You will not wait for the Revolution to carry out the objectives proper to it; you are in too much of a hurry', and so forth. When the Youth of Our Lord Muhammad dissolved, the sheikh founded the Society of Islamic Guidance (*jama'at al-hidayat al-islamiyya*), which strove to avoid repression and to create Islamic centres for teaching the Koran. The best known of these centres were the Mosque of the Martyrs in Suez and the al-Nur mosque in the Abbasiah district of Cairo, which in the early eighties was to become the prime Islamicist stronghold. The sheikh announced its construction in response to Nasser and the negus having laid the first stone for a Coptic cathedral nearby.

Arrested in 1966, Hafiz Salama observed the war of 1967 from his cell. He asked to be released in order to go to the front and analyzed the defeat as 'treason by the political leadership'. After his release, he persisted in believing that only Islam could indicate the path to victory over Israel. A partisan of the global unity of the Islamic movement, Salama travelled to Cairo to catch a plane to Beirut, where he was to meet the Shi'ite imam Musa Sadr; but the war of October 1973 intervened. He was determined to return to Suez, even though the route was closed to civilians, and was arrested on his way there. Yet his preaching moved a young officer to let him through; and thus began the great battle of the sheikh against 'the Jews'. According to Hafiz Salama's analysis, the Egyptian regime had only one objective in the war of 1973: to effect a military balance with Israel in order to make peace with the Hebrew state. The 'Muslim masses', on the other hand, had an entirely different wish: to prevent the realization of this American-Zionist plan. Thanks to their resistance at Suez, 'under the direction of Sheikh Hafiz Salama, they defeated Kissinger the conniver and Sharon the fox'. Day after day the sheikh, invoking memories of his career as activist and saboteur dating back to the forties, organized commando actions from the Mosque of the Martyrs that inflicted large casualties on the Israeli forces; they also lost numerous tanks, and the conquest of the Suez proved long and costly for Israel. Here it is important to note that, in setting up Sheikh Salama as the main architect of the resistance—and that in defiance of the governor of the city, that is, the Egyptian political authority—his Islamicist followers would confer on him a legitimacy which obliterates that acquired by the Egyptian regime in the war of 1973. Furthermore, the biographical booklet on the sheikh appeared in 1984, in the midst of a media controversy sparked by a series of articles by the novelist Yusuf Idris. The pieces, featured in an

Arab journal, criticized the events of the October war, labelling it a farce.

After the upheaval of October 1981, al-Nur mosque in Cairo became all the more notable as an Islamicist centre in contrast to the other great mosques of the capital, whose preachers had assumed a low profile. In addition, its massive yet perpetually unfinished buildings occupy a strategic position at the centre of the Abbasiah crossroads, one of the principal transport nodes of Cairo. Upon the construction of a bridge that was to have one supporting column planted near the edifice, a violent press campaign was launched in the pages of *al-Da'wa* in October 1980, and the mosque became a symbol of an Islam menaced by hostile forces. Michel Bakhum, the Coptic engineer assigned to this controversial public works project, was accused of the darkest designs and treated as a *khawaga*, or foreigner. Thus the mosque won notoriety in 'the struggle against the Crusade', an issue that had already come to the fore in the mosque's founding.

In this same vein, at the end of January 1985, Sheikh Hafiz Salama took the floor at the mosque in company of Sheikh 'Umar 'Abd al-Rahman, the blind 'mufti' from the group *al-Jihad*. It was he who had delivered the *fatwa*s declaring legal the murder of the Coptic goldsmiths of Naj' Hammadi by the militants of this movement in Middle Egypt.[4] Released from prison but not at all shaken in his convictions, Sheikh 'Umar, assisted by his host, emphatically voiced reservations about the return of Pope Shenouda to Cairo at the beginning of that month.

Only after parliament's rejection on 4 May of a motion requesting the immediate application of the *shari'a*, however, did Sheikh Salama take the offensive. In his sermon of Friday the 24th, a few days after the beginning of Ramadan, he made the congregation swear on the Koran not to disperse before the application of the *shari'a* and planned for a 'green march' at the presidential residence if the decision was not in effect on 14 June—or 26 Ramadan, the 'Night of Destiny' in the hegiran calendar.

The regime quickly responded to this challenge, undermining the logic of Muslim solidarity that Hafiz Salama attempted to set in motion. On 13 June, the march was forbidden. In early July,

4. See chapter 7.

Egyptian motorists were asked to remove all decals of a confessional nature from the windows of their cars. These were displayed on some three out of four automobiles, since at the beginning of the year an astute entrepreneur had marketed an elegantly penned Muslim profession of faith, selling for 25 piasters (which, in turn, elicited a plethora of Virgins and Christs on Coptic windshields). The measure nonetheless was implemented, without demurral, in twenty-four hours, much to the surprise of observers.

On 3 July, the government issued a decree placing all private mosques (*ahli*) in Egypt under the supervision of the Ministry of Waqfs and required that the Friday sermons have its prior authorization. Although no one harboured illusions regarding the capacity of a quite undynamic ministry to exert its actual control on the tens of thousands of *ahli* mosques in the country, it was nevertheless clear that the 'whiners of the mosques'—as the Islamicists were nicknamed in hostile circles—were to be the first targets. On Friday the 5th, Sheikh Salama did not preach, but the imam sent by the minister said nothing, either; and Abdallah 'Taha' Samawi, who participated in most of the Islamicist groups of the seventies, delivered the *khutba*. In response to the governmental decree, the sheikh summoned a large demonstration on 12 July at Abidine Square (where the *jama'at islamiyya* were holding prayers for the two holidays). Although authorized by the court, the gathering was called off *in extremis* by its instigator. On the 14th, the police arrested Sheikh Salama in his office at al-Nur mosque, seizing leaflets and court exhibits, and took the Islamicist preacher into custody. There were further arrests on the following days in Alexandria and Fayum. On 19 July, al-Nur mosque was closed. One month later, however, Hafiz Salama was released so that he could take part in the pilgrimage to Mecca.

The failure, at least for now, of the offensive led for the application of the *shari'a* is symptomatic of the political climate of Mubarak's Egypt. Modelled on the Islamicist demonstrations of Sadat's time, which aimed to mobilize civil society against the state in the name of the transcendental order, the offensive could not revive the movement that had developed before October 1981, but simply reassert the existence of groups whose public seems henceforth more limited. Sheikh Salama and his discourse can be truly effective only in the role of the regime's sole challengers. Those who would denounce in the name of Islam the 'hidden agenda' of the war of 1973 need supporting evidence if their stand is to prevail over an identical denunciation, such as that by Yusuf Idris, in the name of principles having but little to do with the transcendental order. And, with the rebirth of a freer press—though it be controlled by politicians' strategies, for which the daily suffering of the people is no central concern— the appeal of Islamicist rhetoric fades.

If Egyptian Islamicist groups seem, in the mid-eighties, to have reached a crux, the regime as well is walking a narrow line. Its looser political style and efficient and discreet use of repression have enabled it, in robbing the Islamicist movement of its role as a surrogate for all challenges to the established order, to effect the uncoupling of Talmasani and Salama, on the one hand, from the young people of the teeming, poverty-stricken suburbs, on the other. But, for the years to come, the real issues lie elsewhere. 'The state, powerless to awaken the national conscience, is reduced to passing out sinecures, increasing salaries, giving full rein to the private sector, and closing its eyes to corruption in the public sector', the novelist Ihsan 'Abd al-Quddus wrote at the end of 1982 in the weekly magazine *October*. This 'awakening of the conscience' was, to many Egyptians in the seventies, embodied in the values of the Islamicist movement. Now, in the following decade, debates and criticisms have become the order of the day; these, at the very least, can shed more light on the problems facing that society.

Paris, 31 August 1985

Sources

Books and Articles

[1] ABUL KHAYR, 'Abd al-Rahman, *Dhakrayati ma' Jama'at al-Muslimin* (Memoirs of the Society of Muslims), Kuwait 1980.

[2] 'ASHMAWI, Hasan al-, *al-Ikhwan wa'l-Thawra* (The Brethren and the Revolution), Cairo 1977.

[3] ARNALDEZ, Roger, *Jésus fils de Marie, Prophète de l'Islam*, Paris 1980.

[4] AZM, Yusif al-, *Ra'id al-Fikr al-Islami al-Mu'asir, al-Shahid Sayyid Qutb* (The Martyr Sayyid Qutb, Master of Contemporary Islamic Thought), Damascus-Beirut 1980.

[5] BAHNASAWI, Salim al-, *al-Hukm wa Qadiyat Takfir al-Muslim* (Power and the Problem of the Excommunication of the Muslim), Cairo 1977.

[6] BERGER, Morroe, *Islam in Egypt Today*, Cambridge, Mass. 1970.

[7] BISHRI, Tariq al-, *al-Haraka al-Siyasiyya fi Misr, 1945–1952* (The Political Movement in Egypt, 1945–1952), Cairo 1972.

[8] BISHRI, Tariq al-, '*Sa Yabqi al-Ghalu ma Baqiya al-Taghrib*' ('Extremism Will Last as Long as Westernization'), *al-'Arabi*, no. 1, Kuwait 1982.

[9] BOURDIEU, Pierre, 'Genèse et structure du champ religieux', *Revue française de sociologie*, XII, 1971.

[10] DEKMEJIAN, R. Hrair, *Egypt Under Nasser*, London 1972.

[11] GARDET, L., and ANAWATI, G., *Introduction à la théologie musulmane*, Paris 1948.

[12] GHAZALI, Zaynab al-, *Ayam min Hayati* (Days of My Life), Beirut-Cairo 1979.

260

[13] GRIL, Denis, 'Une émeute antichrétienne à Qus', *Annales islamologiques*, XVI, 1980.

[14] HAYEK, Michel, *Le Christ de l'Islam*, Paris 1959.

[15] HUDAYBI, Hasan al-, *Du'ah, la Qudah* (Preachers, Not Judges), Cairo 1977.

[16] HUSSEIN, Mahmud, *Class Conflict in Egypt, 1945–1970*, New York 1973.

[17] IBRAHIM, Sa'd al-Din, 'Anatomy of Egypt's Militant Islamic Groups', in *International Journal of Middle East Studies*, no. 12, 1980.

[18] IMAM, 'Abd Allah, *'Abd al-Nasir wa'l-Ikhwan al-Muslimun* (Nasser and the Muslim Brethren), Cairo 1980.

[19] JANSSEN, J.J.G., 'The Voice of Sheikh Kishk', in AL SHEIKH et al., ed., *The Challenge of the Middle East*, Amsterdam 1982.

[20] KHALIDI, Salah, *Sayyid Qutb, al-Shahid al-Hayy* (Sayyid Qutb, the Living Martyr), Amman 1981.

[21] KHALIFA, 'Abd al-Rahman, *al-Ikhwan al-Muslimun fi Sutur* (The Muslim Brethren in a Few Lines), Amman 1980.

[22] LAOUST, Henri, *Contribution à l'étude de la méthodologie canonique d'Ibn Taïmiyya*, Cairo 1939.

[23] LAOUST, Henri, *Essai sur les doctrines sociales et politiques d'Ibn Taïmiyya*, Cairo 1939.

[24] LAOUST, Henri, *Le Traité de Droit public d'Ibn Taïmiyya* (French translation of Ibn Taimiyya's *al-Siyasa al-Shar'iyya*), Beirut 1948.

[25] LAOUST, Henri, *Les Schismes dans l'islam*, Paris 1945.

[26] MARTIN, Maurice P., 'Egypte: les modes informels du changement', in *Etudes*, April 1980.

[27] MARTIN, Maurice P., 'University Expansion and Student Life in Egypt', in CEMAM *Reports*, no. 4, 1976.

[28] MARTIN, M.P. and MAS'AD, R.M., 'Al-Takfir wa'l-Hijra, a Study in Sectarian Protest', in CEMAM *Reports*, 1977.

[29] MAWDUDI, Abul A'la, *al-Mustalahat al-Arba'a fi'l-Qur'an* (The Four Technical Terms of the Koran), Kuwait 1977.

[30] MITCHELL, R.P., *The Society of the Muslim Brothers*, Oxford 1969.

[31] QUTB, Sayyid, *Ma'alim fi'l-Tariq* (Signposts), Dar al-Shourouk, Beirut-Cairo, 1980; (a) edition of the World Islamic Union of Students, no location, n.d. (Kuwait).

[32] RAMADAN, 'Abd al-'Azim, *al-Tanzim al-Sirri li'l-Ikhwan al-Muslimin* (The Secret Organization of the Muslim Brethren), Cairo 1982.

[33] RIZQ, Jabir, *Madhabih al-Ikhwan fi Sujun Nasir* (The Massacres of the Brethren in Nasser's Prisons), Cairo 1977.

[34] RIZQ, Jabir, *Madhbahat al-Ikhwan fi Liman Tura* (The Massacre of the Brethren in Tura Prison), Cairo 1979.

[35] and [36] SABANEGH, Edouard, *Muhammad, portraits contemporains*, Rome 1982.

[37] 'Student Agitation in Egypt', in CEMAM *Reports*, no 1, 1972–73.

[38] (An Egyptian student), 'L'impatience paralysée: réflexion sur le récent mouvement des étudiants en Egypte', in *Travaux et Jours*, no. 42, 1972.

[39] WISSA-WASSEF, Cérès: 'Le pouvoir et les étudiants en Egypte', in *Maghreb-Machrek*, no. 57.

[40] LAOUST, Henri, *Politique de Ghazali*, Paris 1970.

[41] ABENSOUR, Miguel, 'L'utopie socialiste: une nouvelle alliance de la politique et de la religion', *Le Temps de la réflexion*, Paris 1981.

[42] ARISTOTLE, *The Politics*, T.A. Sinclair, trans., Harmondsworth 1962.

[43] BLOCH, Ernst, *Thomas Münzer als Theologe der Revolution*, Munich 1921.

[44] CERTEAU, Michel de, *L'invention du quotidien. 1. Arts de faire*, Paris 1980.

[45] HOURANI, Albert, *Arabic Thought in the Liberal Age*, Oxford 1970.

[46] MARX, K., and ENGELS, F., *Sur la religion*, Paris 1972.

[47] MORABIA, Alfred, 'La Notion de jihad dans l'islam médiéval', unpublished thesis, 1975.

[48] 'UWAYS, Sayyid, 'Sur quelques modes égyptiens de résistance à l'oppression et aux épreuves', in *Modes populaires d'action politique*, mimeographed, no. 2, CERI, Paris 1983.

[49] MORO, Muhammad, *Al-Shaykh Hafiz Salama wa Ma'arakat al-Yahud fi'l-Suways* (Sheikh Hafiz Salama and the Battle Against the Jews in Suez), Cairo 1984.

[50] MORO, Muhammad, *Qissati ma' al-Sadat: al-Shaykh Ahmad al-Mahallawi* (Sheikh Ahmad al-Mahallawi: My Dealings with Sadat), Cairo 1985.

262

Periodicals

1. Egypt
Al-Ahram (daily), *al-Akhbar* (d), *al-Jumhuriyya* (d), *Rose al-Yusif* (weekly), *Uktubir* (w), *Mayo* (w), *al-Sha'b* (w), *Musawwar* (w), *Sabah al-Khair* (w), *al-Da'wa* (monthly), *al-I'tisam* (m), *al-Mukhtar al-Islami* (m).

2. Lebanon
L'Orient-Le Jour (d), *al-Safir* (d), *al-Nahar* (d), *al-Anwar* (d), *al-Nida'* (w), *al-Shihab* (m).

3. Kuwait
Siyasa (d).

4. Saudi Arabia
Madina (d).

5. Britain
Al-Muslimoon (m).

6. France
Agence France-Presse (dispatches of the Cairo bureau, graciously made available to me by Ignace Dalle), *Le Monde* (d).

Chronology:
1928–August 1985

The chronology lists many of the major events in Egypt between 1928 and August 1985. Items in roman type refer to the Islamicist movement itself. Indented items in italics refer to broader events in Egyptian political life.

1928

Foundation of the Society of Muslim Brethren (the Muslim Brotherhood) by Hasan al-Banna in Ismailiyya.

1933

First congress of the Muslim Brotherhood held in Cairo.

1936–39

The Brotherhood collects funds for the Arabs of Palestine.
Anglo-Egyptian Treaty signed (1936).

1937–39

Rapprochement between the Brotherhood and the Palace against the Wafd Party.
1937: Coronation of King Farouk.

1939

Split of the 'Youth of Our Lord Muhammad' group, which denounces al-Banna for his compromises with the regime.
Beginning of the Second World War.

1940

First contact between al-Banna and Sadat to free Egypt from British domination.

1941

Al-Banna banished to Upper Egypt on British orders.
Demonstrations in support of the Axis powers.

1942

Feb.: Wafdist cabinet imposed on the king by British tanks.
Sadat arrested for having contacts with the Germans.

1943(?)

Formation of the 'secret apparatus' of the Muslim Brotherhood.

1944

End of the Wafd cabinet.

1946–47

The government encourages the Muslim Brethren in a struggle against the Wafd and the Communists.
Violent atmosphere. Many clashes between rival political factions. Anglo-Egyptian negotiations to free Egypt from the terms of the 1936 treaty.

1947

Internal dissent and rise in the power of the 'secret apparatus'.
UN votes to partition Palestine.

1948

Jan.: Discovery of arms caches belonging to the Muslim Brotherhood.
War in Palestine. Contacts on the front between Muslim Brethren volunteers and officers of the Nasser group.
March: Assassination of a judge by the secret apparatus.

April: Muslim Brethren volunteers fight in Palestine against the Zionists.

June-Sept.: Anti-Jewish and anti-Western violence in Cairo.

Nov.: Evidence of existence of secret apparatus comes to light.

Dec.: Dissolution of the Muslim Brotherhood on charges of 'attempts to overthrow the existing order, terrorism, murder'.

Dec.: Riots against Arab-Israeli armistice talks.

1949

Feb.: Hasan al-Banna assassinated by the political police on 12 Feb. Salih 'Ashmawi takes over leadership of dissolved Brotherhood.

1950

June: Wafd government in power.

1951

May: Legal reconstitution of the Brotherhood.

Oct.: Egypt unilaterally abrogates the 1936 Anglo-Egyptian treaty. Clashes with British forces stationed in Egypt.

Dec.: Judge Hasan al-Hudaybi becomes Supreme Guide of the Muslim Brethren, formally replacing al-Banna.

1952

Jan.: Hudaybi condemns riots, contradictions between rank and file and the Supreme Guide.

Jan.: Egyptian police barrack attacked by British army. The next day (16th) Cairo ravaged by anti-Western rioting.

July: Coup d'état by Nasser's Free Officers (23rd).

July: Enthusiastic support for coup by rank and file of the Brotherhood.

Sept.: Hudaybi rejects offer by Free Officers to bring Muslim Brethren into government.

1953

Secret apparatus escapes control of the Supreme Guide.

> *Jan.: Dissolution of all political parties and creation of one-party state (16th). Muslim Brotherhood exempted from dissolution.*

Nov.: Sanadi, head of secret apparatus, expelled from Brotherhood.

Dec.: Salih 'Ashmawi, Muhammad al-Ghazali (favourable to Nasser) expelled from Brotherhood.

1954

Jan.: Dissolution of Muslim Brotherhood.

> *Feb.: Nasser-Neguib conflict; the latter, supported by ex-Brethren, Wafdists, and Communists, is last obstacle to absolute power of his rival.*

March: Muslim Brethren legally authorized again.

> *Aug.: Violent press campaign against the Brethren.*

Aug.: Supreme Guide disappears from public life and goes underground.

Oct.: A Muslim Brother attempts to assassinate Nasser in Alexandria (26th). Very violent repression against the Brethren.

Nov.: Speedy trial of Brotherhood leaders.

Dec.: Six defendants hanged (9th), among them 'Abd al-Qadir 'Awda. Hundreds of militants imprisoned in camps.

1955

Bandung conference held.

1956

Nationalization of the Suez Canal.

1957

May: Twenty-one Muslim Brethren slaughtered in Tura prison. Zaynab al-Ghazali and 'Abd al-Fattah Isma'il meet in Mecca to 'relaunch the Muslim Brethren'.

1958–62

Period of Egyptian-Syrian union.

1962

Unification of various Islamicist groups around the nucleus of the reconstituted Muslim Brotherhood. Readings of Sayyid Qutb's book *Signposts.*

1964

Egyptian army sent to Yemen.
May: Sayyid Qutb released from prison.

1965

Aug.: Nasser, in Moscow, denounces a 'new conspiracy by the Muslim Brethren'.
Aug.-Sept.: Repression against the Brethren. Sweeping arrests; Shukri Mustafa among those seized.

1966

August 29: Sayyid Qutb hanged.

1967–71

Formation, in the camps, of an Islamicist current that declares society excommunicated.

1967

June: Six-day war. Arab countries defeated by Israel.

1968

Feb.: Student demonstrations against those responsible for the defeat.
Nov.: Fresh student demonstrations.
Muslim Brethren in Mansura participate in the November demonstrations.

1970

Oct.: Death of Nasser, succeeded by Sadat.

1971

Release of Islamicist militants arrested under Nasser. Shukri and Talmasani are at large.
> *May 15: Sadat eliminates pro-Soviet Nasserists in 'rectification revolution'.*

1972

> *Jan.: Student demonstrations for war with Israel.*
> *Nov.: Fresh demonstrations.*

Nov.: Islamicist current opposes Nasserists and Communists at universities.

1973

Birth of the *jama'at islamiyya*. Arrest of members of Shukri Mustafa's Society of Muslims, pardoned after October.
> *Oct.: War against Israel. Regime encourages the* jama'at islamiyya.

1974

April 21: Attack at Heliopolis Military Academy by Sirriya group.

1975

> *Jan.: Demonstrations organized by the left. Beginning of the policy of economic opening* (infitah).

1976

March: The *jama'at islamiyya* control the congress of the Student Union.

July: Reappearance of the magazine *al-Da'wa.*

Nov.: Shukri attacks 'apostates'; arrest of militants, who are not brought to trial.

1977

> *Jan.: Riots in Cairo against the rise in price of subsidized products.*

July 3: Kidnapping of Sheikh al-Dhahabi by the Society of Muslims. Assassination of al-Dhahabi on 7 July.

July-Nov.: Arrest and trial of members of the Society of Muslims. Shukri and four other leaders are executed.

Nov. 8: Sadat's trip to Jerusalem.

1978

Regime robs *jama'at islamiyya* of their success in student elections. The entire Islamicist movement, all tendencies, violently criticizes the 'shameful peace with the Jews'.

1979

March: Signature of the Camp David accords.

May: Sadat travels to provinces, attacks Islamicist movement.

June: Student Union reformed to end Islamicist control.

June: Publication of *al-Da'wa* suspended.

1980

April: Sadat visits United States and comes under criticism from Coptic exiles.

April: Violent incidents between Copts and *jama'at islamiyya* in Asyut. Meeting between Faraj and Zuhdi, leaders of the two branches of the Jihad group.

1981

June: Confessional rioting in Cairo's al-Zawiyya al-Hamra neighbourhood.

Sept.: *Jama'at islamiyya* banned, Islamicist press suspended. The neo-Muslim Brethren and Sheikh Kishk are imprisoned. Khalid al-Islambuli decides to kill Sadat.

Sept.: Sadat arrests 1,536 oppositionists, demotes the Coptic pope, suspends the opposition press.

Oct. 6: Assassination of Sadat.

Oct. 8: Insurrection in Asyut.

Oct.: Husni Mubarak is elected president of the Republic by plebiscite.

Nov. 25: Thirty-one oppositionists are released from prison and received by the president. (These include Heikal, F. Siraj al-Din, and eleven members of the PUR.)
Dec.: Release of Talmasani and S. 'Ashmawi.

1982

Jan. 28: Fifty-five prisoners are released, including Sheikh Kishk.
March 6: Five death sentences are pronounced in Sadat's assassination trial.
April 15: The five prisoners sentenced to death are executed, Faraj and Khalid al-Islambuli among them.
April 25: All Sinai (except Taba) is restored to Egyptian rule.
May 11: The death sentence is sought for 299 of the 302 defendants in the trial following the Asyut insurrection.

1983

April 12: The State Council confirms the deposition of Shenouda III. The Coptic hierarchy refuses to elect a new pope.
Sept.: Application of the shari'a in Sudan, linked with Egypt by a 'treaty of complementarity'.

1984

March: A coalition between the friends of Talmasani and the neo-Wafd Party is formed.
May: Campaign for the elections to the People's Assembly, which take place on the 27th.
Sept. 30: A lenient verdict is passed in the trial of the Asyut insurrection.
Oct.: Violence at demonstrations in Kafr al-Dawar against inflation leaves three dead and twenty-six wounded.
Nov.: Demonstration by the students of al-Azhar.

1985

Jan.: The decree against Pope Shenouda is annulled on the 1st, and he celebrates Christmas Mass in Cairo on the 6th.
May 4: The People's Assembly rejects a motion demanding the immediate application of the *shari'a.*

June: Sheikh Salama threatens to lead a 'green march' if the *shari'a* is not applied by the 14th (*Laila al-Qadr*).

July: Automobile decals of a confessional nature are banned. All mosques are placed by decree under the control of the Ministry of Waqfs, and the *khutba* is made subject to prior approval. Sheikh Salama and the Islamicist militants in Fayum and Alexandria are arrested (14–17th).

Aug.: Sheikh Salama is released to go on the pilgrimage to Mecca.

Index

274

Isma'il, 'Ali 'Abduh (founder of the
Society of Muslims), 75–76
Isma'il, Muhammad 'Uthman (governor of Asyut), 134, 171
Isma'il, Nabawi (minister of the interior under Sadat), 162, 166
Israel, 83–84, 89, 112–13, 182, 191,
203
—Israeli-Egyptian peace treaty, 70–
71, 114, 116, 121, 148–49, 159, 165,
168
al-Istid'af, Marhalat ('phase of weakness' in the strategy of assuming
power), 74, 78, 202
al-Isti'mar (colonialism or imperialism), 111, 140–41, 203
al-Ita'a (al-Mawdudi's concept of submission to God), 49
al-I'tisam (Islamicist journal), 104, 246

al-Jama'a (community, or especially
group or society of Muslims; in
contrast to political party), 44, 64
—al-Hidayat al-islamiyya (Society of
Islamic Guidance, founded by
Hafiz Salama), 253
—al-Muslimin (Society of Muslims
led by Shukri Mustafa). See
al-Takfir wa'l-Hijra.
—al-Tabligh (Islamicist group
founded by the Indian Nadawi),
184 n
—Islamiyya (University Islamicist
groups), 71, 109, 129–30, 133–34,
136, 138–39, 141–72, 189, 193, 201,
205, 207, 214, 216–17, 231, 234, 237,
240, 249, 256
—al-'Uzla al-Shu'uriyya (spiritual at-
tachment group), 74
al-Jama'iyya:
—Khayriyya (charitable association),
199
—Shar'iyya (charitable association
close to the Islamicist movement),
199
al-Jami' (mosque):
—Ahli (private), 81, 206, 256
—'Ayn al-Hayat (Source of Life,
where Sheikh Kishk preached), 175
—Dome of the Rock, 112

—Holy Mosque of Mecca, 182
—Hukumi (government), 81, 175
—Mosque of the Martyrs, 254
—al-Nur, 254, 255, 256
—Qa'id Ibrahim, 252
—Saladin, 149

Janssen, J. J. G., 242
al-Jazzar, Hilmi (Islamicist student
leader), 160–61
Jews (Jewry), 56, 83–84, 111–12,
114–17, 122, 124, 158, 169, 209, 238
—of Dawnama (Dönme, followers of
Shabbetai Zevi), 121–22
al-Jihad (holy war for Islam), 54–55,
60, 84, 113, 133, 147, 193–95, 198–
200, 202–04, 206–09, 211–18, 230,
236, 240
—group (group that assassinated
Sadat), 92, 102, 146, 164, 189,
191–218, 234, 237, 240, 241, 255
al-Jinn (object of worship), 50
Jirjis, Dr. Fu'ad (Christian university
professor), 167, 170
al-Juhl (state of ignorance), 62

Kardasa (village outside Cairo), 32–33
Khalidi, Salah, 242
Khalifa, 'Abd al-Rahman, 242
Kharijism (Muslim sect of the first
century of the hegira), 58–60, 64,
99, 231
Khomeini, Ayatollah, 11
al-Khulafa', al-Rashidun (the first four
'rightly guided' caliphs under
whom Islam enjoyed its 'golden
age'), 130, 139, 227
al-Khuli, al-Bahi, 36
al-Khutba (Friday sermon), 177–90,
256
Kishk, Sheikh, 'Abd al-Hamid
al-'Aziz Muhammad (Islamicist
preacher), 172–90, 197, 201, 224,
230, 238–39, 244, 246, 249, 252
—mosque of: See al-Jami': 'Ayn
al-Hayat.
al-Kitman (concealment practiced by
some Shiite sects), 75
al-Kuttab (Koranic school), 38, 84, 186

People's Assembly (Egyptian Parliament), 126–27, 172, 184, 190, 193
Pharaoh, 50, 201, 240
Pilgrimage. See al-Hajj.
Power, phase of. See al-Tammakun, Marhalat.
The Prophet. See Muhammad.
Protocols of the Elders of Zion, 23, 115

Qadhafi, Mu'amar, 22
al-Qadir, Abd, 16
Qanatir prison, 31
al-Qardawi, Yusif (leader of the neo-Muslim Brethren), 128, 146, 150
Qutb, Muhammad (brother of Sayyid and Islamicist leader), 61, 64, 66
Qutb, Sayyid, 23, 27–31, 36–69, 74, 83, 90, 98 n, 102–03, 120, 126, 131, 155, 175 n, 180 n, 189–90, 192, 202, 224, 236–37, 239, 240, 242

al-Rabb (lord; one of Mawdudi's four technical terms of the Koran), 48, 50, 63
Ramadan (Muslim month of fasting), 82, 86, 150, 209 n
Ramadan, 'Abd al-Azim (historian), 106, 243
Ramadam, Sa'id, 34
Rectification revolution (of 1971), 54, 134
Retreat. See al-'Uzla.
Richard document, 118, 160–61
Rizq, Jabir (Islamicist historian), 28, 243, 244
al-Rububiyya (divinity), 155

Sabanegh, Edouard, 243
Sadat, Anwar, 27, 52, 62, 85, 92, 94–95, 97, 103, 105–06, 108, 116, 129, 132, 139–40, 147, 155–56, 158–63, 166, 172–73, 191–218, 235–36, 240, 242, 243
—assassination of, 19, 22, 35, 71, 129, 164, 170, 191–218, 235–36, 240, 244
Sadat, Jihan (wife of president Sadat), 184 n
Salama, Hafiz (Islamicist preacher), 249, 252, 253–54, 255–56, 257

al-Salibiyya (Crusade; designates Christians living outside Dar al-Islam), 111, 117–20, 124, 158
Samuel, Bishop (member of the papal counsel of the Coptic church), 160
al-Sayyid, Lutfi (Egyptian intellectual), 234
Sect. See Firqa.
Secularism, 111, 124
Shabab Sayyidina Muhammad (Youth of Our Lord Muhammad), 253
Shafi'i (one of the four legal schools of Sunni Islam), 79
Shah of Iran (Muhammad Rezi Palavi), 17, 19, 158–59
Shahid (martyr), 59, 96, 125
Shaltut, Sheikh (Sheikh of al-Azhar under Nasser), 80
Shamm al-Nisin ('Smell the Breeze', Egyptian holiday), 169–70
Sha'rawi, Sheikh Muhammad Mitwali (Muslim preacher), 80, 173
Shari'at (law of God, based on the Koran and the Sunna), 48, 51, 55, 97, 107, 118, 127, 141, 167, 184, 190, 194, 196–98, 213, 247, 249, 250, 251, 255, 256
Shenouda III (patriarch of the Coptic church), 159–60, 239, 244, 245, 255
al-Sibki, Mahmud Khattab (founder of the *jama'iyya shari'iyya*), 104
al-Sibki, Muhammad 'Abd al-Latif, 60
al-Siddiq, Abu Bakr (contemporary of Muhammad), 181
Siffin, battle of, 58
Sirriya, Salih 'Abdallah Ibrahim (leader of the Military Academy group), 93
Siraj al-Din, Fuad (Secretary General of the neo-Wafd Party, formerly leader of the Wafd), 244
Society of Islamic Guidance. See Jama'at al-hidayat al-islamiyya.
Society of Muslim Brethren. See al-Ikhwan al-Muslimin.
Society of Muslim Ladies, 29
Society of Muslims. See al-Jama'at al-Muslimin.
Spinoza, B., 21

280

Sovereignty. See al-Hakimiyya.
al-Sunan (Islamic customs and attitudes), 207
al-Sunna (collection of texts that establish the Tradition of Muhammad), 79, 107, 126, 184 n
Sura (chapter of the Koran):
—'Cow', 79
—'Joseph', 28
—'Friday', 85
—'Mary', 179 n, 188
—'*Sad*', 182, 189
—'The Table', 196

al-Ta'alluh ('apotheosis', term of Mawdudi), 49
al-Tabshir (term applied to Christian missionary activities), 117, 158
al-Taghut (false gods; name applied to the despot, or to objects worshipped instead of God), 49, 79, 195
al-Tahrir (liberation), 155
al-Takfir (excommunication), 58, 72, 74–75, 77
al-Takfir wa'l-Hijra ('Excommunication and Hegira', name applied to the Society of Muslims), 19, 59, 64, 66, 70–102, 105, 110, 147–48, 156, 158, 181 n, 215, 217, 226, 230, 234
al-Talmasani, 'Umar (editor-in-chief of the magazine *al-Da'wa*), 63, 105–06, 108, 110, 112, 114–16, 122, 124–28, 147, 150, 156, 190, 204, 244, 250, 251, 257
al-Tamakkun (or al-Tamkin: 'phase of power' in strategy of Society of Muslims), 82, 202
al-Taqlid (scholastic tradition of the doctors of Islam), 49, 59, 64, 79, 196, 199, 202
Tartars, 194, 196, 199, 211, 230
al-Tawaghit. See al-Taghut.
Tawfiq, Husain (hired assassin), 33
al-Tawhid (unity; fundamental concept of Islam, which stands in opposition to the Christian concept of the Trinity, refers to the sole source of Islamic inspiration, the Koran), 155, 228

Tradition. See al-Sunna; al-Taqlid.
Tura (concentration camp), 28, 41, 74–75, 116, 175, 236

al-Ubudiyya (adoration, in the writings of Mawdudi and Qutb), 47–50, 155
Ulema (religious scholars), 37, 56–59, 80, 91–102, 107, 126, 173, 193–94, 196, 198, 228–30
Umayyad dynasty, 53
al-Umma (community of believers), 44–46, 55, 66, 80, 83, 129–71, 237
Ummiyyin (illiterates), 85
al-'Umra (minor pilgrimage to Mecca), 198
Usul al-din (origins of religion; one of the four traditional faculties of al-Azhar), 190
'Uthman, 'Uthman Ahmad (Egyptian entrepreneur), 109
'Uways, Dr Sayyid, 232, 234, 243
al-'Uzla (separation; tactic of retreat from society upheld by some Islamicist tendencies), 35, 64, 66, 74, 78, 83, 203

Wafd, neo-Wafd Party, 244, 249, 250–51
Wahhabite. See Ibn 'Abd al-Wahhab
al-Waqf (property whose funds are used to support a religious foundation), 230
—*Minbar al-Islam* (magazine of the ministry of waqfs), 60
—Ministry of (manages Islamic religious property and acts as mouthpiece for government Islam), 60, 89, 100, 106, 175, 177, 184 n, 256
Warda, Majdi Rajab (militant Islamicist author of anti-Christian tract), 168, 170
Weakness, phase of. See al-Istid'af, Marhalat.
Wissa-Wassef, Cérès, 243

Yasa (Mongol law), 196
Youth of Our Lord Muhammad. See Shabab Sayyidina Muhammad.